Thrills and Frills

ALSO BY ANDREW CROZIER

An Andrew Crozier Reader (Manchester: Carcanet Press, 2012) (ed. Ian Brinton)
All Where Each Is (London: Allardyce, Barnett Publishers, 1985)
Utamaro Variations (with Ian Tyson. London: Tetrad, 1982)
Were There (London: The Many Press, 1978)
High Zero (Cambridge: Street Editions, 1978)
Duets (Guildford: Circle Press, 1976)
Residing (Belper: Aggie Weston's, 1976)
Pleats (Bishops Stortford: Great Works Editions, 1976)
Seven Contemporary Sun Dials (with Ian Potts. Brighton: Brighton Festival, 1975)
Printed Circuit (Cambridge: Street Editions, 1974)
The Veil Poem (Providence, RI: Burning Deck Press, 1974)
Neglected Information (Sidcup: Blacksuede Boot Press, 1972)
In One Side & Out the Other (with John James & Tom Phillips.
        London: Ferry Press, 1970)
Walking on Grass (London: Ferry Press, 1970)
Train Rides (Pampisford: R Books, 1968)
Loved Litter of Time Spent (Buffalo, NY: Sum Books, 1967)

ALSO BY IAN BRINTON

(ed.) *'An intuition of the particular': Some essays on the poetry of Peter Hughes*
        (Bristol: Shearsman Books, 2013)
Poems of Yves Bonnefoy 1 (Oystercatcher Press, 2013)
(ed.) *An Andrew Crozier Reader* (Manchester: Carcanet Press, 2012)
Brontë's *Wuthering Heights, A Reader's Guide* (London: Continuum 2010)
(ed.) *A Manner of Utterance, The Poetry of J.H. Prynne* (Exeter: Shearsman Books, 2009)
Contemporary Poetry: Poets and Poetry since 1990 (Cambridge Contexts in
        Literature (Cambridge: Cambridge University Press, 2009)
Dickens' Great Expectations, A Reader's Guide (London: Continuum 2007)

Andrew Crozier

Thrills and Frills

Selected Prose

Edited by Ian Brinton

Shearsman Books

First published in the United Kingdom in 2013 by
Shearsman Books Ltd
50 Westons Hill Drive
Emersons Green
BRISTOL
BS16 7DF

Shearsman Books Ltd Registered Office
30–31 St. James Place, Mangotsfield, Bristol BS16 9JB
(this address not for correspondence)

ISBN 978-1-84861-301-0
First Edition

Details of publication history are provided at the head
of each essay.

Contents

Introduction

Almost without exception the prose of Andrew Crozier—reviews and articles centred upon the close reading of poetry, including fearless debate about the importance of some figures who have either been overlooked by the establishment or given little more than a cursory nod of acknowledgement—has been out of print for far too long. The work, often published in journals or as contributory chapters to other books, has never before been collected together and this seems astonishing. In a letter sent to me in 2006, when I was first formulating the idea of editing a selection of Crozier's work, Michael Schmidt wrote of his admiration for the prose: "He is a magnificent critic, moving with the certainty of a glacier, gathering everything." This echoes the comments Schmidt made to Crozier himself in a letter of July 2006 when he affirmed "the highest regard possible for your critical essays" and suggested that they "dig far deeper and uncover far more than most of the critical writings of writers I admire in our generation." A fuller account of this correspondence can be found in the introduction to *An Andrew Crozier Reader* which Carcanet published in 2012. In that introduction there is also a substantial quotation from a letter written to me, concerning the work on Harry Roskolenko which Crozier was most preoccupied with at the earliest stage of his all-too-brief retirement. This Shearsman collection of prose contains the first publication of that work as well as the full book proposal which Crozier provided for Cambridge University Press for a full-length study of 'The Fate of Modernism', a reappraisal of the British poetry of the 1940s. It also contains the full texts of the essays on Basil Bunting and Louis Zukofsky which Crozier had suggested to me at some point "should be amalgamated".

I see this book as very much a companion piece to the already published *Reader* and because of that I have not reproduced the prose which already exists in that book, such as the substantial article on Roy Fisher's *A Furnace*, the essay on George Oppen's early poetry and 'Resting on Laurels', the contribution to a Routledge compilation of essays *British Culture of the Postwar: An Introduction to Literature and Society 1945-1999*. Neither have I repeated the excellent bibliography which Derek Slade helped me to compile for that book.

It is very important to acknowledge debts and this book could not have been put together without the assistance of Jean Crozier, who gave me unfettered access to Andrew Crozier's papers, my wife Kay who has been ever-patient about my being closeted in the study, and Tony Frazer whose enthusiasm for the project has never been in doubt. My thanks also go to Michael Schmidt whose enthusiasm for the *Andrew Crozier Reader* got the whole venture off the ground and whose belief in the immense value of Crozier's work proved a starting point for me: it permitted me to enter a world that is central to any real understanding of what was happening in the field of modern poetry from the late Sixties onwards.

Trilogy, HD (Carcanet Press, £2.50 cloth, £1. 20 paper);
The Linear Journal, Peter Riley (Grosseteste Review Books);
Acrospirical Meanderings in a Tongue of the Time, Chris Torrance
(Albion Village Press, 75p).

This review was written for *The Spectator*, June 22nd 1974.

It's good that the range of HD's work is finally being made accessible, albeit in counter-chronological fashion; indeed that is probably all for the best since to approach any estimate of her position entails finding some starting point other than that of the *imagiste* HD, disciple of Pound and author of a few anthology-pieces. Following *Tribute to Freud* and *Hermetic Definition* Carcanet Press have now brought together, in one volume for the first time, HD's war trilogy *The Walls Do Not Fall*, *Tribute to the Angels*, and *The Flowering of the Rod*. Each book of *Trilogy* is organised serially in 43 sections and it is possible, reading such details as a form of numerical symbolism (4 and 3 as symbolic entities themselves, added together to make 7, &c.), backed up by the eclectic religious and mythological content of some sections, to see the whole poem as a hermetic work engaged in the manipulation of arcane and occult knowledge. Although there certainly is such a side to the poem it is not its distinctive characteristic, for HD's prescription of the poet's activity has to do with the spinning of a "thread / that binds all humanity // to ancient wisdom." She sees the role of the poet involved in certain mysteries, but they are mysteries which patience and skill can penetrate, like DNA or the conic spiral through a shell, secrets of organisation within superficial form expressed as that form's characteristic, recognisable signature. It is a poetic role which includes the public and the collective, privileged only in the sense of its special attainments, demanding a transcendence of the personal world. In this, set beside her intuitions of perennial wisdom and recreations of archetypal story (aspects of the poem which, I find, provide only a thematic undercurrent to other issues), we have a second reference point, the function and dignity of the poet, the scribe, of language and memory. But there is a third and even more immediate frame of reference in the everyday data of experience which the poem encompasses of wartime London and the author's life in the blitzed city, "when the shingles hissed / in the rain of incendiary." It is the presence of such elaborate coordinates for the poem as a whole that underwrites the sense I have of it, not as an hermetic work, but as a distinctively open and candid achievement of writing.

For one of the distinguishing notes of the poem is of an anguished and nervous sensibility at variance with its environment, both the substantial barbarity of war itself, and the less overt brutalisation inherent in the mobilisation of civilian life and opinion. There is nothing precious in this, nor is it a matter of pathos passively expressed; it is the personal tone, rather, by-product of the attempt to retain value, to hang on to consciousness, to perpetuate an eternal principle and continuity essential to any kind of renewal in such a broken and divided world. There is an intense, wilful optimism inherent in this, the purpose behind which is not irrelevant to our own world. The figures of the poem function in terms of this central desire, and in their particular detail modulate between the privacies of HD's memory and identity, childhood and adult relationships, and the accessible objects of her experience which, endowed with iconic vigour, are interpretive of individual life within a pattern of greater continuity. Thus a burnt apple tree in bloom, or a building ripped open by bomb damage, turned inside out as it were, are more than intimations of the natural cycle of birth and death and an inner life brutally laid bare, they are symbolic vessels which can, in their recurrent deployment, alongside more traditional visionary material, be made to contain meanings which are not gratuitously attached to them but are their valuable and salutary human complement. The modulation between the different details of the poem, that is to say, which occur in a searching-out and discovery of correspondences and recurrences, is an equation for the transition between the individual poet HD and the self-consecrated role she assumes, and it is in the resultant multi-levelled texture that the eclectic doctrinal elements of the poem are tautly and securely held. The central perception of the poem as I see it has to do with a renewal or rebirth of self not in a passive rest-and-recuperation sense but in the more demanding and active sense of a self-created other self, which both affirms the old self as author while transcending it. We can see in this the mode of action of such a poem as *Trilogy*, in which pragmatic details of the poet's life are made part of a hermeneutic, while her "real" life goes on to become an endowment of the work, conferring upon it an experience of psychic intensity which is not spurious or worked up, I would say, because it is an experience for the author before it can be experienced by the reader. I am talking really about fine adjustments of poetic tone which occur when writing is not translation from an entirely different order of experience, but is made to accommodate to itself the conditions, the experience, of its making. HD offers the experience of her own rebirth in *Trilogy*, it is not private, not a fantasy of eternal youth, but an image of self-completion. HD's ancient wisdom has ultimately to do with the attainment, through the instrumentality of language, of an identity which is fully human as the location of an individual in the general life. *Trilogy* is apocalyptic of a psychic integration that is both personal and collective, and although the poem ends climactically with the image of the infant Christ as a fragrant bundle of myrrh in his mother's arms, its energy does not derive from such explicitly doctrinal content but from the processes of language which make such confluences of thought and feeling possible.

The view of human life evinced by HD's poem, the sense of poetic vocation it reveals, and its technical procedures are far from current orthodoxy as to what goes in poetry. Its serial technique places major demands upon the reader's span of attention; its language is unindulgently spare and precise, but does not fall into the rictus of terse brevity which afflicts much of current verse production in England. Neither Peter Riley's *The Linear Journal* nor Chris Torrance's *Acrospirical Meanderings in a Tongue of the Time* falls into this category however. One thing they have in common is the employment of serial form, but the nature of the sequence is different in each case, and I should certainly not like to suggest any very extensive derivation of their work from HD. In Riley's book (his fifth) there is a threadlike extension across actual terrain, connectedness partly a matter of linear continuity as the title suggests. Yet this topographical element, with all its potential for the rich and exotic, is played down throughout; within the poem the actual journey is made the occasion of the poet's apperception of the total world he inhabits. The journey, however, is not made a pretext for metaphorical substitution (turned into a spiritual journey, for instance, with an attainable goal in view) or for a series of reveries upon suitable occasions discovered in the course of travel. The distinct components of an ordinary, disjunctive contemporary life retain their separate modalities—publicity, culture, violence, economics, adolescence, pathos &c.—merging and emerging in a plurality of consciousness which is sustained by a continuous surface of language. The tone is largely dissociated from any sense of the personal, and this is perhaps necessary for the accomplishment of the oblique jumps and elisions or reference which are sustained within the loosely flowing syntax of this writing. The poem might give the appearance of collage, but I think it would be wrong to see in Riley's work any such synthetic or constructive aesthetic. He is persistent rather than inventive in his language, his art very much a matter of renunciation (of what can easily be made, of available feeling) and openness (to echoic incursions which prey upon and disrupt the mind and feelings) in order to be able to write something expressively true to present-day conditions.

Whereas Riley employs various strategies to avoid the inauthenticities which beset the contemporary poet who supposes there exists a natural language directly correspondent to his individual sensibility, Torrance is a poet of a more traditional order whose ultimate concern is the creation of an authentic natural speech. He writes about the life and processes in the midst of which he finds himself (and in this case it is a wild nature, but he has written equally well, in his previous two books, of urban life) in a way which tends towards visionary elevation, yet he works very close in, the perceptive limits of his world are tightly acknowledged and apply their appropriate constraints to the movement of feeling within his work; the shaping influence of weather is particularly registered, and it is out along such systems that Torrance's perceptions travel for their sense of scale. In a sense there is something analogous in its effects here to the deliberate strategies employed by Peter Riley, only in Torrance's case one finds much more the sense of an immediate personal sensibility at work obdurately excluding the unnecessary, yet able to seize and hold in suspension various impinging natural identities without needing to assimilate or subvert them. Both these poets, it seems to me, are engaged in an attempt to write poetry that can be totally inclusive of a man's serious interests. HD's work ought to be *canonical*. Torrance and Riley are part of the real direction of English poetry now. I don't suppose though that very many will notice for some time yet.

The World, The World.
A Reading of John Riley's Poetry

This essay was included in the 1979 Grosseteste publication *For John Riley*, a collection of memories, thoughts and messages to commemorate the life of the poet who had been killed in Leeds in October 1978. Although the book was compiled by Tim Longville, the note at the beginning makes it clear that he did not see his role as that of a selecting editor: "I let people know that the possibility of it existed: what is printed here is what was sent".

John Riley wrote a poetry of what is known and, hence, desired, frequently dogmatic or magisterial in quality, on occasion almost overbearingly so, in which the commonplaces of human experience become realistic emblems of man's spiritual nature. His poems present themselves insistently as an accumulation of statements about the world, and these meanings tend to spread out and join together to suggest an inviolable scheme of authorial confidence. The poems are secular, of course, though not in the narrow sense of contradistinction from the sacred; the ground for that negative distinction is reworked in the appalling gloss provided for the word "planet" in A MEETING—"a word for television-watchers". But although Riley contemns the reductive imagery of screen culture, he follows this with a reduction of his own, "the world, it is the world"; nestling within the embattled assertion of the tautology a pronoun refers world back to planet in the more bare and desperate statement that that is really all there is. The world is neither space-ship not launching-pad as it might appear to be to the astronauts encountered in a much earlier poem, 'After the Music', who "walk in/Slow motion one hundred and eighty miles up", whom the poem locates within the context both of terrestrial weather and a notion of space as musical, so that they are placed, finally, against the imagined provision of "A given time and strict measure to resolve this/Curious involvement, a dominant species."

The dominion of human nature, the disjunction between it and the rest of creation, yet their permanent co-presence, nature plus man, constitute what is for John Riley's writing the world, and entail its existence both as immediate spiritual revelation and as instance of sacred history, uniting past and future. But the implicit concept of the sacral unity of the world hovers over rather than informs the world as it is known by experience, which in its own existence is susceptible to being treated in terms of equally large-scale concepts. The world in the totality of human experience remains an object of renunciation or, at the very least, transformation: "all things must be changed" ('Birthday Poem') if it is not the case that "everything must be done away with." ('Love Poem')

From the point of view of the English tradition of romantic transcendence, extensively bulwarked as it is by a rough-and-ready empiric naturalism, what is least familiar about this and, in its implications, most disturbing, is the absence of any systematic correspondence between experience in the world and spiritual discovery. Percepts do not nourish and encourage concepts; indeed, in John Riley's poems concepts regularly usurp places normally occupied by percepts. "The rainbow colours of becoming,/A rhythm of moving limbs and exchanged glances- // It is a part of this that the time for that is past, / I speak now of a still life." ('A Birthday Poem for One Person, and Hence for Others') But just as man is disjunct from nature, and is the agency by which spirit is introduced into the world, he is also estranged from himself as a natural creature; although man can at moments project a sense of glory into the world, and thus discover in natural forms the tokens of spirit, his more normal experience of the world is of a meagre and reluctant habitation. Indeed, the more the natural world appears, in John Riley's poems, in the aspect of richness and plenitude, the more that world pulls away in its autonomy to emphasise man's separation from it within his experience. Yet the dualism implicit in this attitude to human life does not stop here; if it is not possible to praise man in terms of his participation in an ample nature, neither is it possible to praise him from humanistic motives—therein lies the impoverishment of both astronauts and their spectators. Man gives praise, and discloses his meaning and value when, transfigured by love, his life is revealed to him in the aspects of eternity; there is hope in the untitled poem which begins "I shall not weary you with poems" because "we shall live after/this day, this day." In the doubling of time the moment is imprinted with the eternity in which man lives.

If John Riley's poems were of interest primarily for their theology then even two quite early poems might serve to place terms on the extent of that interest. In 'La Dame à la Licorne' is shown how, despite the beauty of the world, human life does not find its fulfilment there; the lady sets her face against that beauty, while the poem nevertheless acknowledges it as a sign of life's creative force, which the lady must search for elsewhere. The poem refers to an allegory of sexual and virtuous attraction, from which it takes its terms and meaning; the submission of the unicorn before the lady's looking-glass, acknowledgement of her state of grace, directs attention finally to the source of that grace. The connection between the natural and the human is not direct, and points away from each towards their common creative source. In 'The Full Moon is Bathing These Fields', on the other hand, a cosmic yet intimately felt nature is set over against the exclusivity of social existence: "Say, shall we see this sky as an astronaut would see it / ...its floes its continents and depths / So touchingly reduced to dimensions, charted?" (The imaginative strategy here should be compared with that of 'Views of Where One Is', in which the imagination rises over a flat landscape to see "Trees like maps of intricate green continents / Floating in blue oceans", and there occurs "a constant movement / From mechanical habit to consciousness.") But although the astronaut is to be pitied as "that social man happy / Perhaps, to live our lowest fantasy", the poem ends in a contemplation of nature as a place threatened with total colonisation by social man. It is implied that man depends upon that natural portion of the world, under threat from his own species, to provide him with images that can be informed by spirit and convey its presence: "The noise of the wind in a tree / Startled me, it sounded exactly like a conversation."

Between the polar negatives evinced by these two poems whatever John Riley has to say about the character of human life finds a location, and is available to serve specific purposes of textual or doctrinal analysis. But the theology itself is stabilised and potentially reductive, and for the poems to be allowed to exert their existence to the full the question of doctrine should be allowed to cede its place to that of the modes of thought and feeling that articulate doctrine and yet also imply the active presence of other issues in the poems. Those other issues might be expected to be less optional than the theology and, without constituting an autobiography, or serving the purposes of expression, might be expected also to relate in a direct way to the existence of the poet. Indeed, despite their superficial contrast, one extensively dependent upon an existing structure of significance, the other drawing upon more immediate thought and feeling, the two poems just discussed might in each case suggest that they are the product of a careful intersecting of will and condition.

The resumé of John Riley's habitual poetic themes provided in the opening lines of 'Czargrad' is explicit on the subject of their degree of self-reference: "thoughts and memories of lots of people / in a book of hours, meanings, hierarchies / an Easter greeting always, uncertainties / of private death dispelled…". It would be misleading to attempt to identify this self, although it is frequently instanced as wilful and impatient, because although the poems regularly make recourse to a notion of the self as their agency, there is neither projection of a complete persona to take on the whole burden of discourse, nor, on the other hand, is there systematic deployment of a notion of poetic self-identity. One of the means by which John Riley's writing copes with the difficulty habitually encountered by modern poetry in the area of the self, seemingly original if not altogether remarkable, for it must owe something to the theology of secular and sacred time, is to proffer a rough-and-ready distinction between the perceptual and more-or-less immediate, plastic self, on the one hand, and the conceptual, more-or-less continual self on the other. 'Days Times Flowers' is an early and somewhat schematic example of such a contrast in action; intention and recognition are deployed one against the other, partly for purposes of defensive irony, but in a discourse which centres on the question of how to relate to another person. Although the contrastive distinction involves the disparity and adjustment of different time-scales, the poetic activity is not one of reflection or judgement, with automatic advantage conceded to the future, the domain of the privileged self. The future by its nature cannot be secular. The weight of the moral issue is sustained throughout by both parties equally, the displacement of percepts towards concepts a matter of transposition rather than revision.

The framing of poetic discourse around the first person as its central grammatical figure, as found in 'Days Times Flowers', where the temporal discontinuity of the intentional self is contained within the inclusiveness of memory, is not typical of John Riley's writing, and occurs here for the purpose of an ironic emphasis of the self as object, presenting its inconsistency in the eyes of the other. Like many of the other poems in *Ancient and Modern*, 'Days Times Flowers' owns to a ground-text in the relations between the sexes, but the other poems tend to refer to such ground more circumspectly, and with less dramatic immediacy. 'De Rerum Modu', for example, pursues the transactions which occur between events and qualities through a series of juxtaposed conceptual images, using the dissociative syntax of the line end and of spatial punctuation, in order finally to address its question to a "you" which is only located in its occupation of the transactional nexus. 'Moon in my Eye', by contrast, modulates from the third through the first person towards an exegesis of the symbolic imagery of movement, in earth, moon, dream, tide, tree, with which the poem cloaks the sexual relationship. There is in fact no consistent stylistic thread running through the discourse of John Riley's poetry as a whole. Despite its settled, almost monolithic theology, the writing is continually deviant in form and technique; varied in tone and mood despite its restricted range of imagery. Each of the four major books appeared as a deliberate and considered act, a new collection displacing and modifying what preceded it. This sense of vigorous trajectory can, moreover, be induced locally from each book, from a quality of internal fracture and discontinuity of sequence which mitigates whatever feelings might be entertained concerning the particular book's over-determination. In John Riley's poetry at its best, which is to say in much of it, the writing itself pulls clear of the theology, and is not to be thought of in expository terms, but reveals, down to its most basic procedures, the passionate engagement of a realist with experience. It would be a mistake to see the theology enforcing a drive towards iconic fixity; the poems cannot be carried about, but move of their own accord.

At the heart of John Riley's poetry is to be found a preoccupation with knowing, but it is not that erotic knowledge of much modern poetry, with its post-romantic tradition of naturalism, which proceeds through the exhaustion of sensuous detail, or the capture of an essential quality. It is a knowledge, rather, of the placement, within the structure of permanent lexical apprehension, of that to which, in its discursive structure, language seems to testify. An act of naming, in other words, implying recognition rather than invention, to which nature and language itself are partially resistant by virtue of their changing and unstable natures. This urgency of naming, in its problematic usage, is close to identity with that "animal longing" to which the poems often refer, and is the cause of passionate outcry on more than one occasion: "name your realities / on this cloudless day name them what's known / is also not known is lost…" ('Czargrad, III') As a primary emotion, however, it can also merge with the means by which belief itself, because it constitutes a way of interpreting experience, functions as a source of feeling. While 'Days Times Flowers' might be seen as one intuitive foreshadowing of a theology, the several Easter poems stand as examples of the fusion of motives of desire and belief.

But although, throughout John Riley's work, concept is related to percept, belief and the structure of knowledge to experience and sense data, the transactions between these two orders are continually checked, frustrated, or disrupted, both in the process of their utterance and in actuality. The detection of a divine presence, and the eloquence thus occasioned, is at best fitful, and beset by an endemic condition of backsliding. History is not yet perfect. The Church, with its liturgy, ritual, and festivals, is not the place in which man lives; 'Fragments of an Argument about the Feast' and the 'Second Fragment' which succeeds it argue this fully, in their exposure of the inauthentic consolations of history. One man's history, it is remembered, is another's experience. The past tense is an imposition that won't do, it must give ground to the perennial natural phenomenon, "the rain that once beat on Rome / or fell gently on the Galilean hills." The poems of religious observance appear to struggle to contain the bitterness which they articulate within frameworks of symmetrical verbal repetitions, which mark the limits and exclusions of ritual. Love also exists potentially in nature, however, and the love which informs knowledge of landscape or of another person occasions a discourse that is not amenable to such forcing, for it is unsanctioned, fugitive, and unable to contain its objects; it is to be contained by them, rather, and confer form to their constantly changing nature. "...phenomena / I hear her footsteps across the stones , / her footsteps that are sounds but could be made by no one else / and I can time her arrival by the silence." ('Report, Unfinished') It is in the tensions thus set up, desire reaching for images of what it cannot attain, that the energy of John Riley's writing stands revealed. Although the poems attempt to say things simply and clearly, artifice and indirection are enjoined on attempted discourse by the obduracy of changing nature and experience. Yet hope for the future, that plainest of utterances, is not extinguished, for language and writing itself are finally one with nature in their ability to change and accommodate. A longing to possess the embodiments of what is known is felt as the very nature of writing. Not even the recognition that praise and participation have no aftermath, that knowledge and meaning inhabit natural, mortal bodies, which permeates the late poem 'Rough Tor, Cornwall, this landscape what song' as thoroughly as it does the earlier 'Fragment of an Argument about the Feast', can countermand that eschatology:

I look to the end as to the greatest cycle of love a second turn, the greatest in the calculation of our hearts.

Thrills and Frills:
Poetry as Figures of Empirical Lyricism

The essay 'Thrills and Frills' was specially commissioned for inclusion in a 1983 collection of essays titled *Society and Literature 1945–1970*, edited by Alan Sinfield, which formed part of Methuen's *The Context of English Literature* series. In July of that year Michael Schmidt wanted to publish the article in *PN Review* since from his point of view "the essay is of considerable value, exploring many of the themes which have been central to *PN Review* since its inception".

Contexts in canons

If we want to ask questions about the context of poetry, with the idea, perhaps, that the broader our frame of reference the better our knowledge, we should find ourselves at the same time having to ask the question: What poetry? Some modes of contextual criticism commonly encountered avoid this in practice. One, for example, will point to self-evident social factors which can be exhibited in their due place beside a standard choice of texts. Another infers a total historical and social reality determining all literary productions uniformly, able without difficulty to incorporate within itself even those productions that resist such determination: from this point of view the literary productions of a given period are typical and more or less equivalent. Both these positions, even when adversary, treat poetry as an unproblematic unity, knowable as such in a way largely independent of any comprehensive survey. Neither position asks of itself why it attends to this poetry rather than that, for as a result of an inclusive embrace of text and context the only poetry in evidence is whatever is at hand. That other poetry might never have been written. Neither position interrogates its own context (is poetry not part of the context of criticism?) and thus must operate with implicit commitment to unexamined and even disowned judgements of literary status.

Yet there is a quantitative phenomenon (which, incidentally, suggests that notion of status and quality often have more to do with prescription and taste than judgement) that can put into proportion the question of what our critics refer to. It is not often enough remembered that in recent years, and maybe for much longer, poetry has been the art with probably the greatest number of practitioners in this country: entrants to poetry competitions and participants in writers' circles and creative-writing classes are a fraction of the total. The mass of these poets are, of course, without ambition, and the private nature of their activity means that they are not concerned with making a quality product; but this is not the point. Not only do these poets hardly know what the quality product is; when it is pointed out to them they tend not to recognise what makes it so very different from what they write themselves. Unless they are ambitious to win prizes, they certainly do not rush to buy it. If we dismiss these poets as amateur, as self-preoccupied, or of having old-fashioned standards of taste, we do not remove their significance. We have not justified the direction of our attention.

This is not just the question of a distinction between high art and popular culture. Nor are the questions raised here to be resolved by contrasting the critical privileging of literature as high art and the disparagement of popular culture. The pressures behind such an observation are obvious enough, but to proceed from a general point about the social production of literature to a complaint about the élitism of its criticism is to go on too fast. What literature? and What poetry? remain questions unasked within a blanket notion of high art; nor are questions about the relation of criticism, as a mediator of contexts, to the production of its subject allowed to be put. Yet everyone engaged in the academic study of English knows how criticism has redesigned the tradition of English literature throughout this century. Where recent literature is concerned, and criticism shares the immediate context of its production, such relations are intensified. The poetry commonly talked about—the standard, canonical work—cannot be simply located in a non-literary context if it owes not only existence but status to the way in which that context operates in intimacy, through secondary discourse, with its production. Not to proceed too fast, therefore, we should bear in mind that criticism itself is contextually produced, before being an agency through which literature is determined.

The criticism of contemporary literature typically represents cultural values as artistic values, and so governs the perception and status of what is regarded as artistically valid. There is a notional admission that art directs its own discourse, but most criticism, in the guise of artistic judgement, is doing no more than affording its sanction to culturally and socially approved modes of discourse. Present-day criticism of the poetry of the period 1945-70 has its origins, still, within the period itself; indeed, when we examine its origins we see how closely they were involved with a section of its subject. It would appear, specifically, that currently approved modes of discourse established themselves in poetry in the early and middle fifties. In order, therefore, to understand why the canon for our period exists in the form in which it does, we need to consider it in relation to its formative critical context. Two points of focus—the canon as it is received today and as it emerged and was codified—provide the starting-point of this essay: superimposed, they provide an image of the self-consciousness, so to speak, of the canonical poetry of the period. But when we trace the terms by which the canon was defined it becomes apparent that they are also those by which it was validated; controversy never infringed certain agreements, and these largely unexamined positions cover major exclusions of poetic discourse. In terms of the poetic history of the period the present-day reader is ill served indeed, but this problem cannot begin to be overcome until we see it in its critical context.

But what is the canon? Do I make exaggerated claims for its existence? These are questions readers may already have answered from their own knowledge. In his monograph on Seamus Heaney (1982) Blake Morrison provides a current version, registering the status of his subject, placing him in the company of his peers, and marshalling an array of established authorities to underwrite the orthodoxy he describes.

> Seamus Heaney is widely believed to be one of the finest poets now writing. To call him "the most important Irish poet since Yeats" has indeed become something of a cliché. In Britain he is as essential a part of the school and university syllabus as are his post-1945 predecessors Philip Larkin and Ted Hughes; in America scholarly articles reflect a growing interest in his work; on both sides of the Atlantic influential critics… have pressed large claims on his behalf.[1]

It is worth noting, in passing, the slight shiftiness in tone in this passage ("is… believed", "part of the… syllabus"); Morrison is never wholly behind what is being claimed. But this is only local colouring to an argument which, it is clearly felt, need not be made: the constellation of Larkin, Hughes and Heaney is assumed, and it is as "one of the finest poets now writing" that Heaney belongs there.

What we should attend to in particular are the implicit strategies of this argument, which strip from the notion of a canon of excellence any suggestion that the criteria involved might not be universal. First of all, the argument is contained within an unspecified concept of quality, "the finest poets". It accomplishes itself by means of ostensibly neutral chronological markers ("since Yeats", "post-1945"); yet, while 1945 is an important date in social history (the election of a Labour government, the end of the Second World War—although neither was directly an event in Irish history, surely), "Yeats" is a function of literary history. The notion of an autonomous literary history is implied by the concept of succession, Yeats-Heaney, Larkin-Hughes-Heaney, yet such succession is not simply chronological but is concerned with authority and status and, it would seem, relations of descent; a version of tradition, in other words, though not that of Pound or Eliot. Something British perhaps? Whatever the case, the argument derives its force more from its air of unassuming conviction than from anything it says about the poets in question, and it functions rather like those systems of radio interference used to jam other signals. The message that is allowed to come through is the persuasive notion of major quality, quite unbiased, simply the best. It is a salesman's message (seeking in fact to develop the market for a series of primers on "Contemporary Writers"), appealing to a variety of tastes, a variety of English-language cultures, but appealing above all to the taste for quality. (It should be remembered that the appeal of quality is always pitched towards the individual consumer.)

The most compelling strategy of the argument as a whole is the way it associates the authority of period and tradition with the generosity of contrast and internal diversity. The canon, within limits, is able to evolve. Some years ago, before the decisive advent of Heaney, it was usual to encounter the name of Ted Hughes twinned with that of Thom Gunn. Larkin and Hughes are frequently perceived as antithetical, the one tame and insular, the other barbaric and invoking elemental powers. Heaney is Irish. There is a host of subsidiary poets available to be conscripted by exponents of the canon if they are keen to diversify. Morrison himself mentions Geoffrey Hill, and is bravely revisionist in his account of Heaney, arguing that in the more recent verse his sympathies are Republican.

Morrison has the merit of providing us with the canon in pure, concentrated form: Larkin, Hughes, Heaney. But he appears somewhat halfhearted in his commitment to it, and it might appear that the critical position it embodies has become decadent, the terminology a codified, rhetorical strategy. If we look at the canon nearer the moment of its inception the difference in tone is striking. In the next section of this essay I show that, while proponents of the canon initially exploited the notion of period much as Morrison does today, they used the notion of contrast

Thrills and Frills

in order to dissociate, to signal protest rather than catholicity. In a similar protestant manner, far from any suggestion of an apostolic succession, it was implied that they were renewing connections with an older tradition disrupted by recent literary events. Donald Davie, for example, who has seen himself as the theorist of that moment of protest (the "Movement", as it was commonly known) wrote about Larkin with committed rhetoric.

> I think that everyone knows, really, that Philip Larkin is the effective laureate of our England. Other poets may criticize what Larkin does with the truths he discovers, what attitudes he takes up to the landscapes and the weather of his own poems; but those landscapes and that weather—none of us, surely, fails to recognize them? And this is just as true if we think of landscapes and weather metaphorically; we recognize in Larkin's poems the seasons of present-day England, but we recognize also the seasons of an English soul—the moods he expresses are our moods too, though we may deal with them differently.[2]

"Everyone", "our England", "our moods": the collective pronouns are powerfully attached; even the question of Larkin's special distinction is placed in terms of a native institution. Davie published these remarks in 1963, when Larkin's reputation still effectively rested on a single book, published in the provinces.

The appeal to Englishness may reinforce values placed on the concrete and specific (and, indeed, Davie goes on to say of a poem by Ted Hughes that its landscape lacks such local definition: it could be England but it might equally be Ireland), but at the same time the argument annexes poetic quality to an exclusive sense of cultural possession. Clearly, the present-day canon, although its values are no less exclusive, is not possessive in quite this way. But to what extent might Davie's praise of Larkin address the qualities of the Movement as a whole? Does Movement poetry in fact elaborate and celebrate the recognition and enjoyment (however wistful) of common cultural property? In the next section of this essay I consider the arguments put into play following the theoretical and polemic initiatives of Robert Conquest's anthology of Movement verse *New Lines* (1956)[3], but it will be as well to preface that discussion with some consideration of the qualities there disclosed by the Movement in its most vigorously codified form.

A recurrent impulse of the poets associated in *New Lines* is to apprehend or, at least, allude to the discrete: this impulse centres both the topics and the mode of discourse of their poetry. The art object or the cultural site (both generally foreign) or the moment of experience (again, often in a remote setting) furnish occasions for the majority of their poems. 'Afternoon in Florence', 'Baie de Anges, Nice' (titles of poems by Elizabeth Jennings and D.J. Enright respectively) exemplify one aspect of this preoccupation with the discrete. The type of occasion for moral-aesthetic reflection found by Davie in 'A Head Painted by Daniel O'Neill' is modified and brought closer to contemporary life (as we might expect) in Philip Larkin's 'Lines on a Young Lady's Photograph Album'. In 'The Minute', by John Holloway, "He scarcely saw the moment when... make one bright / Minute: and then the thing was done." Such discrete occasions are partially seen as potential with expressive discourse; what they might say to the poet is taken up and considered in a poem. But—and this seems inevitable in view of the poets' lack of intimacy with, even estrangement from, whatever it is that provokes them—their own discourse does not readdress the worlds of discourse to which they allude. It does quite the opposite, in fact. Occasions, however necessary that may be to poets, are not felt to be trustworthy. They are not full with a world of realized experience. The components of the moment of realization in Holloway's poem can, without misrepresentation, remain obscured by my ellipsis, for the point is that experience of them was wryly deficient. In Enright's 'The Interpreters', "those critics for whom the outside is a dreadful bore" are condemned, while a reality of surfaces is esteemed, both the grass which covers a "senseless" mess, and the "really" meant.

> Good lord, if a poet really meant what he said,
> we should all be out of a job – why on earth
> would he sing of the merely real? – the papers have taken
>   up that chorus –
> 'the agonies, the strife of human hearts'? – why,
>   Hollywood will do that for us.

But the irony of Enright's "merely real", a reality that is exclusively human, rebounds, surely, from the allusion to Keats, for Enright's reality ("the peasants look at their rotting cabbages, / a gang of clods are building a block of flats") is conscientiously remote and diminished.

In these poems we detect in the poet's authority a relentless determination of poetic discourse and foreclosure of its intended audience. The discourse is emphatically singular in many cases: the first-person pronoun "I" is characteristic, we notice, in Thom Gunn as well as in Larkin; while "we", as uttered by Davie, for example, implies a restricted group, and is far from being generously inclusive. If we include ourselves we do so by self-election. "How dare we now be anything but numb?" concludes his 'Rejoinder to a Critic', a poem of casuistic argument in which Davie figures the effects of "Love" as the radioactive fallout from an atomic bomb burst, and suggests—since love and hate are both "versions of / The 'feeling'" that the critic enjoins—that a modern answer to Donne's question "Who's injured by my love?" would be "Half Japan!" It is hardly possible to feel that "we" here implies a communal injunction, so beset is it by the thickets of feeling conjured up by the critic. Furthermore, numbness is a state of such nullified response that communication might seem out of the question. No, the discourse here is set, typically, towards a few others who can be imagined as sharing the moments of privileged contemplation such poems envisage. "We" is not "us", the English, but rather "you and I", English poets. Donald Davie and John Donne.

It might be supposed that a poetics of objects, sites and moments placed its exponents in the tradition of enfeebled Romanticism, the decadence of conventional poetic emotions; and to a certain extent the poets of the Movement are to be understood in this light. But at the same time they place themselves outside that tradition by earnestly demystifying its conventional occasions, by finding nothing there, nothing below the surface. The profound or sublime are closed options. In 'Near Jakobselv' Robert Conquest is able to contemplate the unfamiliar, alien landscape of an Arctic summer not with horror but in a mood bordering on complacency. Here, as elsewhere, the expressive discourse potential in the occasion is found to reside less in the occasion itself than in its conventional status. This bifurcation—in which ostensible occasions are virtual fictions—is recognized and exploited by Kingsley Amis in 'Here is Where'.

> Here, *where the ragged water*
> *Is twilled and spun over*
> *Pebbles backed like beetles,*
>
> *Bright as beer-bottles,*
> *Bits of it like snow beaten*
> *Or milk boiling in saucepan...*

Going well so far, eh?
But soon, I'm sorry to say,
The here-where recipe
Will have to intrude its *I*…

But this irony, which becomes increasingly emphatic ("Scream the place down *here*, / There's nothing *there*") cannot elude its dependence on the very conventions it rejects. We might attribute this ambivalence to the social origins of the Movement poets (reference to which is made, in passing, in the next section of this essay), suggesting that the cultural institutions around which they sustained their careers were not theirs by birth. Be that as it may, it will be apparent that ambivalence of this sort is likely to be attended by an incongruity between poetic occasion and motive that is fraught with disruptive pressure in need of containment.

It is in these terms, I believe, that the formal characteristics of Movement verse, which Conquest makes prescriptive, are best understood, rather than in a straightforward congruity of form and content. The high regard for regular rhyme and stanza displayed throughout *New Lines* does not engage notions of finish, of the polished object; the poems are not discrete events in the sense that they correspond as such to their discrete occasions. They are discrete, rather, in the way they wrap around their author-subject. Their occasions are for the most part treated with scepticism, and the texts distort and buckle as a consequence of inner tension. Traditional forms are invoked not so much for the freedom they can confer as for support. They define the space in which the self can act with poetic authority, while at the same time, in the absence of assurances provided by conventionally felt poetic experience, they secure the status of the text.

From our retrospective point of view our questions concern not only how best to read Movement verse but also how to explain its success in determining and underwriting the emerging canon. Within the constraints operating in Movement verse we would expect to find that individual poets wrote with different degrees of flexibility and inclusiveness. I would suggest that Larkin exploited Movement ambivalence most fully, and was thus best able to retain the terms and formal procedures of its discourse without exhibiting them as limits. Davie's remarks, I think, implicitly recognized this, although I might put the point another way, and say that Larkin's objects, sites and moments are English and thus intimately his.

To summarize the argument so far, I might say that the present-day canon has its roots in the Movement. But if Blake Morrison were to owe anything to Donald Davie, say, his position nevertheless exhibits a falling away from the rectitude and seriousness of Davie. Yet, were I to mount a dispute, across almost two decades, between two such opponents—in the knowledge, for example, that Davie's praise of Larkin involves some rather damaging remarks about Hughes—it would amount, I fear, to no more than an internal, sectional difference. Both are positioned, in relation to what they admire, towards the same mode of poetic discourse: a necessary response to actual pressures at one time, no doubt, but now very much a preferred manner.

The Movement as controversial nexus

We no longer see the Movement as a pressure group or a publicity stunt; it has acquired historical status. Blake Morrison has published a useful survey (*The Movement: English Poetry and Fiction of the 1950s*, 1980) which offers a representative account of the literature of the decade. His treatment of the Movement falls in line with frequent claims that the term itself is a misnomer—that there was no membership, no push or direction, no common programme or general agreement on principles. All this is quite helpful, even if it stands in the way of any reconstruction of Movement networks and tactics we might wish to make, for if no Movement as such can be said to have existed, and we can only approximate the typical features of its poetry and not judge individual departures from a standard, the way is open to seeing the work of a particular poet as typifying the poetry we think of, however vaguely, as being Movement. Many signs point to Philip Larkin as an appropriate choice: not only does he figure largely in much Movement documentation; his writing confirms and clarifies much of its polemic. In other circumstances I might not treat the Movement and Larkin as in some sense commutative, but here my concern is with the extent to which the Movement's self-definition was set strategically against the poetry of the previous decade, and the concurrence of this Movement disposition with polemics otherwise directed against the Movement. Larkin's career, with its early, rejected affiliations with the rhetoric of forties poetry, is exemplary in the way it incorporates and stabilizes such antagonisms.

It is not necessary to go into circumstantial detail here—the series of pamphlets published out of Oxford by the Fantasy Press, the role of the

Spectator. Morrison documents it all fully. But it will be useful to remind ourselves of his account of the Movement's ideological characteristics: the Low Church and middle-class origins; the concern with classlessness and upward social mobility; the hostility to the "posh" and the "phoney", and the nostalgia for traditional order; the connection with provincial universities. All these bespeak a high degree of social rootlessness, and a complementary degree of personal isolation and self-dependence. They also imply a social matrix largely made up of males. Certainly, the Movement provoked a number of squeamish reactions to what was felt as its posture of tough and aggressive philistinism. More forcefully, it was also argued against the Movement that the refusal of ideas, the empirical derivation of poetry from exclusively personal experience, made for a socially conservative poetry, uncommitted and without dedication.

But if Larkin provides a standard for Movement poetry, and inaugurates the canon of post-war English poetry, it is in Robert Conquest's propaganda that Movement positions are generalized and made exclusive. The Movement effectively demonstrated its existence to the general reader in 1956 with Conquest's anthology *New Lines*. It was reprinted within months, and again the following year. It was sharply attacked by Charles Tomlinson in a 1957 review article in *Essays in Criticism*,[4] and provoked a counter-anthology of "poets unafraid of sensitivity and sentiment", *Mavericks*, edited by Howard Sergeant and Dannie Abse (1957),[5] intended to demonstrate that the Movement did not have a monopoly in poets born after 1920. (Typical "mavericks" were Jon Silkin and W. Price Turner.) A. Alvarez's anthology *The New Poetry* (1962; revised in 1966 and still in print)[6] engaged the Movement from a rather more up-to-date position but included five of Conquest's nine poets. Conquest brought out a revised and updated *New Lines II* (1963),[7] with many more poets, to produce an even greater overlap between *New Lines* and *The New Poetry*. Both include Ted Hughes, Alvarez's strongest anti-Movement contender. It has been argued that *New Lines* appeared after the Movement had shot its bolt, and that it should not be taken as definitive—both nice points which I would not try to dispute. Conquest claimed considerable achievement already for the poets in his first anthology, while noting that several of them had yet to publish substantial collections of their work. By any accounts *New Lines* was able to reach a considerable and new audience, and most of the poets went on to establish careers for themselves, if they had not done so already.

What we see in the sequence of response and reaction following the publication of *New Lines* is not, needless to say, the internecine feuding of small, conspiratorial groups of poets, let alone the successful dominance of a single group (the event feared by the editors of *Mavericks*). It is something much more like the establishment of a new kind of literary professionalism, utilizing the cultural prestige of poetry to diversify into new markets—universities, the media, the secondary education syllabus—in a manner already established in the USA, with the poet playing the role of cultural entrepreneur. As in any boom (the professionalism I describe was more a feature of the sixties than of the fifties, of course) such an economy rolled forward under its own momentum, and Movement poets, unless they were especially recalcitrant, found themselves merged with their successors. Davie's 1963 remarks about Larkin, or his 1962 polemic dialogue with Alvarez in *The Review*,[8] in which he advocates the moral and aesthetic resistance of objects (very much with Tomlinson's poetry in mind) against Alvarez's insistent personalizing of experience, can be seen as attempts to resist such dispersals of poetic energy.

Because he served as the major publicist of the Movement, although declining to invoke the authority of its unofficial name, Conquest's Introductions to his two anthologies are of special interest. He may vulgarize ideas put forward by Davie in his occult role of theorist in *Purity of Diction in English Verse* and *Articulate Energy*,[9] he may not have a very generous appreciation of the poets he brought together (distinguishing Amis and Wain by name, say, rather than Davie and Larkin), but he provides the Movement with an immediate and polemic frame of reference by asserting its newness, and in doing so initiates the present-day canon attributed to finely made judgement. In 1956 Conquest starts from the journalistic proposition (somewhat disingenuous in hindsight) that each decade has its characteristic poetry, and stakes a claim to the fifties, asserting of *New Lines* that it represents "a general tendency… a genuine and healthy poetry of the period". But he claims more than this: not only is *New Lines* contemporary; fifties poetry, as represented by *New Lines*, is better than the poetry of the previous decade. In addition, as "healthy" might have warned us, even more is at stake. Uncovering the pathology of the forties in terms of its "images of sex and violence", Conquest remarks that to "combat this trend was not a purely artistic task". How the task was conceived, whether in moral or political terms, will emerge later. What Conquest goes on immediately to say, however, suggests that his quarrel is not just with the poetry of the forties but with most of twentieth-century writing: "When a condition of this sort takes hold it sometimes lasts for decades. The writers remembered later are odd eccentrics—the Kiplings and Hardys." Announcing "a general tendency, perhaps of lesser talents", rather than a collection of individual eccentrics, Conquest is implicitly claiming that the Movement, the poetry of the fifties, represents a return to literary standards inscribed in social normality.

Conquest sets the poetry of the fifties in reaction to that of the forties through a series of binary contrasts: empiricism versus theory, intellect versus feeling. The forties poets gave the id too much of a say in things; they attempted to delete everything from their writing except emotion and submitted to the "debilitating theory that poetry *must* be metaphorical". Even more than "technical and emotional gifts", poets must have "integrity and judgement enough to prevent surrender to subjective moods or social pressures". What distinguishes fifties poetry is that it "submits to no great systems of theoretical constructs nor agglomerations of unconscious commands. It is free from both mystical and logical compulsions and—like modern philosophy—is empirical in its attitude to all that comes." Reference is also made to "reverence for the real person or event" and "refusal to abandon a rational structure and comprehensible language". None of this is argued through; positions are affirmed as though their truth were self-evident. We might consider that any view of "social pressures" that presents them in an invariably negative light is likely itself to have developed in response to social compulsions, and that corollary notions of integrity and the person will equally have unconscious social derivation. The proclaimed affinity with "modern philosophy" (a rare instance of Conquest's claims to representative status involving reference to contemporary non-literary concerns) does little more than seek prestige for uncommitted attitudes. The reference to rational structure, on the other hand, seems to echo the ideas of the American critic Yvor Winters (whose Thomist logic we might expect Conquest to disdain) to which Davie had responded with enthusiasm in the late forties.

It need not concern us much that Conquest's arguments in 1956 were incoherent and question-begging; what matters is that he codified a successfully assertive group position based on exclusion and prejudice. His arguments in the introduction to *New Lines II* show how the needs of the situation had changed. "The influences making for distortion in poetry are now different from what they were seven years ago." It was no longer necessary to take up a position against the previous decade, nor to claim attention as representative of the moment. (It was, after all, no longer the fifties, and part of Conquest's intention now was to forestall new claimants.) In retrospect, Conquest argues, the importance of *New Lines* was not topicality but rather its demonstration that "as against the work of the past few decades, a good deal of contemporary poetry had returned to the cardinal traditions of English verse". Conquest's rejection of the modern tradition is now explicit. The authentic English tradition is still vulnerable, however, for "a great deal is still being written which affects to be founded on new, or at least different, attitudes".

This disclosure of position, while it confirms what was implicit in the Movement's beginnings, also serves to underline divergences within it at a point where poetry and criticism peel away from one another. The point might be put thus: when the Movement lost whatever poetic integrity it initially possessed, its polemic apparatus was detached and naturalized as critical commonplace—that the modern movement was over, the need for experiment no longer existed. (In his conversation with Alvarez, on the other hand, Davie could remark, referring to Pound, Eliot and Yeats, "Let's go back, then, to them, and go forward from there.") Conquest does not pause to define his tradition but says that it has fallen into decline from time to time through the impositions of critical fashions. What he objects to are pretensions to extend the range of that constant tradition, and the concomitant esteem of novelty, as he sees it; the poet's relationship with tradition is normally unselfconscious. Such arguments allow Conquest to generalize the authority of *New Lines*; it is more appropriate, now, not to appear embattled, but to lay claim to as much as possible.

His polemic in 1963 is directed primarily at arguments put forward by Alvarez in his Introduction to *The New Poetry*, and the dispute is no longer between generations (within the perspective of history) but internal (within "the traditions of English verse"). Conquest reinforces this internalization both by taking pains not to identify his adversary and by presenting his adversary's position as that of a critic (i.e. wilfully modish) rather than an anthologist. Alvarez's arguments thus appear as those of a depraved taste and its prescriptive criticism—as another example of that systematic criticism which pretends to make its judgements "derive rigorously from the nature of the poem discussed". (Judgement, in other words, derives from the critics, and we judge of critics by their taste.) What Conquest objects to is the demand for powerful feeling at the expense of "balance and proportion", suggestions that "the circumstances of modern life…open up hitherto unsuspected psychological depths", and the recommendation of European and American poets as models for English poetry. Against these, Conquest argues that

> the human condition from which the poetry of one country springs cannot be readily tapped by that of another. The British

culture is receptive to immigration, if not to invasion: but it remains highly idiosyncratic. It is part of our experience, and for that no one else's experience, however desirable, can be a substitute.

The adaptability of Conquest's polemic was its great strength; the care not to identify too precisely what was argued against, and to make it instead a projection of the case in hand, pre-empted many possibilities of disagreement. The assertion of an unspecified, native tradition underpinned claims to be authoritative and inclusive, so that the most disabling argument against Alvarez was not that he sanctioned bad poets but that he might corrupt or mislead good ones. To disagree successfully with Conquest—to forestall, that is to say, the possibility of any disagreement being reconciled and generalized by the inclusiveness of the terms in which he argued—would have entailed taking issue with his version of history. Any disagreement about "modernism", for example, would remain a matter of recuperable detail if it failed to challenge his view of tradition. Yet this polemic strategy, so absorptively coercive, was so little substantiated in detail that its pretensions seem hardly to have commanded notice. On the other hand, both Tomlinson and Alvarez were ready, with Conquest, to write off the poetry of the forties as "vicious" (Tomlinson), "English poetry... at its nadir" (Alvarez).

The differences between Tomlinson's and Alvarez's opposition to *New Lines* are worth attention; neither of them, however, denies its coherence (as, in a sense, the editors of *Mavericks* did by challenging its claim to be representative). Furthermore, the particular qualities they object to—for Tomlinson its "suburban mental ratio", for Alvarez its "gentility"—are roughly identical. But although this pinpoints something about Movement poetry in general there is no broader agreement between them. They do not share a point of view. Tomlinson considers the "myth" surrounding the Movement poets, that they represent the average man and write for a middlebrow public, but concludes instead that they are making for themselves "another cosy corner... in our watered down, democratic culture", and that they thus hardly differ from the forties poets (he instances Tambimuttu's editorial line in *Poetry London*) who propounded an artistic democracy of the unconscious. He objects to the Movement's parochialism, failure of nerve, and merely negative virtues, and deplores the lack of "high and objective criteria" that allows *New Lines* to be taken for "a significant literary fact". This lack of objectivity, in self-awareness as much as in critical standards, is Tomlinson's main concern, the key to all

Thrills and Frills

the Movement's deficiencies. The poets in *New Lines* "show a singular want of vital awareness of the continuum outside themselves, of the mystery bodied over against them in the created universe".

Regard for the presence of the object, in Tomlinson's own poetry, was the issue which prevented Davie and Alvarez reaching agreement in their 1962 conversation. What Tomlinson objects to as the imposition of a poet's "mental conceit of himself" (their "suburban mental ratio" in the case of the *New Lines* poets) on "that which is beyond itself" might be seen, moreover, as the very thing argued for by Alvarez in *The New Poetry*, with the difference only that risk and extremity are the "mental conceits" preferred to gentility. Alvarez's hope for poetry, a combination of the "psychological integrity and insight" of D.H. Lawrence and the "technical skill and formal intelligence" of T.S. Eliot, need not detain us; nor need the inconsistency of his explanation of the failure of the experimentalism of "Eliot and the rest" to "take on" in England—both because it had been "an essentially American concern" and because of the operation of a series of "negative feedbacks". (By this he means, I think, that English poets reacted against experimentalism, although to say this doesn't tell us why they did so.) Alvarez, with some circumspection, can justify experimentalism when it is able to "open poetry up to new areas of experience", but the distinction implied between this and unjustified experiment is not explored. (As usual, we wonder why such distinctions need not apply to writing in conventional forms.) His argument is that "negative feedbacks" (which presumably have kept English poetry closed to those "new areas of experience") can be short-circuited without having to go back to Eliot: American poetry in the forties, unlike English poetry, had assimilated the experiments of the twenties, and this new poetic generation, represented at its best by John Berryman and Robert Lowell, exemplifies a "new seriousness" English poetry sorely needs. The revised edition of *The New Poetry* (1966) added Anne Sexton and Sylvia Plath to Alvarez's model of the American vanguard. (It is worth noting, while American influences on English poetry are in question, that Alvarez had no truck with many American poets who emerged in the fifties. Charles Olson, Robert Duncan, Robert Creeley and Edward Dorn, for example, heirs to the practices of Ezra Pound and William Carlos Williams, were noticed with interest by Tomlinson and Davie, among others, although generally disdained by English critical opinion.)

Alvarez's argument may depend on the notion of new experience, but he is not setting up as an advocate of experiment; nor need he, since although English poetry has not assimilated the experiments of "Eliot and the rest" American poetry has. In an important sense, therefore, his disagreement with the Movement is less radical than Tomlinson's. Tomlinson does not employ any such crude notion as "the experimental", but he goes beyond rejection of the personal and social values implicit in Movement poetry and argues that a willed or manipulated self-image (a failure of objectivity) impedes the realization of a work of art. Alvarez, on the other hand, objects to the inadequacy of the self-image of the English poet ("the post-war Welfare State Englishman") rather than its aesthetic consequences. Gentility, he argues, the "belief that life is always more or less orderly", is "a stance which is becoming increasingly precarious to maintain" in the face of "the more uncompromising forces of our time", "forces of disintegration which destroy the old standards of civilization". Alvarez, pointing to the scale of twentieth-century evils, concentration camps, genocide, the threat of nuclear war, looks back as far as the mass slaughter in trench warfare of the First World War. This might strike us as powerfully persuasive evidence were it in fact the "new experience" he had in mind. What Alvarez is in fact impressed by are parallels between modern experience of these evils and perceptions derived from psychoanalysis, and "our recognition of the ways in which the same forces are at work within us". The forces of disintegration, that is to say, are not social, political or economic, but psychological; but what this psychological insight is made to require of poetry is that it treat of all events as projections of the poet's psyche. "Dominant public savagery", "the full range of his experience"—the import of such phrases reduces to the statement that "the writer can no longer deny with any assurance the fears and desires he does not wish to face".

Alvarez's espousal of what is commonly termed "confessional" poetry, his advocacy of personal risk and extremity, even suicide, are notorious but consistent with his argument that psychoanalysis constitutes an unavoidable new area of experience for poetry. His praise of Robert Lowell, particularly the Lowell of *Life Studies*, is understandable, for Lowell is pre-eminently a poet in whom the confusions and violence of the age (these are question-begging notions, of course) are figured out in terms of his own disturbance. But, leaving aside any misgivings this may provoke— for example, that in such poetry the poet takes rather too much (of our experience, say) upon himself or herself—Alvarez's special pleading should not obscure the fact that he shares a broad agreement with Conquest about the proper mode of discourse of poetry. The agreement is so fundamental, in fact, as to be in danger of passing beneath notice. Both Movement and "confessional" poetry share a discourse which operates through the personal lyric, often dramatic in its presentation, and employs an elaborate figurative language to draw together the self and its objects. The site of Conquest's disagreement with Alvarez, therefore, suggests that his "English tradition" is concerned less with any maintenance of traditional poetic decorum than with an ideological preference among self-images.

When Alvarez contrasts Larkin's 'At Grass' and Hughes' 'A Dream of Horses', in order to consider the "kind of success" different styles allow, the distinctions he discovers are less convincing if we pause to consider the similarities between the two poems. Both are surfeited with extended figurative devices which tie the things referred to—horses, in each case— to the speakers of the poems: in Larkin's poem the speaker is an implied observer whose presence is reinforced by interjected qualifications and reservations, "perhaps", "what must be"; in Hughes' poem the speakers are a chorus of stable lads. In both poems the horses are allegorized by the speakers' double view of them: in Larkin's poem racehorses retired to grass are seen against after-images of their fame and glory on the course; in Hughes's poem the speakers dream of powerful, overwhelming horses unlike the pitiful hacks they mind. Both poems are allegories of an absent fullness of being, although Larkin, as we might expect, is the more ambivalent in his treatment of this conventional theme. His devices undercut the glories associated with the race meeting, and imply that the horses, although approaching the end of life, have more authenticity in their anonymous retirement than in any role they played in racing and its annals. Hughes, by contrast, uses his devices for emphasis and amplification, in a way that deflects the suggestion (rather commonplace, nevertheless) the poem might be making that the grooms' relations to their charges are inverted in dream. Alvarez's conclusion that Hughes's horses, unlike Larkin's, "have a violent, impending presence" may indicate a preference but is not very much to the point. What presence there is in Hughes's poem is a presence of dream images. But this is a minor issue. Both poems, as allegories, ask to be read not for their presentational immediacy but for what they say about life. What differentiates the poems is their approach to the nostalgia of diminished being (and here, possibly, remarks about suburban mental ratios and Welfare State Englishmen have some bearing). Larkin suggests that although we may experience such feelings we should not allow ourselves to be too affected by them, whereas Hughes, I take it, suggests that we can imagine or dream ourselves out of them. Neither poet questions the sources or conditions of such feelings, but takes them for granted. Arguably, however, the personal lyric is not a mode conducive to asking such questions; nostalgia is, so to speak, fully naturalized within the mode, and irony the only restraint able to be applied against it.

Twenty years after Davie's recognition of Larkin's effective custody of "our England" as poetic subject-matter, Larkin is being seriously canvassed as the next poet laureate. The only cynicism such views admit is the suggestion that the laureate's official duties are now excused. Davie's bestowal of laurels was, by comparison, tongue-in-cheek and mildly subversive. He was not looking for official recognition of England's most distinguished poet. It cannot be disputed, surely, that this is how Larkin is perceived today—not only distinguished but quintessentially English, insular almost, and not easily appreciated by American readers. His common sense has moved from being that of the common man, as Alvarez recognised it, to that of the political Right. He puts pretentiousness and the second-rate in their place. But these are no more than the terms in which his general esteem has been negotiated. (What strikes me most in Larkin's poetry is a torpid apprehensiveness about death in the living moment, and a refusal of any compensations for this; it's a moving but idiosyncratic affective conformation.) His recognition of "our England", polluted rivers, cheap consumer goods, and relics of spiritual and national grandeur, is uniformly marked by regret. He is far from being a documentarist, however. Instead, his poems seek to reinsert the values of which they collect the residual signs within the unconscious lives of ordinary people. It is as though, if the landscape and institutions of post-war England are the dumb reminders of a better past, that past at least lives on in its people, latent but unexpressed.

The lyric self cannot stand for either term of this transaction, though it can to an extent collude with both. In 'Church Going', for example, Larkin's speaker aligns himself ("Bored, uninformed") with those for whom a sacred edifice can have little meaning, and a secular wit plays ironically over his account of a sight-seeing visit: "Hatless, I take off / My cycle-clips in awkward reverence". But, for all the ignorance he claims, this visitor displays in passing some knowledge of church fitments—font, lectern, plate and pyx. Such ambivalence disturbs much of the language of the poem, which runs a gamut of plainness, sarcasm and portentousness, so that we are uneasily aware of the incomplete adjustment of the poet's intentions and the serviceability of his persona; at best we might feel "his" wit is a form of discomfort. The poem appears to intend an optimistic assertion of spiritual persistence, "someone will forever be surprising / A hunger in himself to be more serious", but what that seriousness might mean, what it is that is never "obsolete", is expressed in a frigid mixture of abstractions: "all our compulsions meet, / Are recognized, and robed as destinies." Compulsion may turn into destiny, the profane become sacred, but the process seems to be automatic, dispensation perhaps rather than discipline. The poem does well to end, on an altogether less transcendent note, affirming the secular, graveyard wisdom that everyone must die.

'Church Going' uses comparatively little figurative language and instead adjusts its tone to expository shifts of feeling. Although it is an established anthology piece, and did much to get Larkin noticed, it is not really typical of his work in its discursive procedures. What is typical (and, as I argue, is typical in one way or another of what is perceived as the canonical poetry of the period) is what we saw in 'At Grass', the use of verbal figures as devices to readjust the observer's position towards the objective relations perceived. (This is the same type of substitutive device, but more extendable and controllable, as the grammatical figure "Hatless, I take off my cycle-clips", and like that, too, as often as not produces an effect of aloof wittiness.) In 'The Whitsun Weddings', another anthology piece, the mode is fully developed. The poem details events on a train journey from the provinces to London, and this synoptic trajectory might be considered as an emblem of the poem's theme; we see the commonplace view from the carriage window but also, exceptionally, a series of departing honeymoon couples seen off at successive stations by their wedding guests. It is all unremittingly "our England", with a sense of hallucination in the heat and sun, and the people are generalized through grotesque detail which is always on the verge of registering distaste. But the poem's figures, starting with those which present the passage of the train through the landscape, emphasize meeting and incorporation; the people observed may be coarse and vulgar but they are included within a greater figure than themselves, marriage is still ritual and sacrament despite its secular trappings.

But only the poet sees this (in this poem we hardly feel it necessary to observe a formal distinction between poet and speaker), and he sees it not only as observed event but also as complex simile ("I thought of London spread out in the sun, / Its postal districts packed like squares of wheat") replete with connotations of sexual surrender and fecundity, dispersal and unity ("spread", "packed"), the whole and the part. (Yet what exactly are "squares of wheat"? Fields? Not English fields, surely? Grains? Breakfast cereal?) Like 'Church Going', 'The Whitsun Weddings' is expository, yet in this case the different stages of the poem are drawn together by the consistency of the figures. Furthermore, the figures accomplish the poet's participation in what is observed. But at the same time we might feel that his participation is also imposition, a projection in the face of alternatives too appalling to contemplate ("An uncle shouting smut; and then the perms, / The nylon gloves and jewellery-substitutes"). Moreover, we might also feel that just as the description of the ordinary, secular life of these people is selective (and admonitory), so the redemptive figures are somewhat worked up, fanciful rather than felt. In the television programme 'Philip Larkin at 60' (*The South Bank Show*, ITV, 30 May 1982) Larkin, appearing only as cuffs and hands, took the viewer through his notebooks to show how, searching for an expression of "fruitfulness", he arrived at "packed like squares" from "spread like fields" via "packed like fields". Not that there is anything necessarily wrong with such a derivation; it merely goes to show how Larkin's plainness conceals a studied indirectness. But this example also confirms the way the creative energy of the personal lyric is focused in its invention of figures; and the energy of the figures, the rewriting of the world as it is, is made to guarantee the authenticity of the person, the subject. But such guarantees hold good only for the subject, not for his experience; we are asked to trust the poet, not the poem.

Beyond controversy

Since 1945 the major poetic controversies, through which current poetic concerns have received their most effective public exposure, occurred within the decade bracketed by the publication of the first *New Lines* anthology and the revised edition of *The New Poetry*. By and large our sense of the situation of poetry today is conditioned by the arguments of 1956-66. The extent to which those arguments still determine our sense of poetic achievement since the war underscores the suggestion that, for all the differences and disagreements implied by those arguments, certain basic, undeclared—even unrecognized—agreements bound the controversialists together. Positions taken up on behalf of the Movement had the power and flexibility to absorb and merge with those of its successors; the non-partisan, individualist strategies of Movement poets enabled them, when the time came, to transcend their collective moment in the mid-fifties. (Donald Davie, apparently, suggested "Divergent Lines" as an apt title for the representatives of the old guard in *New Lines II*.) *The New Poetry*, once it is conceded that the qualities of the American models it advocated were not reflected in the work of its English poets, is *New Lines* thinned and agitated.

It is surely worthy of consideration—to set against the notions of variety and pluralism and vital difference which controversy might seem to substantiate, of different poetic discourses pursuing different goals—that our three canonical poets, Larkin, Hughes and Heaney, share the same publisher, are apparently thought to possess similar market potential, and imply the same sort of readership. If we accept unreservedly the proposition that they are our best poets, if perhaps we feel it appropriate that Faber and Faber, with their prestigious backlist including Eliot and Auden, should dominate the poetry market, then what notions of continuity and pure quality are we dealing with? Might we not find, in view of the resolution and incorporation of the controversialists' differences within our current view of the period, that their unreflected agreement that the poetry of the forties was an unmitigated disaster is also not to be taken at face value? Should we not question the notion of a homogeneous "poetry of the forties", and might we not also suppose that such a myth possessed advantages for its promulgators? Yet from what position, in relation to any view of what is canonical, can we begin to ask such questions? What is the evidence to consider? At this point I do no more than propose a few materials as a start to answering such questions.

The two most important events of the forties were the war and the Labour government which administered the return to peacetime conditions. As far as publishing was concerned, both books and periodicals, it seems correct to see both these events as largely similar in their effects: the war encouraged an audience for the arts, and publishers, despite economy measures, were able to carry on their business. On the face of it there was a boom in literary publishing, of poetry especially, which benefited not only established firms such as Faber and Faber but also smaller, speculative enterprises such as the Fortune Press and the Grey Walls Press. There was a rash of magazines, anthologies and annuals. Post-war austerity seems to have perpetuated the conditions in which this sort of publishing flourished, whereas the relaxation of austerity (the availability of consumer goods and the new patterns of spending that ensued) seems to have reduced the market for poetry, even while publishing in general expanded. Within a comparatively short period of time a number of small literary publishers and magazines either went out of business or found themselves forced to operate on a considerably reduced scale: Grey Walls Press, Falcon Press, *Poetry London*, *Poetry Quarterly*. The mass-market *Penguin New Writing* folded. It was reported that Routledge could not continue Geoffrey Grigson's book-format periodical *The Mint* because they overestimated sales by thousands. Depression in the poetry market seems to have lasted into the mid-fifties: Conquest makes the point, in *New Lines*, that less poetry was published than formerly, and that contributors to the anthology had, for the most part, published only in pamphlet format with small presses. But if this reminds us, parenthetically, that the Movement was an attempt to win recognition for new writers, it was an attempt upon virtually abandoned territory. Many poets who began their careers in the forties had found themselves without publishers in the fifties.

For other reasons, too, the Movement's ambitions met with little resistance. Many poets of the previous generation had stopped writing, or had put their literary careers on ice (while establishing themselves in new post-war jobs, for example), or were in the process of remaking their style. In the latter category we might mention Roy Fuller (although the changes are less drastic than is sometimes suggested), Norman MacCaig or, rather later, W.S. Graham. In the former categories, not always possible to distinguish exactly, we might think of Charles Madge, Kenneth Allott, F.T. Prince, Nicholas Moore, David Gascoyne and J.F. Hendry. (An even earlier generation, that of Spender and MacNeice, was able to maintain its impetus. Arguably, it was sufficiently well established to receive little effect from the war or its aftermath.) The most prestigious career to terminate, however, in the way that seemed to mark the end of an era, was that of Dylan Thomas. The Movement, of course, held Thomas in particular disrepute, and gave the impression that it thought his premature death a deserved consequence of lifestyle and poetic style combined. He and his "followers" (a somewhat mythical company of scapegoats), and the mindless romanticism for which it was held they stood, were made to bear the burden of responsibility for the low standards of poetry in the forties. Leaving such judgements to one side for a moment, it is worth noting that whereas Movement poets often reflect their times in more or less direct ways—in their individualist concept of the "ordinary" man, for example, or their tentative recognition of consumers' pleasures—and repudiated any connections they may have had with the poetry of the forties, the poets of the forties were, for the most part, poets of the late thirties in the first instance, and responded to the war not in an empirical fashion, as though it were some unprecedented novelty, but as the fulfilment of their worst fears and predictions. Many of these poets, albeit in rather an obscure way, saw the transition to peace as requiring a search for solutions to the same set of problems for which the war had failed to provide a solution.

According to such a logic, while 1945 may be a date of the first order in our social and political life, it may not serve us as well when we try to reconstruct a context for poetry. But, equally, we may find no other date which serves us better. If we think in terms of generations, however, it is possible to argue that poets born after 1920 (the threshold adopted for *New Lines*) were able to repudiate their war experience, that having had their careers delayed by wartime conditions they set out to make up for lost time. Donald Davie says as much for himself in his recollections *These the Companions* (1982).[10] Poets born after 1908, on the other hand, but before 1920, would tend to stand in a very different relation to the war. (And in many cases their regular careers were postponed not only by wartime but by pre-war conditions.) The post-1920 generation would all, in one important respect, begin as survivors. The poets of the earlier generation, on the other hand, would have experienced war in part as a threat to survival, in part also as a prolongation and culmination of their pre-war experience. If, briefly, we can imagine Roy Fuller and Donald Davie as mess-mates (naval service took Fuller to East Africa and Davie to Russia), then we might see how, although empirically their wartime experience would be similar, their respective stances towards it must have been different in ways having little to do with personality.

But this in itself would not explain why the generation of 1908 had such a poor hold on the post-war poetic world. Indeed, to all appearances that generation flourished in the late forties. It was extensively documented, for example, in the USA by Kenneth Rexroth in his 1949 anthology *The New British Poets*,[11] but yet significantly this remarkable anthology was not brought out in an English edition. If we wished to make a representation of the diminishing presence of this generation of poets, its rapid acceleration towards vanishing-point in the fifties (ignoring, that is to say, the re-emergence of some of its members in the late sixties, at a time when other poets of an even earlier generation were breaking silence), we might note the rapid eclipse of Dylan Thomas's reputation after his death, and the publication of probably the last collection of forties poetry, in the "bad" sense, W.S. Graham's *The Nightfishing* (1955). In the same year Philip Larkin's *The Less Received* was published by the Marvell Press in Hull, and further impressions were very quickly called for. Graham, by then, must have seemed to Larkin's readers very much a back number. It would appear that in 1955 vested interests in the publishing of poetry no longer addressed the most promising market. We should bear in mind, also, the charges made by Tomlinson, that *New Lines* was the culmination of a sustained publicity campaign, and consisted only of OK names. If the Movement took issue with what it conceived of as the "London literary racket", then perhaps we should see the Movement as, in turn, not only an academic literary racket but also the creator of a new audience for poetry, in schools and colleges and among teachers of English.

When we look at the poetry of the forties we find that the collective and interlocutory manner of address which we associate with Auden, and the phrase-making habit, are strongly persistent. We might feel that these are modes of candour and generosity, but equally we might note that neither the mode nor the associated quality of feeling is characteristic of Movement poetry. If we consider Roy Fuller as an example of such persistence, we might also note that his attempts to detach himself from his pre-war politics (Marxist) and aesthetics (mildly surreal), and to establish his themes as those of the poet as private citizen, although they direct much of his subsequent career, remain liable to the pull of contrary experience and of an imagination that cannot wilfully forgo its past. His best poems are those in which such conflicts are played out. In '1948', for example, (*Epitaphs and Occasions*, 1949) panic overtakes the poet while he reads in his garden.

> I hear behind the words
> And noise of birds
> The drumming aircraft; and am blind till they have gone.

But although his panic subsides ("blind till they are gone") the poet goes beyond the personal occasion of the poem to consider our tenure on peace ("behind" is exact and anticipatory in its perceptual and moral ambiguity).

> It is as though the lease
> Of crumbling peace
> Had run already and that life was as before.[12]

But this is not the kind of forties poetry so powerfully objected to in the fifties and sixties. It may be irresolute, and it may end with a trope ("The gnawed incredible existence of a dream") which seems persuasively to refer to normality as a dream from which we will be woken, but it is civil and decorous none the less.

When Robert Conquest deplored "the theory that poetry *must* be metaphorical" he was being caustic, but not using his terms with any exactitude. (Larkin and Hughes, as we have seen, rely on figurative devices, on metaphor and simile.) What Conquest was gesturing towards, I think, was the extensive use in forties poetry of images and symbols, and we can best understand his objections to such procedures in the light of his claimed empiricism. Dylan Thomas' images, and the connections he establishes between them, cannot be empirically verified by appeal to a world independent of the poem—independent in theory, though sanctioned in practice by the poet's warrant that it is that real world, shared (but at a distance) with the reader, to which the poem refers. Such verification requirements, which lie behind objections to Thomas' poems, do more than assume the incompatibility of language and reality; they require that poetry observe the prevailing contractual usages in language and hence that it be bound by the common-sense meanings of the times. (Alvarez's arguments, for all their radical posture, failed to address themselves to the preconditions of poetic meaning, which involve the position of discourse within language. Any language use, even the most unconsidered or apparently nonsensical, entails some immediate seizure of reality.) Hughes' 'A Dream of Horses' observes a clear-cut distinction between real world and dream world; we may move between one and the other, as we wake or sleep, but we know which is which. (Such knowledge, of course, is not operative in both worlds and implies a confident demarcation of reality.) In Fuller's '1948' the distinction, for him and for us, is more in doubt. Thomas, on the other hand, insisted that his poems should be read literally; to take him at his word would be to commit a serious assault upon the empirical sanctions of meaning.

The collective and interlocutory manner, as I have called it, does not assume the need for empirical verification; it looks no further than the experience and expectations of the group implied or addressed. Hence the power of phrase-making, the group acting as the poet's resonating board; hence, also, the tendency to semantic drift, commonly noticed in Auden's pre-war poetry, for example. But if we see this manner as a compromised attempt to restore to poetry a social reference without, at the same time, reintroducing the authority of the poet's subjectivity, as I believe we must, we can see other attempts to redefine the subject matter of poetry which go further in their displacement of the discursive centrality of the self. It is in this light that we should approach the work of the poets associated with the "New Apocalypse", the poets most typically associated with the vices of the forties. The term "Apocalyptic", broadly used to refer to the poets influenced by Thomas, now has exclusively pejorative overtones. I will not begin to describe the Apocalypse as a movement, but it is important to note in passing that it emerged in anticipation of the outbreak of war, and that the poets most closely involved with its publications and responsible for its programme (in so far as their critical writings can be said to constitute a programme)—J.F. Hendry, for example—tend to deny Thomas' influence. Instead it makes more sense, for the time being, to think of the Apocalypse in terms of a style and its practitioners, bearing in mind Conquest's objections to what he thought of as metaphor. The mode is lyric, but treats the person as a site in which experience is to be acted out as conflict. It presents a dense, often violent rhetoric, from which the guiding and controlling presence of a speaking subject—constructing the poem's framework of interpretation around its personal authority, and furnishing its empirical experience as the horizon of the poem's range of reference—is excluded. The self (the subject, the poet) does not stand at the centre of and mediate the reader's experience of the poem. That which, in grammatical relationships, is consigned to the role of the predicated, defined and subordinate, is afforded scope for its own resistance and counter-action. We might think of this as occurring in the space vacated by the figures of conventional rhetoric. (Hence, I believe, some of our experience of difficulty and obscurity when we read such poetry.) This theory does not, needless to say, suggest that such poems have written themselves, that they have no human author, but rather that the poet does not constitute at one and the same time the poem's protagonist and boundary. No surrogate enactment of the poet's intelligence is provided as part of the poem's interior, and instead the poem claims to represent the whole person. Through such a mode the things referred to in the poem participate actively in what is imagined, they are not merely figurative devices, and the poet is acted upon as well as acting—an experiencing creature rather than a mastering intelligence.

In this passage from *The Nightfishing*, for example (chosen because it is a late example and because Graham stood somewhat on the fringe of the Apocalyptic movement, and thus illustrates the diffusion of the manner), sea, fishing boat and fisherman exist in a relation one to another of active resistance.

> See how, like an early self, it's loath to leave
> And stares from the scuppers as it swirls away
> To be clenched up. What a great width stretches
> Farsighted away fighting in its white straits
> On either bow, but bears up our boat on all
> Its plaiting strands. This wedge driven in

To the twisting water, we rode. The bow shores
The long rollers.[13]

These relations are not simply observed, they impinge upon and constitute themselves through the writing. So there are moral as well as formal issues in question here: the personification of the natural world; the vigorous, energized language; the release of individual words ("shores" in the passage above) into equivocal syntactic and semantic relations, which are consequences of the way the poem's discourse marginalizes the self. We may think, with Conquest *et al.*, that these are examples of poetic vices, but that does not allow us to think that they are devices employed for their own sake, rather than means employed to accomplish a distinct mode of discourse. In the poetry of Nicholas Moore or David Gascoyne the commonsense data base of the empirical self is eluded by less overtly disruptive means, in particular by presentation of a non-authoritative self, socially marginal or suffering. If we wish to recuperate their poetry (and I do not see how we can afford to neglect it), it will entail severe criticism of the terms in which the accepted canon of post-war poetry has been constructed.

Different examples

In the poetic tradition now dominant the authoritative self, discoursing in a world of banal, empirically derived objects and relations, depends on its employment of metaphor and simile for poetic vitality. These figures are conceptually subordinate to the empirical reality of self and objects, yet they constitute the nature of the poem. Poets are now praised above all else as inventors of figures—as rhetoricians, in fact—with a consequent narrowing of our range of appropriate response. Poetry has been turned into a reserve for small verbal thrills, a daring little frill round the hem of normal discourse; objects and relations in the natural and social worlds have an unresistant, token presence; at its most extreme, they serve as pretexts for bravura display. It does not wish to influence the reader's perceptions and feelings in the lived world: its intersection with that world is attenuated and discourages reading back; transformation is confined within the surprises and routines of rhetoric. The poems written by Craig Raine (in whom the Larkin-Hughes-Heaney canon extended itself in the late seventies) are the appropriate illustration s of this argument.

It may be felt that the case I am advancing depends on more substantiation than has been provided so far. By way of further example, therefore, here are some lines from Heaney's poem 'The Barn' (*Death of a Naturalist*, 1966), a poem which deals with the transference of enclosure and menace from a building to the intimacy of one's own feelings.

> Threshed corn lay piled like grit of ivory
> Or solid as cement in two-lugged sacks.
> The musty dark hoarded an armoury
> Of farmyard implements, harness, plough-socks.

The figures are applied in this opening stanza as an enrichment of description, but the same figurative technique is used to produce the space in which to effect the transfer from the elaborate figure of the barn itself to the speaker's affective life.

> Then you felt cobwebs clogging up your lungs
>
> And scuttled fast into the sunlit yard.
> And into nights when bats were on the wing
> Over the rafters of sleep, where bright eyes stared
> From piles of grain in corners, fierce, unblinking.

Here the figure is functional ("the rafters of sleep, where"); elsewhere figures project the speaker's terror.

> I lay face-down to shun the fear above.
> The two-lugged sacks moved in like great blind rats.[14]

The tropes proliferate and are uniformly highlighted, like consumer goods in a shop window, but they are uncoordinated (unlike Larkin's, say); the effect is gratuitous and draws attention finally to the poet's rhetorical ingenuity. Everything is of a piece, irrespective of what is being said. Our sense that the details bind together into a more complex meaning derives not from the figures but from the attenuated presence of autobiographical anecdote.

By way of contrast, here is an example of poetry from the middle of our period in which figures play a minor role. The following lines are from Charles Tomlinson's 'Geneva Restored' (*Seeing is Believing*, 1960), and we might note the careful, sustained description of the city's environs, with its suggestion that language might be compatible with what it refers to rather than necessarily appropriated to the special register of the poet's sensibility.

> Limestone, faulted with marble; the lengthening swell
> Under the terraces, the farms in miniature, until
> With its sheer, last leap, the Salève becomes
> The Salève, juts naked, the cliff which nobody sees
> Because it pretends to be nothing, and has shaken off
> Its seashore litter of house-dots. Beneath that,
> This –compact, as the other is sudden, and with an
> > inaccessible
> Family dignity: close roofs on a gravel height,
> Building knit into rock; the bird's nest of a place
> Rich in protestant pieties, in heroic half-truths
> That was Ruskin's.[15]

We might feel that the poet has his imagination reined in here; alternatively we might feel that his attention has been directed to good purpose. We might also feel that he is satisfied to let his language become so identified with his material as to court the risk of tautology, until we notice that the repetition of "the Salève", coming as it does at the beginning of a new line, transforms the thing into its proper name by the formal capitalization of the first letter of the definite article: "The Salève". Not only is the poem's point of intersection with the world realized in detail, and in terms of particular, local qualities, the place is also remembered to possess a history, to be charged with it indeed as associations, with Protestantism, with Ruskin, which feed into the present. Yet none of these, it can be argued, owes its presence to the poet's intervention; they occur because the poet finds them interesting and they sustain the poem accordingly.

Tomlinson's poem, highly literal, informed by respect for the presence and character of things, is one example of a discourse unlike that of the dominant canon. But his is not the only one. In *Thomas Hardy and English Poetry* Donald Davie, although from a somewhat exclusive concern with landscape, writes about other poets, from the sixties, who conduct their writing in ways quite independent of the norms of the canon. It is a comment on the narrowness of our critical culture that such challenges have not been more fully recognized and taken up.

Notes

1   Blake Morrison, *Seamus Heaney* (London: 1982), p. 11.

2   Donald Davie, *Granta*, 68, 1229 (1963); repr. in *Thomas Hardy and English Poetry* (London: Routledge & Kegan Paul, 1973).

3   Robert Conquest (ed.), *New Lines* (London: Macmillan, 1956).

4   Charles Tomlinson, in *Essays in Criticism*, 7, 2 (April 1957).

5   Howard Sergeant and Dannie Abse (eds), *Mavericks* (London: Editions Poetry and Poverty, 1957).

6   A. Alvarez (ed.), *The New Poetry* (Harmondsworth: Penguin, 1962; rev. 1966).

7   Robert Conquest, *New Lines—II* (London: Macmillan, 1963).

8   *The Review*, 1 (1962).

9   Donald Davie, *Purity of Diction in English Verse* (London: Chatto & Windus, 1952) and *Articulate Energy* (London: Routledge & Kegan Paul, 1955).

10 Donald Davie, *These the Companions* (Cambridge: Cambridge University Press, 1982).

11 Kenneth Rexroth (ed.), *The New British Poets* (New York: New Directions, [1949]).

12 Roy Fuller, *Epitaphs and Occasions* (London: John Lehman, 1949).

13 W.S. Graham, *The Nightfishing* (London: Faber, 1955).

14 Seamus Heaney, *Death of a Naturalist* (London: Faber, 1966).

15 Charles Tomlinson, *Seeing is Believing* (London: Oxford University Press, 1960).

Introduction to *A Various Art*

A Various Art, the anthology of contemporary poetry edited by Andrew Crozier and Tim Longville, was published by Carcanet in 1987 and consisted of work by Anthony Barnett, David Chaloner, Andrew Crozier, Roy Fisher, Veronica Forrest-Thomson, John Hall, Ralph Hawkins, John James, Tim Longville, Douglas Oliver, Peter Philpott, J.H. Prynne, John Riley, Peter Riley, John Seed, Iain Sinclair and Nick Totton.

This anthology represents our joint view of what is most interesting, valuable, and distinguished in the work of a generation of English poets now entering its maturity, but it is not an anthology of English, let alone British poetry. We did not begin with this distinction in mind; indeed, had we done so it might have appeared that there were no operative criteria by which to proceed. We knew this was not the case. Why, then, make such a distinction, as though the work of English or British poets did not belong to the general category of their national poetry?

The answer to this question will refer to culture rather than art, and must draw attention to the history of perceptions of English and British poetry since the 1950s. It is helpful to bear in mind, for instance, that polemic anthologies during this time, while laying claim to pre-eminent achievement, have done so within the inclusive reference of national representation. As in the phrase 'the best of British', the frame of reference of national culture and the notion of quality have been brought into uncomplicated mutual alignment, as though the prestige of national origin constituted a claim on the world's attention or, at any rate, was seal of approval enough for us. Successive anthologies of this type have also asserted their contemporary novelty of style and taste. Hence the inclusiveness of national poetry, in the possessive embrace of a sectional view of change and difference, takes on the exclusivity of fashion. The longer this show runs the less it exhibits the organicism implicit in the notion of a national poetry (however complex and dividedly other the nation has become) and the more it bespeaks new Imperial suitings. Pre-war anthologies, for some reason, had no need of such clothes, and contained a less complacent style of polemic, as though some cultural positions still remained to be stormed.

Most of the poets in this anthology began to publish in the 1960s. Most of them were university educated, many in departments of English.

Their social formation, in other words, had much in common with that of the poets who generated and were the beneficiaries of the shift in taste in the 1950s, but this did not enable them to see the position thus publicly secured for poetry as a point of reference. Instead, in various places, in Birmingham, Bristol, Cambridge, London, and Manchester for example, several of them became aware of one another's presence and a shared reaction to current taste. The notion of reaction does not itself, of course, explain the event it describes, but one or two motives can be suggested in hindsight.

For one thing, poetry, if it is an art, is an art in relation to language in general; its artifice is various, and its rules apply to specific rather than to general occasions. But the poets who altered taste in the 1950s did so by means of a common rhetoric that foreclosed the possibilities of poetic language within its own devices: varieties of tone, of rhythm, of form, of image, were narrowly limited, as were conceptions of the scope and character of poetic discourse, its relation to the self, to knowledge, to history, and to the world. Poetry was seen as an art in relation to its own conventions—and a pusillanimous set of conventions at that. It was not to be ambitious, or to seek to articulate ambition through the complex deployment of its technical means: imagery was either suspect or merely clinched an argument; the verse line should not, by the pressure its energy or shape might exert on syntax, intervene in meaning; language was always to be grounded in the presence of a legitimating voice—and that voice took on an impersonally collective tone. To its owners' satisfaction the signs of art had been subsumed within a closed cultural programme.

But in addition, the redefinition of taste in the 1950s had had to be enacted by means of a wholesale rewriting of and reorientation towards the history of modern poetry, and this included the virtual suppression of parts of it. When they began to write, therefore, many of the poets in this anthology, confronted with such a depthless version of the past, found that as English poets the ground had been pretty well cut from beneath their feet. To accept the version of English poetry then sanctioned would be to become like a fly on a wall that had just been built. The general character of this moment and the types of choice it provoked cannot be separated from the wider context of English interest in the 1960s in American music, painting, and writing. Certainly, at the time, one of the means by which many of the poets in this anthology were identifiable to one another was an interest in a particular aspect of post-war American poetry, and the tradition that lay behind it—not that of Pound and Eliot but that of Pound and Williams. But more immediately important than this, perhaps, American examples provided lessons in the organisation and conduct of a poet's public life, indicating how poets might take matters of publication and the definition of a readership into their own hands by establishing their own publishing houses and journals. Most of the work collected here was published under such auspices. In the 1960s, as well, the publishing of poetry did not command much prestige in the media, let alone represent significant turnover; what little prestige it had, it appeared, attached to the publisher's privilege in being able to afford to subsidise a small portion of high culture.

We do not refer to the 1960s in order to invoke the spirit of a regretted golden age. Nor do we assert the claims of some speculative counter-culture, alternative or underground, an Albion in place of England perhaps. Our views concerning the constructed totalities that represent national culture, however defined, forestall temptation of that sort. Most of the poems collected here were, in fact, written in the 1970s and 1980s, and bear witness, in a way that sets questions or reaction or influence beside the point, to a developed confidence in the poets' own creative resources. But reference to the 1960s serves several purposes nonetheless. It indicates the time-span we have in mind when we speak of a generation of English poets. It defines a formative moment. And it draws attention to the decade in which an attitude to writing not represented here both reached its apotheosis and lost its vitality.

The last point is of curious interest because current constructions of British poetry, to our amusement though not to our chagrin, persevere with the stylistic remnants of that attitude. The poetry generally on offer is either provincial or parasitically metropolitan, and furnishes the pleasure of either a happy nostalgia or a frisson of daring and disgust. Or so we find. Our comment is not intended, however, to be harsh so much as cautionary. The poets represented here are, we suppose, unlikely to be familiar names to many readers of anthologies—those imaginary beings at whom we aim, and to whom we hope to introduce a range of poetry that has not easily been accessible. For this reason we provide a more than usually full bibliography. We have not attempted to provide a polemic apology or manifesto because no claim is advanced here for the existence of anything amounting to a school. Many of the poets represented have read and responded to one another's writing, but what impressed us most, while we made our selections, was the degree of difference that existed between individual poets, and the extent to which each poet had accomplished a characteristic and integral body of work, with its own field of interest and attention. What we claim is both the possibility and presence of such variety, a poetry deployed towards the complex and multiple experience in language of all of us. This is by no means, of course, ever one and the same thing, and the poets collected here will be seen to set their writing towards a range of languages, ordinary, scientific, traditional, demotic, liturgical, and so on. These denote topical and intellectual reference of different sorts, different procedures and affective states of language, but their variety and mixture equally point to the important common characteristics of these poets, commitment to the discovery of meaning and form in language itself.

As editors we have not, we hope it is clear, set ourselves the task of charting a general poetic milieu or recording its history. In order to make what seemed to us the best use of the space available we have had to make some difficult decisions and, in some instances, to agree to differ; had we been left to our separate devices each of us, no doubt, would have made a somewhat different choice. But we have, nevertheless, made an anthology of poems we could agree to admire.

Styles of the Self:
The New Apocalypse and 1940s poetry

This essay was published in *A Paradise Lost: The Neo-Romantic Imagination in Britain 1935-1950* (ed. David Mellor), London, Lund Humphries, 1987.

WAR AND POETRY

Poetry in the 1940s was inevitably affected by war, but the Second World War did not inspire "war poets", new Owens, Sassoons, and Rosenbergs, in the sense of that term already implicit in the forlorn cries that went up for the poets of this new war to reveal themselves. The "war poets" of 1914-18 were produced, as much as by their experience of warfare, out of their reaction against the romantic and genteel idealism of their own pre-war verses, and this in itself set them apart from their modernist contemporaries, such as Pound, Eliot, and Rosenberg's friend John Rodker, whose reaction against the decadent tradition of nineteenth-century Romanticism was more deliberate and technically motivated—a reaction which post-war social and cultural circumstances made increasingly difficult to sustain except in severe artistic isolation.

Between the two world wars poetic innovations and counter-innovations occurred in startling confusion, to an extent unparalleled, certainly in the decades preceding 1914, so that the situation of poets in 1939 followed out of a hectic continuum which the war itself did not obliterate. Furthermore, war did not now confront a generation ignorant of its nature and social causes, for the political struggles of the 1930s, and foreign wars, in Abyssinia, Spain, and China, had all, though at a distance, made their mark on poetry. In enemy countries artistic avant-gardes had been suppressed or exiled, while in England, it almost seemed, the defence of culture was a war aim. To the young poet two preceding poetic generations would have appeared firmly in place, those of Eliot and of Auden, in alliance with one another to an extent but both, at the end of the 1930s, off the boil. It was a moment in the history of English poetry which appeared to offer many models and precedents, even to permit, in some cases, the revival of the poetic as a romantic cultural icon, but which disclosed no clear indications of future direction. And, indeed, in retrospect such a state of affairs might seem to have been the best prognostication of the poetry of the coming decade, for the 1940s saw both the re-emergence of some modernist poets (Eliot's *Four Quartets* and H.D.'s 'War *Trilogy*' were published), and the emergence of others (Roy Fuller and Norman MacCaig for example) who were not to reach their full maturity until the 1950s and 1960s, alongside but not directly aligned with "Movement" poets such as Larkin and Davie. There were, too, poets such as Alun Lewis and Keith Douglas (and Fuller himself, of course) whose writing engaged directly with their experience in the armed forces.

But retrospect also commonly attributes to the poetry of the 1940s its own special identity, to which none of the instances just cited contributes. Before the end of the decade, in fact, Geoffrey Grigson could already deplore the effect of the war on poetry, and contrast it to the good effects brought about by the previous war. For Grigson it appeared that the poetic renovations of the inter-war years had been abandoned recklessly, and lessons of aesthetic hygiene forgotten. In the 1950s condemnation was more general, the poetry of the preceding decade was seen to have been confused, self-indulgent, vicious even—"Apocalyptic". The name of the most vital poetic movement of the 1940s had become a term of abuse. "The New Apocalypse", to give its name in full, was short-lived, its adherents separated and dispersed by the war, and its coherence dissipated by aggressive overexposure. Yet it provided, briefly, a belated theoretical context for the poetic style that had emerged to compete with that of Auden. Degenerate versions of both style and theory provided the basis for most poetry written during the remainder of the decade and, in particular, for that written out of a sense, often spurious no doubt, of participation in the significance of the historical moment, of engagement with the experience of the war and post-war reconstruction.

STYLES OF THE SELF

The sense of consciousness as something complex, even multiple, that is characteristic of Modernism, is absent in both the poetry of the Movement and that of Auden and his peers: the self is represented, instead, as a site of singularity, and the discourses of their poetry are governed accordingly. The self-consciousness of the subject establishes the framework of poetic utterance, whether it concerns the subject's awareness of its own self-identity, or the subject refers propositionally to things outside itself. In both cases meaning is conceived as objective, and the subject is the mediator of the experience or knowledge from which meaning is held to arise. The singularity of the self goes hand in hand with its role as mediator, so that it becomes an abstraction, radically apart from whatever else enters the field of poetic discourse. But this mediation takes place between meanings and their objective sources, is short-circuited, so to speak, within the subject, whose role, both in the utterance of the text, and in the relation between text and reader, is directive. The reader is directed to respond to the poem in only a receptive spirit, not in the spirit of dialogue.

Such a view of Auden might seem strange in the light of both the range of tone and manner in his writing in the 1930s, and the themes it discloses: the role of the unconsciousness, repression, guilt, and betrayal; the collapse of a culture and the struggle between classes; the need to transcend the present, however privately attractive, in commitment to a better future. Here, surely, is a poet who shows the difficult complexity of life. But that it is shown, as though by a poetics of containment, is precisely the point. Auden achieves this by a process of displacement from the self, on to heroes, victims, friends, lovers, and landscapes, carried into effect by dazzling series of concrete images, in a tone of voice which maintains its self-possession equally in intimate and public address. This assurance of manner, with all its calm and lucidity, was a great achievement, but it was a manner nonetheless.

Auden's 'Spain' illustrates the point made here: vast catalogues of imagery represent the developments of history, the different forms that responsible and irresponsible choice confer upon the person, the types of revolutionary activity and their contrasted civic pursuits. The elaborate machinery of all this concrete particularity is held in place only by a triad of implicitly objective declarations about yesterday, today, and tomorrow, which issue from a subject that neither articulates itself nor belongs with the specifics of the poem's imagery: complexity is displaced across them in a way that reinforces their helpless otherness, and least of all are they symbols of an inner life. The self remains singular in its undisclosed authority; the voice that rises to affirm "I am Spain" does not speak for the poet.

This displacement of complexity from the self on to objective imagery was what enabled Auden's notorious revision of 'Spain'. Furthermore, it was the control of objective imagery by a self-possessed discursive centre that constituted the basis of the style that he made generally available during the 1930s, a style that seemed up-to-the-minute both poetically and for the range of allusion to contemporary life that it permitted. But concurrently, and even in such a magazine as Grigson's *New Verse*, which decisively fostered Auden's reputation and influence, a quite different style was being developed by poets such as Dylan Thomas, George Barker, and David Gascoyne. To think of this other style in terms of Surrealism is helpful only up to a point, despite the fact that Gascoyne, for one, explicitly espoused Surrealism for a time, and his Surrealist poems represent, typically, objects behaving and associating in unusual and impossible ways, as images of the unconscious mind, in a mental landscape disobedient to ordinary laws of space and time. But this was only one aspect of Surrealism in England. Another, closer to Auden in its treatment of objective imagery, and sharing some of the motives of the Mass-Observation project, sought to examine the appearances of the contemporary world as manifestations of a collective, popular unconscious: the objective thus took on the qualities of hallucination. Yet again, it could be argued, as did Hugh Sykes Davies, that the Surrealist project was already developed in English Romanticism. Nevertheless, what these English versions of Surrealism all have in common is a preoccupation with the self more far-reaching than that signified merely by the textual authority of the subject.

This is the case, certainly, in the poetry of Thomas, Barker, and Gascoyne. Their work begins and ends with the question of personal identity, and through this pass all their apprehensions of history, psychology, and contemporary life. It is writing that is sedulously disruptive of its own poise and composure, and which pre-empts any simple foreclosure of the disorders produced within itself; the authority of a singular consciousness is not invoked. It might appear that such poetry is beset by its authors' invasive egotism, by reckless objectification of the body image in terms, especially, of violent organic processes, by insistent possessiveness towards whatever exists outside the self, and by an unconsidered proliferation of imagery quite unlike Auden's calculated and orderly lists. But these would not be pure and disinterested literary judgements, for they point not merely to motives but also to refusals—of the supposed propriety and rectitude of the discrete, objective image, and of the use of grammar that attributes to it the positivist virtues of fixing things in a finite temporal order and establishing their hierarchy of being and action. Such refusals were concomitants of the imagination that concerned itself with the nature of identity in opposites, and the resemblances between different orders of existence, and designed to represent the self as dramatic and participative rather than reflexive. Such a self would be, so to speak, turned inside out upon the world and enacted through it, but it would be the world organised according to internal and unpredictable laws of the mind.

Such is the pattern to be observed in Barker's 'Elegy on Spain', but it would be wrong to suggest that the grandeur and pathos of the Republican struggle, not to mention the issues at stake, are internalised, in some way appropriated by the poet as images of his own psychopathology. Far from it. They do issue independently in the poem, but not in such a way that the poet has only to deploy his own polemic intention toward them: he is implicated in them but equally implicated by them in a sense that takes the issue of selfhood beyond the reach of the singular. It is the unconstrained movement of the poem's imagery, sustained by thematic variation and a rich fullness of sound, that enables the value of the human, and of the Republican cause, to be affirmed irrespective of the vicissitudes of history. If this is to be thought of as providing at best a form of compensation then it needs to have set beside it the one word, "Alas", that Auden's History has for the defeated at the end of 'Spain'.

THE NEW APOCALYPSE AND 1940s POETRY

The general style of Thomas, Barker, and Gascoyne quite rapidly provided its own mannerism, a formula for making poems. It did not, of its nature, possess very exact demarcation, and if it was perceived more in terms of the type of imagery it disclosed than the way its images operated across their discursive content, it then imperceptibly merged with degenerate modes such as symbolism and pastoral or mythological romance. Thus broadly considered it can be seen to constitute the common style of 1940s poetry, easily adopted because it catered to a need for self-expression at a time when the lives of many were disrupted and thrown out of their usual course. Nevertheless it would not be possible to understand the starting point of such a poet as W.S. Graham, one of the most distinguished to emerge in the 1940s, except in terms of a careful attention to what this style might accomplish. The style also came to be associated with Welsh and Scottish literary regionalism, or nationalism, less on account of its supposed Celtic qualities than because it was constructed against the metropolitan culture signified by that of Auden. Its significance in this respect went further, indeed, for radical social positions—critical attitudes to the war, pacifism, even revolutionary defeatism—had now crossed over to it. The attempts by Julian Symons and some others to maintain a politically radical position inside a version of the Auden style had little success.

But this counter-style, dominant as it came to be during the 1940s, initially lacked coherent identity of the sort that arises from a sense that a style is identifiable with its epoch. It tended to be identified, instead, in terms of the qualities of individual poets, of Dylan Thomas perhaps above all. This might be thought appropriate, after all, in view of the significance assigned to the question of personal identity, but it would be to mistake the point, which concerns a mode of self-representation rather than the identities of specific individuals. A series of anthologies, however, published in 1939, 1941, and 1944, assembled the work of several writers under the collective identity of 'The New Apocalypse'. The name caught on, to stick in the end like mud. After these anthologies, edited by J.F. Hendry and Henry Treece, came a small flood of other anthologies and literary annuals (a type of publication encouraged by wartime conditions of book production), largely fostered by Treece, who sponsored successively "Personalism" and a catch-all "New Romanticism". Here were, in different versions, identities not only for poetry but for other arts as well. The overall coherence, however, was less than the publicity amounted to.

"The New Apocalypse", strictly considered, does possess its own sort of cohesion, but as a group movement it cannot bear the weight of representative significance attached to it in retrospect. The poets it brought together were, from the start, a mixed batch; what provided the main grounds for their association was reaction against the poetry of Auden and followers of his such as Kenneth Allott. The best among them, Hendry himself, and Nicholas Moore, developed very differently even during the brief period of group association. The group manifesto, primarily the work of Hendry, was circulated privately in 1938, but did not appear in full in any of the anthologies. The term "Apocalyptic" was itself ambiguous, serving to label the writing of those who published in the three anthologies but, in Hendry's theoretical writings, denoting also writing of a kind that emerges under certain social conditions. What held "The New Apocalypse" together, for even so short a time as it lasted, were Treece's energies as a publicist, and Hendry's vigour in polemic.

Hendry's Introduction to *The New Apocalypse*, the inaugural anthology, both abbreviated and extended the 1938 manifesto. Ideas about organicism and wholeness, influenced by D.H. Lawrence's *Apocalypse*, find their complement in the concept of technological society as a "mechanistic structure" derived from Edward O'Brien's *The Dance of the Machines*. Hendry's polemic was addressed to his sense of a deepening social crisis which political action alone, since the idea of politics itself had become mechanical, could not remedy. "Apocalyptic writing" was concerned with "the collapse of social forms", and occurred where "expression breaks through the structure of language" and "the structure of social convention" so that "man stands forth as the ultimate reality". Such arguments still possess their interest, but the significance of Hendry's polemic as theory lies in the development of his ideas about Myth, the third of the manifesto's terms of reference. Hendry's thinking here is subtle, for he distinguishes between collective and individual myths of the self, between myth as social ideology and the mythic projection of the self as personality into everyday life. The distinction is not evaluative, for in each case, Hendry argues, myth can lead to the integration of personality, and the social expression of human needs, or it may destroy them by a false projection.

The importance of Hendry's argument is that it provided a theory for the poetic style that reproduces the objective world within the projection of the self, including its unconscious content. It will be clear why for him the "mechanistic-materialism" of Auden offered no purchase on the movement of history towards totalitarianism and war, and could only become its victim: that style of the self by which it is projected as the focal point, so to speak, of the sum of objective existence, could not provide a means for the integration of the human world and the world of things that Hendry sought. It is against the background of this theory that G.S. Frazer's account of "The New Apocalypse" as a dialectical development of Surrealism, in which unconscious imagery is brought under conscious poetic control, makes best sense, but in Hendry's theory questions of style and extra-literary motive are more intimately connected.

What Hendry's theory accomplished, however, far from legitimising a widely used style, had the effect of restricting the uses to which it might appropriately be put by denying it purely stylistic autonomy. Moreover, as Hendry's poetry developed, and that of Moore also, both drew away from the congestion of language associated with Thomas, and its suggestion of the dissolution of the self in its strenuous, even violent effects. Both concerned themselves more with the inscription of public events on the texture of personal life: the self lived through the experience imposed by wartime conditions, but the images of that experience derived from its personal location. By contrast, Treece's attempts to enlarge the significance of "The New Apocalypse", by generalising and broadening its context, were counter-productive, and effectively dissolved it back into the general poetic style of the decade, a style which became increasingly moribund in the post-war years.

Hope and Distrust

This article appeared in *PN Review* 88, 19.2, November/December 1992.

"It will have happened to that other / The survivor"
(George Oppen, 'The Occurrences')

"The harm that history does us / Is grievous but not final"
(Donald Davie, 'Wild Boar Clough')

If what makes a poem memorable includes the memory of its first reading then I can think of a number of poems by Donald Davie that belong to that category: 'Homage to John L. Stephens', for example, in *Events and Wisdoms*; or 'Emigrant, to the Receding Shore', in Robin Skelton's *Memorial Symposium* for Herbert Read; or 'Wild Boar Clough', in *Three for Water Music*. More recently, in 1985, there was 'Recollections of George Oppen in a Letter to a Friend', in the *London Review of Books*, but this poem is memorable for the shock with which it left me speechless, "and with a sort of fury", as I re-read those lines, and then read to the end of the poem, in a spirit of offended repudiation.

> Poetic Justice
> I swear made her appearance in a toga.
> Alzheimer's, yes—the diagnosis was
> all very well, but surely George's dealings
> with language had for years anticipated,
> almost provoked, the visitation? Such
> pains as he had been at—in verse, in prose,
> in conversation—to subvert, discount,
> derange articulation. Destiny
> strikes, and for months before he dies
> he's inarticulate. A hideous justice.

If there is a dividing line between shocking and offensive behaviour— and among other things Davie's poem concerns itself with manners and behaviour, and Anglo-American differences (in *Collected Poems* the 'Friend' becomes an 'English friend')—then I think that Davie's lines are shocking, but deliberately so because he has a serious topic in view, in which he feels closely concerned. But it is an unrelenting critique of Oppen, which "hideous justice" is surely not intended to mitigate. Yet it is also ingenuous as a mode of advocacy, and those readers of Oppen who find that he speaks to them will think that Davie has tipped the balance by a shameless play on words. Although Davie backs away from "playing God like this" the judgement is not subsequently reversed, so that, if the reader is not to register only the shocking effect of those lines, to feel them always out of context, it is important to discover what it is that engages Davie so closely, as though it has caught him off his guard.

It is an error to see justice visited on the sick; as a student of the 18th Century Davie will know this very well. In our own century we know that whatever the statistical probabilities when it comes to cases nemesis strikes by chance. But if Swift did not deserve to expire "a Driv'ler and a Show", the aetiology of his disease might, we can suppose, furnish a history for linguistic analysis. In 'Two Aspects of Language and Two Types of Aphasic Disturbances' Roman Jakobson cites the case of the Russian novelist Gleb Ivanovich Uspensky to correlate speech disorder and literary style.

> His first name and patronymic, *Gleb Ivanovich*, traditionally combined in polite intercourse, for him split into two distinct names designating two separate beings: Gleb was endowed with all his virtues, while Ivanovich, the name relating the son to the father, became the incarnation of all Uspensky's vices. The linguistic aspect of this split personality is the patient's inability to use two symbols for the same thing, and is thus a similarity disorder. Since the similarity disorder is bound up with the metronymical bent, an examination of the literary manner Uspensky had employed as a young writer takes on a particular interest.

Theoretical expectations are borne out: analysis of Uspensky's style reveals that he had "a particular penchant for metonymy, and especially for synechdoche". Jakobson does not say that Oedipal conflict involves a predisposition to the realist novel, but will say that "the personal stamp of Gleb Ivanovich made his pen particularly suitable for this artistic trend in its extreme manifestations and finally left its mark upon the verbal aspect of his mental illness". The formula might be that Oedipal conflict plus metonymic bent leads to split personality: unable to reconcile his virtues and his vices Uspensky displaces them by metonymic attribution. Who can say? The point to remember is that in Jakobson's classification of two types of aphasic disturbance similarity disorder is "bound up" with the metonymical bent by antithesis: relations of contiguity persist while those of similarity lapse. Contiguity disorder is, conversely, bound up with the metaphorical bent.

At this point Davie's candid reader might hasten to interject that his poem does not refer in general terms to speechlessness or aphasia. Do not its more specific terms "articulation" and "inarticulate" indicate contiguity disorder in Oppen's case? Is not Jakobson's theory, indeed, precisely what we need to take Davie's point? There are several objections to this. In the first place, Jakobson's main bearing on what is being discussed is to shift its ground from justice to disease. Beyond that, we should be sceptical about attempts to take the terms he borrows from rhetoric to denote the two axes of linguistic relations and bend them back into literary criticism with the same binary logic. And finally, the word "inarticulate" is used of speakers in a very loose sense; its relation to "articulation", in the rather special sense we associate with Davie, involves a deliberate play on words. It is precisely the support this wordplay provides for the figure of Justice, however quaintly garbed, that is so shocking when set beside the figure of the stricken poet. Speechless, aphasic, inarticulate: they can all mean the same thing. The painful details of human affliction deserve respect: it would be impertinent to enquire more closely into the particulars of Oppen's demented utterance.

Yet the charge against Oppen, that he was at pains "to subvert, discount, derange articulation" remains in place. Davie's "articulation" and Jakobson's "relations of contiguity" might be near enough the same thing, for purposes of description, and we might try to read Oppen, in the light of Davie's charge and Jakobson's theory, to see if his writing does reveal a metaphorical bent. This need not commit us to any headlong flight towards medical diagnosis. But a glance at some of the very things Davie has noted in Oppen, as we will see, is enough to show that theory will not bear out the charge. Oppen's proclivity for bald and disconnected statement (the ability to propositionalise depends on relations of contiguity), and his non-metrical verse (meter is a relation of similarity), already establish the presence to some degree of the metonymical process. This is not the place, however, to establish for Oppen's verse the proportions of metaphorical and metonymical processes which, in "normal verbal behaviour", says Jakobson, are both "continually operative".

Nevertheless, if Jakobson's theory will not account for Davie's case against Oppen, it cannot discount it. But Jakobson has served to clear the air in order to turn to Davie himself to establish in greater detail what the issue is between Oppen and articulation. Davie's 'Recollections' include very little reminiscence of Oppen; instead he is inserted in a history of reproach and self-reproach, distrust and self-distrust; it is, indeed, a rumination on vexing and unfinished business: "often as I have settled George's hash / to my own satisfaction / ...still he.../ won't go away, nor let me be, reproachful / as always the dead are"; "Not a bit / of help to me was George, or George's writing; / though he achieved his startling poignancies, / I distrusted them, distrust them still." Something of this history can be gathered from Oppen's *Selected Letters*, but more pertinent to the topic of articulation is Davie's review of Oppen's *Seascape: Needle's Eye*, 'Braveries Eschewed'. The charge that Oppen subverts, discounts, or deranges articulation is here referable to his "suppression" of punctuation, although the point is made in relation to "obscurity", and although this is one of several observations made by Davie to place Oppen before an "oldfashioned reader", the points he makes are brought together finally in an argument in which "articulation in and of the marvel that is human language" is axiomatic of any achieved rhetoric, Oppen's included.

Not much to argue with there, it might be thought, indeed Davie quickly says that his argument is not "with Oppen or with Oppen's poems". But he has already stated the corollaries of the "shabby argument" against which his confessedly "lack-lustre phrase", "the marvel that is human language", was advanced.

> If we truly want or need to cut loose from our inherited past, then we should discard not just poetic figurations of language but any figurations whatever, including those which make it possible to communicate at all, except by grunts and yelps.

The argument comes in two parts, and needs to be considered in two ways. If we attend to the argument as a whole it is apparent that its two parts are combined in the word "inherited": we cannot pick and choose amongst our inheritance, but must accept it as a job lot. What this means in terms of language is that if we reject poetic figurations (the "braveries" of Davie's title) we must reject words and the rules of grammar as part of the bargain. The weakness of this argument is that it makes no distinction between a specific set of "traditional splendours and clarities" ("our inherited past") and the structure of ("human") language generally. We might also remind ourselves that figures of grammar and figures of rhetoric, to use an old distinction, are not to be seen as continuous, if we are mindful of Jakobson's schema, but are in fact opposed. Quite possible to have one without the other. We can also, on the other hand, consider the two parts of Davie's argument separately, to see that the position attributed to Oppen only becomes a shabby argument if the inferences drawn from it are admitted within limits (the range of corollary figuration extends a long way down to grunts and yelps) and Oppen is found not to act in good faith. These points do tell against Oppen and will not dissolve into the "untenable positions [William Carlos] Williams's obtuseness trapped him into" appealed to by the admirers of Oppen Davie presents himself as arguing against.

But if all that remained at issue was that "all that is happening is that a new rhetoric is being preferred before an old one" the position attributed to Oppen would cease to be objectionable; he and Davie could agree to differ. But clearly more is at issue: the pitch of Davie's argument suggests that he feels coerced by Oppen's rhetorical practice; treat it as domestic or intimate as he may, it presents itself to him as historically overdetermined. It is not just that he sets out to rebut such arguments; at the start of his review he draws attention to Oppen's attempt to understand the present as an historian, and the act of willed choice by which he is closed to the past. Such a distinction between history and the past is valid in Davie's hands, its significance is evident in his poems, most notably the *Six Epistles to Eva Hesse*, and he is no doubt in the right to place Oppen as an historian in terms of the Marxism "in his background and his past". But it is surely wrong subsequently to ask "are we Marxist enough, historical determinists enough, to agree that the time is gone for so many of the traditional splendours and clarities as this poetry wants us to dispense with?" The association is wrong (only a historicist argument will enforce such abnegation—Marxists, in my understanding, see cultural production as mediated), and the question is falsely put, for it is addressed ambivalently to poet and reader alike. Nevertheless those braveries on behalf of which Davie appeals with such vivid eloquence belong to our past rather than to our place in history, and quite clearly the distinction between the past and history can underwrite different definitions of art.

It will also be clear by now that by "articulation" Davie means rather more than syntax (indeed he can include "fractured and disjointed language" within the articulation of rhetoric); that the term embraces the whole range of traditional poetic devices; and that this totality of effect belongs with an understanding of poetry's public role as fullness and range of utterance. It is also clear I think that it is articulation in this sense that

Oppen subverts, discounts, and deranges—it must be so if the verbs are deployed with precision, for these are ways of acting not on grammar so much as on the institutions of inherited tradition. But if this is so the relation between "articulation" and "inarticulate" becomes all the more remote, available only by means of the same ambiguous punning that enables Davie to assert that Oppen refuses the "traditional braveries... because they would testify... to a bravery (in the other sense) about his vocation and the art he practices".

Before I return to Davie's poem—it will be understood that the purpose of my discussion is to do it justice—something needs to be said about *Seascape: Needle's Eye*. It cannot be assumed that either in his review or in his poem has Davie given a complete account of his reading of Oppen. It is only necessary to turn to his essay 'English and American in *Briggflatts*' to find him dealing with Oppen in very different terms. The contrast between Bunting's "social and public note", associated with normal punctuation which clarifies "the articulate structure of sentences", and the "characteristically intimate and private" note of American Objectivists such as Oppen, reiterates, under different conditions, distinctions already met with. However, behind both the English Objectivist and his American peers Davie points to "a conviction that is wholesome":

> ...that a poem is a transaction between the poet and his subject
> more than it is a transaction between a poet and his readers. This
> is to make the poet once again more than a rhetorician; and on
> this showing the reader, though the poet cannot be oblivious of
> his presence, nevertheless is merely "sitting in on" or "listening
> in to" a transaction which he is not a party to.

Backing this conviction (and here Davie is quoting Oppen) is "the necessity of form, the objectification of the poem". As a transaction a poem is not at all the performance Davie, in 'Braveries Eschewed', insists against Oppen it must be. I draw attention to these other views of Davie's as differences, not as contradictions; they are, surely, more in the nature of unresolved but productive antinomies. In order, finally, to approach Davie's poem it is necessary to see it not in the light of his reading of Oppen but over against one's own.

I will confine myself to just two points. The first is that Davie's review of *Seascape: Needle's Eye* is perplexingly out of character: it is Oppen's most Poundian collection and yet Davie, of all critics, ignores this, so much so that the references to Williams seem to be a blind. Not only do we hear Pound in his phrases ("glass sea shadow of water", "the tide / brimming / in the moon-streak"), there are allusions to his work ("obstinate islands"), and in 'Of Hours' the figure of Pound is invoked on the occasion of a tense, belated reunion in 1979 ("why did I weep / Meeting that poet again what was that rage"). The second concerns the seventh of 'Some San Francisco Poems', which Davie takes as his warrant for the assertion that for Oppen both the past, and the past of art, are irrelevant, and here of course I shall not merely assert the contrary. I do suggest, however, that Davie's distinction leads to a misreading of the poem, since history and the past need not be opposed in the way he suggests. They are brought together in Oppen's poem in the figure of a wrecked Steinway piano, which serves both as a figure of a specific historical present (the history of our culture's destruction of its own goods and inheritance) and as an emblem of cultural tradition (it is not, after all, a Yamaha electronic keyboard). The thing is both agent, motive, and effect.

> The keyboard gone in the rank grass swept her hand
> over the strings and the thing rang out

"Mr Steinway's / Poem", Oppen says, "Not mine", and comments "A 'marvellous' object / Is not the marvel of things". I think this comment lurks behind Davie's phrase about "the marvel that is human language"; what precedes it is certainly the object of his cryptic remark that "no Mr Steinway manufactured the instrument, language, on which Oppen performs". But I also think that Davie has not taken Oppen's point. His distinction is between the poem as a found object and the poem as a modification and contextualisation of the object, but his point concerns things in general, as the groundwork for particular objects. And it is the groundwork which interests Oppen the more; in this (as I have argued elsewhere) he is fundamentally unlike Williams, as he has always been. And if indeed Oppen's poem is also a marvellous object (as I think it is) it is not so *sui generis*. It is a poem grounded in the history of poetry in which the past can ring out as part of history.

My two points come together to find in Oppen a view of art (as both cultural inheritance and technical practice) which takes its measure more critically than does Davie in 'Braveries Eschewed' (where he suggests that Oppen's poetry will not be able to help Californian youth ignorant of its past) but which is perhaps not very far from the view taken by Davie in

Hope and Distrust: On Donald Davie

Czesław Miłosz and the Insufficiency of Lyric. By that I mean among other things that art is not the solution to our immediate problems. In 'Of Hours' Oppen, by means of his Janus-headed syntax, connects his response to Pound and his response to battle as a response to art: "…what was that rage // Before Léger's art poster / In war time Paris", and although rage is glossed in the comment "perhaps art / Is one's mother and father", it is striking that here the communist soldier responds to the communist artist as—under certain circumstances—irrelevant. Davie's word is the one needed to state what is at issue. But this is not Oppen's last word on the ethical bearing of life on art, and indeed the Oppen who fought in the Ardennes was closer to the political activist who had abandoned poetry as an irrelevance in the depression than to the poet of 1972. In place of the categorical irrelevance of art that poet proffers a discrimination of art based on an empirical test of truth, a fidelity to looking, touching, saying and loving: "Old friend old poet / If you did not look / What is it you 'loved'". That goes home to Pound, and it also grounds the empirical test in the self, not some grand ontological security. Oppen's sense of "precariousness", heightened we may be sure by the history of his own times, is figured throughout *Seascape: Needle's Eye*, in ways which nevertheless acknowledge a debt to Pound, in terms of wind, water, and the durability of cultural products, but it is a poetry grounded in its own metaphysical enquiry.

Davie's poem about Oppen consumes a great many braveries, and it is by their role in a textual economy of flagrancy that the shock of the lines I began by quoting can be absorbed. In invokes and parodies Coleridge's 'This Lime-tree Bower My Prison' and, as in Coleridge's poem, a friend named Charles is addressed. But if the site of Coleridge's poem is wittily conjured up (Davie makes play with his ignorance of botanical names except as poetic appurtenances) the bower is reminiscently displaced, just as the poet's self-communing is self-conscious and decentred. Nevertheless it is a poem (rather as Davie would have us see Oppen's poems) intimately addressed to himself and another of Oppen's friends, and must remain closed to readers who know nothing of Oppen's poetry. Given such a restricted public Davie's shocking lines are a hostage to fortune, indeed they brave the reception of the friend to whom Davie's remarks are addressed, who is only implicated in conversational malice about Oppen to the extent of having joined in mockery of his style of public reading. But Davie's description of this ("his unpretentious chuntering monotone / that could not mark where a poem began or ended") will strike anyone who heard Oppen read by its accuracy. (Not that clear and varied enunciation is what Davie subsequently means by articulation.)

"Poetic Justice…in a toga" is another bravery, as is "playing God", which erases the former—and this is surely to Davie's credit—only after he has exposed himself to the risks that came in its train. But the supreme bravery, I want to suggest, is the figure Davie invents of Oppen himself: it is not the real person and social being, briefly recalled at the beginning of the poem, but the imaginary antagonist in Davie's inward debate about poetry. A figure of Davie himself. It is as his "gaoler" that Davie's recollections of Oppen warrant the co-option of Coleridge's poem, but it is at this point that Davie deviates most remarkably from his predecessor, who was immobilised in consequence of some piece of domestic clumsiness, and this is marked, I think, by Davie's subsequent quotation of lines 6-10 of Coleridge's poem. For surely, in the context in which Davie is writing, the line "Friends, whom I never more may meet again", denotes contingency rather than possibility. It is only beyond this point in the poem that Oppen is ushered securely into the past indicative, his shade laid to rest. At this point also a crisis has passed, and the poem is able to return to the bower and dell at Charles' cottage in a fresh start.

What remains to be noticed is the poem's termination in antithetical distrust and hope, which follows and confirms a harshly drawn self-portrait: "snapping branches of morose / inspirations, aspirations, habits / held up to the weak light, scowled at." For while Davie distrusts Oppen's poignancies he amply recognises his capacity for hope.

> But hope, such hope he had, such politics
> always of hope! Hope is a strenuous business;
> I hope the roar of it enlivens your
> west-country dell, as a whisper of it mine.

The cadence at the end is very fine. To pitch hope against distrust is strenuous, even resolute, but nothing is resolved, nor can it be on account of the ligature between poignancy and Davie's figuration of Oppen as avant garde—"Pathfinder", "Trailblazer"—the role in which he returns as Davie's antagonist. For Oppen's poignancies, which Davie accords him in full measure in 'Braveries Eschewed', all the while measuring the cost by which they are obtained, must be distrusted if Davie reckons they have been paid for at too high a rate. How are poignancies paid for? What we find poignant must first have pierced us, wounded us. Does not Davie fear these poignancies (surely fear properly belongs with hope) as much as he distrusts them, and been pained by them? Is his distrust not levelled, fearfully, at his own response? Perhaps I go too far. In Ronald Aaronson's *The Dialectics of Disaster: A Preface to Hope* the politics of hope begin with the person, as a kind of absurdity, and this is poignant indeed. For the figure of the avant garde Oppen we might substitute that of the survivor, for it is in narratives of survival that Oppen's hope is anchored, and in which, though wounded, the poignancy of old age and youth are discovered. And Davie's reader can propose this because his poem—and this is the bravery (in his second sense) in which it is grounded—invites dialogue and dissent by addressing the reader as the friend to whom he communicates his thoughts.

The Fate of Modernism:
English Poetry 1930-1956

Crozier's idea for a book which would examine the neglected world of 1940s English poetry was initially presented to Cambridge University Press in late September 1992 but faced its first hurdle in the spring of the following year. The referees to whom the proposal had been sent admitted to the problem of not really knowing enough about the poetry referred to, partly on account of its unavailability, and therefore felt insufficiently qualified to be able to recommend its being presented to the Press Syndicate. However, by July 1993 the positive and critically enthusiastic comments of Geoff Ward (Liverpool University) enabled Kevin Taylor, Editor of the Literature list, to present the book proposal to the Syndicate. In August the book proposal was, however, rejected as it currently stood since there was clearly a feeling that since the book was to be about poetry that had been previously neglected there would be some significant difficulty in convincing buyers to purchase what had been, in effect, a lost cause. The importance of market forces had to be considered when one realised that if a book were to sell only 300 copies in its lifetime then a journal might serve its contents better and, as Kevin Taylor put it rather convincingly, a book which began with Auden (dealing with his work in some detail) and ended with Larkin would make a title such as *English Poetry, Auden to Larkin* something which could be marketed more forcefully. A new proposal might produce a book which not only discussed writing between 1938 and 1956 but which would also be a work accessible and of central interest to scholars and teachers of twentieth-century poetry who had not read J.F. Hendry and who might not be persuadable to do so even after reading Crozier's book. A revised proposal was presented to C.U.P. in October 1993 and was accepted in the following month with the provisional title of *The Fate of Modernism: English Poetry, 1930-1956*. A contract was issued on November 24th which included a completion date of 30th September 1995 and an all-inclusive word limit of 90,000 words. However, the book was to remain unwritten. The revised proposal is included here in full.

Under this new title my initial proposal has been revised to take into account and accommodate various ideas expressed when, with a more narrow monographic intention, it was presented under the title 'The New Apocalypse and English Poetry in the 1940s'. The revision is designed in particular to circumvent the major problem of the canonical marginality of "The New Apocalypse", and of 1940s poetry in general, by situating both in relation to literary historical contexts which are better known and frequently discussed. From this it follows that in its revised form the proposal establishes its discursive division of topics on a larger scale, and this meets the persuasive remarks about the freedom of manoeuvre afforded by fewer but longer chapters made in Dr. Ward's report. In addition, since it is focussed less on individual poets, the revised proposal affords greater scope for reference to institutions and histories of publication, aspects of my preliminary research which Dr. Ward wished to see retained. Nevertheless the primary motive of the initial proposal and the research which preceded it—critical rehabilitation of a neglected generation of poets, and elucidation of their position in the history of modern English poetry—remains the same. However, this purpose is now to be served, as a consequence of the longer span of time taken to frame it, by a necessarily more direct polemic engagement with critical consensus and the ways in which the history of English poetry in the 1930s and 1950s has been written. This will also bring into the foreground what was scarcely more than an ancillary motif in the initial proposal, namely the role and character of modernism in English poetry after Pound and Eliot. By arguing that, even while its formal identity was mediated and transformed in complex ways as the consequence of a double marginality (that of modernism itself, and that of English culture in relation to international modernism), the significance of modernism in English poetry has been more sustained and pervasive than has been recognised, the proposal also aligns itself with other current re-evaluations of modernism, and raises questions that are pertinent to the English poetry of the late 20th Century. In this revised proposal, therefore, the limited interest of a study of a marginalised poetic decade is counteracted by the double strategy of situating it more centrally in terms of history, and deploying this broader historical framework to examine theoretical and cultural topics of a more general order.

In its revised form the major alteration to the proposal is that it is no longer focussed on a single decade (indeed, problems arising from the construction of poetic epochs by decades were referred to in the initial proposal) but instead deals with a period of approximately 30 years. Important shifts of emphasis and treatment arise from this, and hence the revised proposal can reasonably be claimed to be an entirely new proposal rather than the modification merely of a previous one. Nevertheless the initial proposal might usefully be retained for purpose of reference in order not to reiterate information about 1940s poetry contained in it. I assume that the salience now accorded to the poetry of the 1930s and 1950s requires no special bibliographical or critical gloss in view of comments suggesting that the scope of the initial proposal be enlarged.

The new proposal takes as its field of enquiry a phase of English poetry marked at its boundaries by two figures of acknowledged major significance, W.H. Auden and Philip Larkin, but it is a phase which has not hitherto been regarded as possessing epochal unity. There are various reasons for this (including the tendency to treat poetic careers and poetic history separately), principal among which is that the phase includes an episode (designated in the title of the initial proposal) which has been treated as exceptional and marginalised. In this proposal it is regarded less as an episode, more as one component and symptomatic strand in the poetry of a 30 year period, and imbricated also with earlier and later English poetry of the 20th Century. In addition to arguing that this strand or episode needs thorough re-evaluation I will maintain that such re-evaluation raises important critical questions about the consensual ordering of 20th Century English poetry. In the light of the helpful comments elicited by the initial form of my proposal I am now persuaded to my own satisfaction that a specifically focussed and detailed study of the sort initially proposed, although still desirable, will not be feasible until the legitimacy and interest of the topic have been established both in terms particular to itself, and in terms which are of wider critical and cultural bearing. The proposal as here revised is intended to accomplish both requirements. Within the larger epochal configuration now deployed it will be possible to map differences and developments on a significant scale without allowing local chronologies to overdetermine the major set of discursive topics to be treated; at the same time it will be possible to focus on specific moments of particular significance without needing to mark these, again in an overdetermined manner, as moments within the significant chronology of a decade. It seems to me, therefore, that the proposal as now revised possesses distinct advantages both as historical interpretation and as theoretical and critical account of its subject.

In the outline of chapters in the synopsis which follows the underlying purpose is to establish the significance of a poetic avant garde ("The New Apocalypse") and its associated style (henceforth referred to as Neo-Romanticism rather than, generically, the poetry of the 1940s). This is undertaken in the context of English poetry as a whole between 1930 and 1956, in order to educe both the formative processes which produced the style which was briefly dominant in the 1940s and the condition of its occlusion and eventual critical suppression (along with earlier modernism) in the 1950s. The historical reinsertion of this style calls into question consensual views of the period's poetry and, since such views underwrite the critical reception of contemporary poetry to a significant extent, also raises questions of immediate and current importance. The first two chapters frame the period historically and also in terms of the study's major critical and theoretical concepts: Chapter 1 deals with the negation of Neo-Romanticism in the 1950s by the polemicized discursive practices of Movement poetry; Chapter 2 establishes a taxonomy of the modern in English poetry circa 1930 on the basis of a significant but overlooked configuration of books by poets of a new generation which were issued in a deliberately innovatory (but short-lived) format. The argument is developed by interrogating the adequacy of reading W.H. Auden as the symptomatic poet of the 1930s, and the diversity of poetic writing in that decade will be examined in order to suggest that such diversity is in fact characteristic of and persistent throughout the period from 1930 to 1956; here and in the concluding chapter the lack of congruence between the historicising of poetry by decades and broader cultural and historical contexts will be addressed. Neo-Romanticism will be read as a codification of various non-Audenesque features of 1930s poetry, but will also be described, and its discursive practices analysed, <u>across</u>, so to speak, its rhetorical antithesis in the 1950s: this provides the centre around which the argument of the study as a whole is arranged. The introductory account of Movement rhetoric, modified by the account of the developments of modernism in English poetry circa 1930, will frame the analytical and discursive account of the 1940s. As a framing device this is only incidentally possessed of chronological symmetry. The protocols of Movement rhetoric will provide a basis for comparison and contrast, and the critique of Movement notions of poetic discourse will open a space for discussion of the modes of signification and textual formation of Neo-Romanticism; modernism, on the other hand, provides points of reference in the form of historical and cultural antecedents modified in and frequently occluded by Neo-Romanticism's privileging of the person. The study will conclude by examining the range of poetry—not exclusively Neo-Romantic—overshadowed by the Movement, and will consider as exemplary in this respect the work of a number of poets (for example F.T. Prince and Roy Fuller) whose careers span most of the period studied.

Title: *The Image and the Fate of Modernism: English Poetry 1930-1956*

Modern poetry has been theorised primarily in terms of the image, its bearings taken from Eliot's notion of the "objective correlative" and, prior to that, Pound's instantaneous "intellectual and emotional complex". In "The New Apocalypse" the image is proposed as a cognitive event and the site of a critique of conceptual knowledge. Despite important differences in the way the image is defined in modernism and Neo-Romanticism it is deployed in both as a primary discursive formation, and thus provides a principal nexus for my argument. Nevertheless, it will be assumed, the image cannot provide a sufficiently differentiated theory of modernism, which requires that non-metrical prosody, diction, and the relation of text to utterance (in which Eliot and Pound differ crucially) be taken into account. These supplementary terms are necessary to bring to light the dynamic in modernism which moves it between lyric and epic frames of discourse. Hence the title proposes a view of modern poetry more generally which both valorises the image and, at the same time, regards its theoretical and textual privilege as a cause of the attenuation (rather than "failure") of modernism. A brief Introduction will set out this case as a speculative extension of existing critical opinion.

CHAPTER 1. 'The Rhetoric of the Movement: The Figure of the Aesthetic and the Discourse of Common Sense.'
This chapter argues (and is positioned accordingly) that it is necessary to take a backward view of the period to be studied because the theory of poetry implicit in the aesthetics and discursive practices of the Movement constitute still the theoretical entailment of English criticism of 20th Century poetry. It will enlarge and focus arguments outlined in my essays 'Thrills and Frills: Poetry as Figures of Empirical Lyricism' (1983) and 'Signs of Identity' (1992), namely that in Movement poetry the literary figure provides the privileged sign of the poetic, but is marginalised in the discursive structure of poetry, and that in consequence poetic language becomes the representation of a rationalised social and cultural identity projected as the mode of the private self. Discussion will focus on the inaugural Movement anthology *New Lines* (1956) and refer extensively to the poetry of Philip Larkin and Donald Davie, but will additionally refer to the work of Geoffrey Hill, Ted Hughes, and Seamus Heaney

in order to demonstrate the persistence of Movement paradigms of the figure. Deconstruction of this prevalent set of discursive practices and the taxonomy of values it encodes is regarded as the necessary preliminary for any discussion of modernism and Neo-Romanticism which is not to be determined by those values.

CHAPTER 2. 'Modernism in English Poetry after Pound and Eliot.'

In 1930 Faber and Faber "devised a format… both convenient and cheap" to publish the work of "the youngest of our poets" who "without being directly derivative" of the poets "who perfected their weapons and who became established during and immediately after the war" had "profited by their rebellion". The publicity material quoted, presumably written by T.S. Eliot, establishes a model of modernist derivation and generational difference which will be used to examine the modernist identity of this younger generation of poets by reference, in the first place, to three volumes issued in this special format. W.H. Auden's *Poems* is frequently cited (although discussion is more commonly referred to the revised and reformatted edition of 1933), but will be discussed here in association with two other little-noticed volumes: J.G. MacLeod, *The Ecliptic* (1930) and Clere Parsons, *Poems* (1932). It thus becomes possible to trace modernist derivations in English poetry in the early 1930s with reference not only (in the case of Auden) to Eliot but also to Pound (MacLeod) and the international modernism of the late 1920s represented by *transition* (Parsons). Reference will be made to the influential *Survey of Modernist Poetry* (1927) of Laura Riding and Robert Graves, and John Sparrow's attack on modernism in *Sense and Poetry* (1934). Other English mediations of modernism (the Cambridge journal *Experiment*, for example) will be cited. This chapter will point forward to discussion of Auden in Chapters 3 and 4, and of MacLeod (writing as "Adam Drinan") in Chapter 5. The poems of Clere Parsons were published posthumously but his work continued to be advocated by Geoffrey Grigson, whose post-war critical stance will be mentioned in Chapter 6.

CHAPTER 3. 'A Low, Dishonest Decade? Varieties of Poetry in the 1930s.'

This chapter will examine the status accorded to Auden as symptomatic and representative poet of the 1930s, a role in which he was first cast during the decade and which subsequent criticism still has him playing. It will enlarge the discussion of Auden and George Barker in my essay 'Styles of the Self' (1987) and extend its range to refer to Dylan Thomas, David

Gascoyne, Charles Madge, and others. However, its focus will be less on single volumes as repositories of authorial style (since such an approach, in consequence of publishing history, inevitably privileges Auden and the poets historically associated with him), more on the range of poets whose work circulated through the poetry journals: *New Verse*, *Contemporary Poetry and Prose*, *Twentieth Century Verse*, and *Seven* will receive particular notice. In addition attention will be given to the journal *Life and Letters* during the editorship of Robert Herring, in which in the late 1930s a version of Anglo-American modernism continued to be promulgated, and which was also hospitable to some of the poets of nascent Neo-Romanticism.

CHAPTER 4. 'The New Apocalypse.'

This chapter draws on the discussion in Chapter 3 to examine and contextualise the critique of Auden, and what was identified (conspicuously in the work of Kenneth Allott) as the socially determined imagination associated with his style, developed by J.F. Hendry around the various manifestations of "The New Apocalypse". It will discuss the development by Hendry and others of manifestos and programmes drawing on Surrealism, Psychoanalysis, and Marxism, and correlate these with aspects of the surreality of everyday life which constituted one of the motifs of the Mass Observation project, with which a number of Apocalyptic writers had been associated as diarists. The chapter will assess the cohesion of "The New Apocalypse" as an avant garde grouping on the basis of its three anthologies (1939-1943), and consider the implications of its effective termination in the cessation of the editorial association of Hendry and Henry Treece.

CHAPTER 5. 'The Rhetoric of Neo-Romanticism.'

This chapter traces and discriminates the different vectors (of which 'The New Apocalypse' was one) of the Neo-Romanticism which established itself as the dominant poetic style of the war years, with which the wartime poetry of Eliot and H.D. possessed affinities. It will analyse its failure as a style as well as the reasons for the rapid historical and critical marginalisation of the poets associated with it. As a style Neo-Romanticism will be examined in terms of its imagery, syntax, and prosody, and their frequently emphatic coalescence in the work of Hendry, W.S. Graham, and Nicholas Moore; as a rhetoric it will be examined in terms of the relation of the self to the body and to history. In conjunction with Chapter 4 it will set out the case for reading the poetry of the 1940s in the theoretical context of modernism.

CHAPTER 6. 'Conclusion: Outside the Movement.'

This chapter takes a broader view of the period as a whole by considering the work of poets whose careers continued from the 1930s into the post-war period, the later careers of some poets associated with Neo-Romanticism, and the work of certain poets close to the Movement whose careers deviated from it. It will argue that the Movement's polemic repudiation of the poetry of the 1940s in effect occluded not only the Neo-Romanticism which was its object of censure but also a poetry of civility and urbanity represented by the work of Roy Fuller, F.T. Prince, Keith Douglas, and the later Norman MacCaig. MacCaig's abandonment of his early Neo-Romanticism will be juxtaposed with the later work of Gascoyne and Graham, which in turn will be juxtaposed with the work of Charles Tomlinson and Donald Davie with reference to the former's exclusion from *New Lines* and the latter's divergence from Movement assumptions following his critical studies of Pound and modernism.

Introduction to *The Works of Andrew Marvell*

Crozier wrote two introductions for the Wordsworth Poetry Library;
both were published in 1995.

Andrew Marvell could be numbered, we might suppose, with Alexander Pope's "mob of gentlemen who wrote with ease" during the reigns of Charles I and Charles II. Pope's phrase is not, in fact, the compliment we might easily take it for (indeed, the word "mob" should have prompted unease enough to put us on our guard), but a professional's comment on an age of amateurs. Although we might assume those gentlemen to be royalist cavaliers, whereas Marvell—as we see from his panegyrics to Oliver Cromwell—adhered to the other side, Pope's judgement might equally seem to apply to him. Marvell himself published few poems, and acknowledged fewer: the poems which comprise most of the poetry accepted to be by him, and which can in most cases be confidently attributed to him, were published posthumously as his *Miscellaneous Poems* in 1681, three years after his death. This collection appears to have been put together from papers left in his London lodgings, and published as a ploy by his landlady, or servant, to pass herself off as his widow—unsuccessfully, as it turned out. For those so inclined the very survival of the poems on which Marvell's modern reputation chiefly depends can seem to owe much to chance. If so, the survival of his Cromwell poems owes even more to chance, for they were suppressed in all but one or two copies of the book.

But it was as a commonwealth's man, an upholder of religious toleration, and an opponent of the political advisers of Charles II, that Marvell was known in his day, on the basis of his public life, his skill as a writer of controversial prose, and as an author of anonymously circulated satires on public events in the 1660s and 1670s. This Marvell was cherished well into the nineteenth century, and we find him in Wordsworth's sonnet of 1802 in which he is numbered with other seventeenth-century upholders of liberty.

> Great men have been among us; hands that penned
> And tongues that uttered wisdom—better none:
> The later Sidney, Marvel, Harrington,
> Young Vane, and others who called Milton friend.

Marvell's connection with Milton was widely known from his commendatory poem on *Paradise Lost* (first published in the second edition of 1674), and was of long standing. There survives from 1653 a letter written by Milton which is, in effect, a testimonial on behalf of a young man looking for a government post, in which he describes Marvell as a gentleman "both by report, and the converse I have had with him, of singular desert for the state to make use of; who also offers himself, if there be any employment for him. His father was the minister of Hull and he has spent four years abroad in Holland, France, Italy and Spain, to very good purpose as I believe, and the gaining of those four languages; besides he is a scholar and well read in the Latin and Greek authors, and no doubt of an approved conversation; for he comes now lately out of the house of the Lord of Fairfax, who was General, where he was entrusted to give some instructions in the languages to the Lady his daughter." This is a good summary of the known facts of Marvell's early life. He had been tutor to General Fairfax's daughter, Mary, at Nun Appleton House in Yorkshire from 1650 to 1652, and became tutor to Cromwell's ward, William Dutton, in 1653. It was probably as a tutor that he went abroad in the early 1640s, after leaving Cambridge, and so was out of the country for most of the Civil War years. In 1657 he became Latin Secretary to the Council of State (he performed other diplomatic roles in the 1660s), and from 1659 until his death was a member of Parliament for Hull. The record is of discreet, conscientious, private and public service. It is understood that as a member of parliament he effectively defended Milton when retribution was exacted on the men associated with the execution of Charles I.

It is commonly supposed that many of the poems in Marvell's *Miscellaneous Poems*, and most of those poems of his which are most admired, were written during his period of rural retirement at General Fairfax's house in Yorkshire, where Fairfax himself had retired after resigning command of the army to Cromwell. 'Upon the Hill and Grove at Bilbarrow' and 'Upon Appleton House', commendatory poems in which his patron's private and public merits are refracted through the properties of his house and estate, self-evidently date from this period, and it is reasonable to associate with them Marvell's other poems on gardens, flowers, grass and fields. Certainly, when they were published in 1681, such poems would have seemed dated, period pieces, as more than one critic has observed. But it can be convenient, as well, to see what may well be Marvell's best poetry as in some way also the genuine article, written in a short space of time preceding his entry into public affairs, as though he then gave up the life of a poet. To do so is a matter of taste as much as judgement, and possibly of false taste, for it allows us to admire as finely poised equivocation the treatment of Charles I and Cromwell in 'An Horatian Ode upon Cromwell's Return from Ireland' (datable to 1650, between Cromwell's Irish and Scottish campaigns) but merely to take note of 'The First Anniversary of the Government under Oliver Cromwell' and 'A Poem upon the Death of Oliver Cromwell', to glance indulgently at the Restoration satires, and to ignore altogether the prose writings. Whereas Pope conveniently ignored the interregnum, this view of Marvell tends to associate him with the pre-Civil War culture of courtliness and grace lamented in 'To His Noble Friend, Mr Richard Lovelace, upon His Poems'.

This is unfortunate, for it deprives us of a possible view of Marvell's consistency, and leaves us surely in something of a quandary when we read the lyric poetry so much admired in the twentieth century. How is it that the speaker—even in 'To His Coy Mistress', ostensibly persuasion to sexual surrender—can remain so calm, so equable in tone while in a state of rapt or intrigued contemplation, so lucid in the exhibition to the understanding of the reader of the complexities of argument and individual plight? It is not a question of what Marvell thought, or where he stood, but rather of how we are able to follow his speakers and recognise an impassioned but disciplined train of thought without a concomitant sense of a dramatized and fully present person speaking. We begin to doubt the basis of our experience of having read Marvell. One way of addressing this difficulty is to see Marvell as primarily a literary poet, writing out of but remaining within his knowledge and experience of the themes and conventions of Renaissance poetry, and it is not difficult to make a start in this direction by detecting affinities with Ben Jonson and John Donne. There is no doubt that Marvell was learned and well read, and used his learning and reading in his poetry (as he did in his controversial prose), but to see these accomplishments as the basis of his lyric poetry is to see the poems as literary exercises, when they are plainly more than that; indeed the doubt that they may be no more than such exercises occurs only when we begin to wonder if we have grasped what we have understood. It is surely the case, rather, that Marvell uses his learning, as well as his wit, and his powers of presentation and argument, to engage with his reader on terms of equality. These are poems to be read in our calm and lucid moments, or to induce those qualities in us by calling into play our own powers of thought.

In his poems about Cromwell, Marvell distinguishes between power and arbitrary personal rule, and the distinction concerns the good of the body politic rather than legitimacy. In the 'Horatian Ode' the things regretted in the poem to Lovelace are more vividly realised in the composure displayed on the scaffold by Charles I, but Marvell passes on, almost without regret himself, to matter of more pressing concern to the republic. In the 'First Anniversary', Cromwell is poised between political wrangling at home and Catholic despotism abroad, but the power he wields represents a nation stabilised by the counterbalancing of contrary interest. The fascination Cromwell had for Marvell is the fascination of power, but for Marvell power is political and calls into question relations between the public and private spheres: they are different but not separate. Politically Marvell appears as a pragmatist interested in the public actions of individuals, concerned for the value of the person but in the recognition that individuals cannot live solely on their own account. He was thus adaptable, as of course were many others who made the transition from serving the Protectorate to serving the restored monarchy, but with a core of consistency. What put him in opposition to government under Charles II were issues of freedom of conscience in religion, and of arbitrary and corrupt conduct of policy. In satires on public events which Marvell is known to have written, but not quite so many as were attributed to him when such writings could be published after the deposition of James II, mock-encomium is used to object to the appropriation by the court of public revenues and, spectacular evidence of this, England's naval humiliation by the Dutch. Corruption at court, and conspicuous consumption, went hand in hand with assertions, in some quarters, that individual conscience should be subservient to royal and ecclesiastical authority, which Marvell opposed in *The Rehersal Transprosed* (1672, Second Part 1673) in a style of *ad hominem* raillery which, we are told, so amused the king that its publisher was able to evade censorship.

Marvell's consistency, therefore, lies in a refusal to be doctrinaire, and what amounts to the recognition that the good cannot be won by force or power of argument. His cast of mind is detached and independent; his public stance involved but non-partisan. This can bring us back to the distinctive and difficult qualities of his lyric poetry. Marvell's imagination, it is invariably noted, is strongly visual. The death of Douglas in 'The Loyal Scot' is realised as an extraordinary emblematic tableau, almost as if he is consumed by the fires of love. In 'To His Coy Mistress', Time's chariot has wings. But in this poem, and in the others in which we catch his distinctive lyric tone, his imagination is perhaps more characteristically kinaesthetic, it registers effort and resistance. Pursuing time is apprehended not as a pictorial emblem (indeed, the speaker cannot see it) but as sound and movement (the beating of its wings), and it is in a hurry. And in an ideally timeless world would not space also be contracted, a lovers' amble take in the Humber and the Ganges? It is a daring conceit to draw these two rivers into a single scene, but the wit would remain illustrative if we did not also know what lovers would do in such circumstances. (She, in fact, is not gathering rosebuds but fine rubies.) The special quality of Marvell's imagination, what we are unprepared for, is his mastery and distribution of kinaesthetic effects, achieved by a frequent use of verbs, carefully chosen and contrasted. The word needed to describe this strenuous exercise of the imagination, I think, is speculative, including its almost forgotten sense (which Marvell would have understood) of looking into things within the mind. Marvell does not affect to speak his mind, or open it for inspection, but draws us into its workings.

Introduction to Andrew Marvell

Introduction to *The Works of Alexander Pope*

One reason for reading Pope—I will suggest several more—is that he was the first poet of the modern epoch, when wealth and power in the state and in society changed from realty to money. Charles I fought and lost because the crown revenues could not support the needs of a modern, expansive nation state, but by the end of the seventeenth century the needs of government, in its foreign wars with the French or the Dutch, could be met by new institutions of public credit—the Bank of England, and the great imperial trading companies, the East India, the South Sea (of the notorious bursting Bubble, when the values of its stock soared and fell catastrophically). Why pay taxes on property when money could be rented out? This financial revolution brought an expansion of credit, everything (and everyone, cynics suggested) had a price. New types of people were being produced, in London especially, the seat of government and commerce; not only a pauperised and criminalised labouring class, but more conspicuously makers of money, new-moneyed people, financially uninhibited, private people with new leisure and consumer needs. Such people had most to fear (or thought they had) from Jacobite attempts to restore Stuart legitimacy which, in England at least, stood for an old order of values, the land, custom, domestic peace and harmony (in *Windsor Forest* "a Stuart reigns"), the social bases of which the new financial arrangements for trade and state eroded. Ideologically such conflict represented itself as between an oligarchy of public men (public because they had an interest in the country in the form of landed property, and hence the independence to serve the public interest as their own) and the competitive interests of private individuals unmotivated by public spirit. Politically, however, there was no contest: the ideologues of the old order were notoriously vague in matters of personal religion, if not scandalously atheistical, whereas the protestant religion was guaranteed by the Hanoverian succession, and this dynasty of frequently absentee kings (more at home in Germany) was also the guarantee of the legitimacy of private interest, of acquisition and display, in an order consolidated by the nice regulation of political corruption by its chief minister, Walpole.

It was precisely the management of financial opportunity for courtiers and politicians, whose interests were thus aligned with those of trade and finance, that produced the political stability which marked the last two decades of Pope's life, the 1720s and 1730s. But if there were to be no more revolutions, or changes of ministry of the sort that drove Pope's friend Bolingbroke into exile, this was the stability of a new sort of business-as-usual, to which Pope reacted with indignant sarcasm and disgust as a spectacle of inverted or destroyed values.

> Hear her black trumpet through the land proclaim
> That NOT TO BE CORRUPTED IS THE SHAME!
> In soldier, churchman, patriot, man in power,
> 'Tis avarice all, ambition is no more!
> See, all our nobles begging to be slaves!
> See, all our fools aspiring to be knaves!

The 'Epilogue to the Satires' (these lines occur at the end of the first Dialogue), written in 1738, almost marks the end of Pope's productive life as a poet. Indeed, this late poem casts doubt on the efficacy of satire in a world in which Vice (the black trumpet is hers) has triumphed over virtue. But Pope supposes that Walpole, the architect of this triumph, privately shared his judgement of the nation.

> Come, come, at all I laugh he laughs, no doubt;
> The only difference is, I dare laugh out.

Pope's knowledge is out in public; Walpole keeps his private and is rewarded with power, but its cynical exercise has corrupted public and private life, and the great man is also somewhat cowardly. He and Pope take different sorts of risk. Indeed there is no advantage in Pope's public boldness, and his satirical laughter reveals the powerlessness of his sort of truth.

Pope approached the end of his career, then, as a disabused patriot. But there is also a recognition of his own greatness, parodically, in what amounts to an act of self-recognition in Walpole, whose private virtues have been conceded. And by implication he has parodied the cynical justification of private interest of Bernard Mandeville (*The Fable of the Bees*, 1714), that private vices are public benefits. Private and public virtue do not exist in inverse ratio if public men have venal motives. However, if at the age of fifty Pope was aware of his genuine eminence (lack of false modesty is one of his amiable qualities), his eminence was partly that of isolation: "Yes, the last Pen for Freedom let me draw," he exclaims at the end of the second Dialogue.

Introduction to Alexander Pope

What was this freedom for which Pope went armed with his pen, if more than nostalgia? It was no, certainly, the abstract freedom of property, for Pope considered that the desire for riches was a form of unfreedom, as indeed was any other immoderate desire or passion. In this sense freedom is a condition of the person, of psychological balance. But it is also a British freedom, of a sort celebrated by Pope's contemporary James Thomson in his ode 'Rule, Britannia' first performed in 1740)—that national conceit that Britons were not subject to the absolute power of church or state. Such freedom is both political and personal, a matter of status rather than of rights, and its celebration is ideological. Pope's insistence that this freedom has been bought grates against Thomson's triumphalism: "Britons never will be slaves."

But if Pope utters this national ideology as it were solely on his own account (his pen gives it a negative inflection, critical of the nation's state: it separates rather than unites) it might appear surprising that he should ever uphold it, for in important respects he was born and lived on several of the nation's margins. His father was a retired merchant, a Catholic, and Pope retained the family religion. His family lived in retirement in Berkshire, perhaps in compliance with measures excluding Catholics from London; he was largely self-educated (Catholics were excluded from the universities). When he first appeared in London he cut a rustic figure; he was also, with his spinal curvature, small and physically grotesque, easy prey for spiteful caricature. On all counts he was hardly cut out for public life, for however that might be defined it would be in terms of power. But Pope's self-education had been in poetry, and poetry, by the end of the seventeenth century, had come to occupy ideological space: the public space of writing had moved from the theatre to print, in a way that politicised writing of every sort, and disrupted the hierarchy of *genres*. As a writer Pope could be nothing other than a public man, but as a poet he was also committed to values which were hostile to these new arrangements. In 1709, when he was just twenty-one, his *Pastorals* were published in one of the poetical Miscellanies popular at the time. That the inferior *Pastorals* of Ambrose Phillips, in the same volume, received better notice left a lasting impression on Pope: he was self-critical, but the ill-founded criticism of others made him the scourge of the world of letters. He never forgave poor Phillips.

The *genre* of pastoral was the focus of a contemporary critical controversy of "Ancients" and "Moderns", which turned on the questions of how closely classical writers should be followed and how realistically shepherds might be portrayed. What was truth to nature if classical writers provided standards of both truthful representation and literary art? The very deadness of classical languages lent permanence to their exemplary primacy. Pope inclined to the Ancients, in so far as he was prepared to take a stand in this pseudo-controversy, but in other respects was a sedulous moderniser, as his versions of older English poets show. He was aware that as a living language English was subject to change, and accepted that his own language would not be permanent, but his versions of the older poets were not motivated solely by the sense that their language had become difficult. They wrote in unpolished times, when men were less free, and Pope applied to them the standards he applied to his own work: verses should be *correct*. (This is the key to understanding Pope's reliance on the heroic couplet, a verse form readers suppose to be hidebound and tedious before they have read Pope at any length.) Correctness lay in "bringing sense and rhyme together", but it also lay in improvement: "it was as pleasant to me to correct as to write". (Both remarks are from Pope's Preface to his *Works* of 1717.)

The young Pope was, then, a highly literary poet, his pursuit of correctness a pursuit of consummate and supreme style. But these qualities were also to be the source of the poetic and moral authority of his later work. If in *An Essay on Criticism* he finds true wit in the best expression of "what oft was thought", it is merely a later notion of originality that he appears to flout; and if thought makes no claim to originality it is not thereby negligible: thought, like wit, should be true, and that is the matter of judgement. It is not possible to separate in Pope precisions of style and meaning, discriminations of wit and judgement. They combine in *The Rape of the Lock*: this really is a quarrel about nothing. *Genre*-parody and the imaginative machinery of the sylphs please us with their wit as much as they judiciously place the events recorded, yet this is also the poem in which Pope makes some of his hardest and most direct comments on manners and values. But even here Pope relies on wit and judgement: on what scale of values do we compare husbands and lapdogs, or compute the punctuality of the jury's dinner and the jury's verdict? This is not yet satire, for Pope has too much sympathy for his victims (as well as sympathy for victims of the law), and his first intention was to mend a rift in the thin social fabric of the polite world. Yet the poem is damning, for it reveals a world in which good order has given over to extremes of artifice and convention, stumbling over trifles.

Pope was somewhat of this world, of course; he was capable of nursing a grievance and spiteful retaliation. His wit was to be feared. But when

Introduction to Alexander Pope

his satire is personal rather than general its tendency is to make persons representative. The reader may grasp the action and catch the tone of *The Dunciad* without recourse to annotation; if anything, the poem has imbued historical nonentities with posthumous vitality. What the reader needs rather more is to be able to see the poet of *The Dunciad* together with the poet of *An Essay on Man* and the *Moral Essays*, for these very different works of Pope's maturity comprise his greatest achievement, in which is explored his conviction that there is an order in things and his vision of present disorder. This is the central contradiction in Pope, displayed more fully by his experience as a poet than in his experience of the polite world, and what inscribes throughout his work the patriotic ideology of freedom upheld, stubbornly and disdainfully, in the 'Epilogue to the Satires'. For Pope's correctness, the aim both to be correct and to correct, is a public virtue, as well as, in Pope, an historical achievement. He had followers but no successor. But Pope's historically achieved correctness coincided with the moment in a different history when writing became a commodity, literature a means of social aspiration, and writers might be political hirelings. Pope benefited from this: his translation of Homer (1715-26) secured his financial independence. He was independent of party. In him were combined literary status and success, but the culture he represented was that of the aristocratic oligarchs whose independence embodied public virtue and the public good. For all his success, therefore, Pope belonged to an oppositional culture. On his terms a poet had to. The press attacked him, and *The Dunciad* is his counter attack on the literary marketplace, a chaotic world of commerce which circulated the new values of private interest. Whatever Pope's personal motives, they are not what motivates the poem.

Pope is more personal in *An Essay on Man* and the *Moral Essays*, in which he writes from conviction, and with the social ease of confidence in being understood by his equals. Pope could be convinced because the argument of *An Essay on Man* is not fresh: its ideas were current, and the poem, published anonymously at first, was greeted with rapture by some of his detractors. What animates the poem is Pope's sense of urgency, that men might disrupt the order of which they were part. Pope's appeal to order is conventionally to a higher agency, to a providential deity intelligible through his works and specifically through man. His theodicy is thus also a justification of the natural order—there is a harmony and connection between parts and the whole—and inevitably, also, of social hierarchy, but it is not a justification of individuals. Individual vagaries might work themselves out in the whole order of things, but that can be of no import to the person. Pope's account of the use to be made of the individual life is developed in the *Moral Essays*, the choice to be made between an orderly balance and the disorder of excess. The issues are posed in terms of ethics, but for Pope and his contemporaries what was finally at issue was the fate of the individual soul.

Pope's theoretical optimism is admirable, and I am less inclined than some other readers to find it self-contradictory. It utters itself, if anything, in contradiction of both the poet's own crippled body and his society, and its poise and certainty of utterance are an achievement not dependent on mere ideas. Pope's social knowledge, it is apparent, did not provide the empirical evidence for such optimism, rather the reverse. But the pessimism of the 'Epilogue to the Satires' is anything but glum, and Pope's management of the push and pull of the two dialogues is almost jaunty in its finesse. And he had one last trick up his sleeve. What remained for Pope was to add, in 1742, a fourth book to *The Dunciad* of 1728, in apocalyptic fulfilment of what, in the earlier culmination of the poem, was figured as prophetic dream. Pope's pessimism, if that is what this is, is realised through the active performance of his imagination, for the triumph of Dulness, transferred to the new conclusion of the poem, is realised in the same terms of fantasy as before. It makes no difference that the fantasy no longer purports to be a dream, although it is much worse than now "Darkness buries" rather than merely "covers all". But it is also surely a recovery that this triumph, unlike the triumph of Vice, is the work of unfettered imagination. Here, finally, we have Pope free of ideology.

Paper Bunting

In a draft note dated April 1995 Crozier outlined his discovery of the true authorship of an essay that had been attributed to Basil Bunting. In a summary he declared that "The essay 'The Written Record' attributed to Basil Bunting by Peter Makin, and published as his in Basil Bunting, *Three Essays* (1994), is not by Bunting. It is the essay 'Paper' by Roger Kaigh, pseudonym of Irving Kaplan, the friend of Louis Zukofsky, unpublished and supposedly lost, which Zukofsky considered bore a pertinent relation to his own early critical writing." This article was first published in *Sagetrieb*, 14.3, February 1997. As a result of Crozier's detective work Richard Caddel and Diana Collecott, Directors of the Basil Bunting Poetry Centre at the University of Durham produced the following response titled 'The Written Record':

"Evidence brought to light in April by Andrew Crozier (University of Sussex) now demonstrates that this essay—on the unreliability of the written record—is not in fact by Basil Bunting, but by 'Roger Kaigh', the pseudonym of Louis Zukofsky's friend, Irving Kaplan. Dr. Crozier will publish his work on the origins and ascription of this paper in due course—meanwhile the Directors of the Basil Bunting Poetry Centre issue this statement to avoid further confusion.

The essay was purchased, together with a group of papers by Bunting, Zukofsky and others, from the Bunting estate in 1988. Its initial identification was made by Peter Makin, Peter Quartermain, and Richard Caddel at that time, on the strength of the circumstantial evidence of its discovery, and its contents. Any confusion caused by this premature judgement is very much regretted. The essay has been available in the Basil Bunting Poetry Archive—where it has been consulted by numerous Bunting and Zukofsky scholars—since 1988, and since 1994 it has been available in published form in the Centre's publication *Three Essays*. At no time has its ascription been questioned.

We are therefore grateful to Dr. Crozier for identifying the piece as 'Paper' by Roger Kaigh (referred to and quoted from by Louis Zukofsky in his own essay 'American Poetry 1920-1930'), and for his work on the Kaigh/Kaplan-Zukofsky connection. It still remains a matter of conjecture how the piece, without its title page, or any authorial statement, came to be in Bunting's possession—but its importance to him—demonstrated in the other pieces in *Three Essays*—is evident.

We are pleased that the piece has now been correctly identified, and that an important unpublished paper which had been thought lost is now identified and accessible. We are of course also eager to contact Irving Kaplan or his heirs at an early stage."

When Crozier's article was published it was followed by the following note:

I wish to acknowledge scholarship's debt to the dog as aid and model: it was my wife's whippet bitch Amy whose nocturnal insistence on being let out brought on an insomniac episode employed to check the Zukofsky 'Paper' paragraph against 'The Written Record…', and whose persistence on the scent later afforded the leisure in which doubts about Bunting's authorship were formed.

The following notes correct a mistaken attribution and announce a discovery. They do so at some length because the matter amounts to rather more than reattribution of a known work. Identification of the text recently published as 'The Written Record…' in Basil Bunting, *Three Essays*, as Roger Kaigh's 'Paper'—supposed lost—throws new light on the intellectual context of Louis Zukofsky's writing while he was developing the critical concepts which defined his writing practice and the idea of the "Objectivist" poet.[1] In addition, identification of 'The Written Record…' as not Bunting's reveals more fully, by contrast, the significance of his essay 'Some Limitations of English' as an example of the attention paid by poets to the cultural theories developed by Durkheim, Frobenius, and Lévy-Bruhl through the study of "savage" or "primitive" societies and, more particularly, to the ethnological reports from which their work was derived.

The research on which these notes are based was carried out over several months in 1995, the notes themselves having their own role to play in this since the deductive activity they record served to frame subsequent empirical enquiries. Rather than recast my findings synthetically to suggest a completed outcome I have retained the form of my original notes, which as they stand are the result of continual redrafting, for two reasons. The first is that lines of speculation and investigation which followed the initial discovery, in an essay attributed to Bunting, of a paragraph cited by Zukofsky as from 'Paper' by Roger Kaigh, can tell a story, though not the whole story by any means, and I think it is important to glimpse the complex of wishes and exchanges, the network of relationships, which surrounded 'Paper' and constitute its forgotten history. The second, already hinted, is more important. It would be rash to suppose that I have been able to locate all relevant evidence, and hence presumptuous to offer my findings in a more determinate form. My hope is, rather, that others may be able to add to the evidence presented here, and thus enable more definite conclusions to be reached, or discover broader implications in this episode. Some readers may, nevertheless, find it helpful to start with a summary of the information these notes adduce.

Early in 1929 Zukofsky made plans for a quarterly magazine, *The States*, to include in its first issue 'Paper' by his Columbia classmate Irving Kaplan, writing under the pseudonym "Roger Kaigh". 'Paper' draws a distinction between formulaic and particular meanings of words, and its intellectual background includes the use by early 20th Century writers such as Lucien Lévy-Bruhl of the work of 19th Century ethnologists. (Kaplan thus shares a source with T.S. Eliot, whom elsewhere in his essay he attacks.) Later in 1929, when plans for *The States* were abandoned, Zukofsky sent some of the intended contents, including 'Paper', to Ezra Pound. Concurrently he discussed his own plans for critical essays concerned with what he termed the vitalization of words. A paragraph from 'Paper' quoted in his 'American Poetry 1920-1930' (completed June 1930) is pertinent to this. Later in 1930, writing to Pound from Berkeley where he was spending the summer with Kaplan, Zukofsky mentioned a scheme to publish 'Paper' together with four of his own essays; it would be stated that "Roger Kaigh" was the pseudonym of an Arunta aboriginal.

Two manuscripts of 'Paper' are now known to exist: one, at Durham University Library, formerly the property of Bunting, and recently published as by him; another, at the Harry Ransom Humanities Research Center, University of Texas at Austin, formerly the property of Zukofsky. The latter is a later typescript (though virtually identical textually with the Durham manuscript); the Durham manuscript is the major remnant of an earlier typescript from which preliminary matter has been excised, but was not the copy text for the Texas manuscript. The Texas manuscript also states that "Roger Kaigh" is the pseudonym of an Arunta, and dates the essay 1922-23; the Durham manuscript does not identify author or title.

There are significant affinities between 'Paper' and Bunting's 'Some Limitations of English', written in the Autumn of 1930. It is not known when or how he acquired a copy of 'Paper', but the supposition must be that he obtained it from Zukofsky, and there are good grounds to suppose that this was in 1930, while on a visit to America, when he met and corresponded with Zukofsky, and when 'Paper' was fresh in Zukofsky's mind. These grounds do not include the essays' affinities, since Kaplan and Bunting may well have worked independently using Lévy-Bruhl and similar writers; if, indeed, Bunting did know 'Paper' when he wrote his essay we may assume that its interest for him lay in his familiarity with its topics, and the different inflection he gave them. But it might also be surmised that Bunting acquired his copy, along with later Zukofsky manuscripts now at Durham, after he returned to America in 1938.

THE STATE OF CRITICISM IN AMERICA

Zukofsky's essay 'American Poetry 1920-1930' is a polemic statement of what was currently of value in American poetry. It was written from within the perspective of his own generation of poets in America, and its critical discriminations turn on a strategy designed to show that the London-based Imagism of the 1910s had been superseded in the later work of Pound, which had gone from an Imagist "isolation of the image" to "the poetic locus produced by the passage from one image to another."[2] We are to understand this specifically as an American quality found also in the work of William Carlos Williams and Marianne Moore, for example; Zukofsky comments contrastively on the ill effects of English cultural influence on the writing of H.D., Wallace Stevens, and T.S. Eliot.

In the second section of his essay Zukofsky adapts the Poundian categories phanopoeia, melopoeia, and logopoeia to his own purposes as image, cadence, and idea, and insists that in poems these are inseparable. But for more detailed commentary of exemplary American work of the 1920s he substitutes for cadence and image the terms music and diction, terms in an equation which allows him to indicate just how they are inseparable in poems: "Music of word in a poem is to a great extent a matter of diction", and "the diction of these poets remains their fully varied material".[3] Still to be brought into the equation is logopoeia, idea, or its third terminological variant, and indeed at the conclusion of this section of the essay we find Zukofsky opting for the new term, meaning. He adopts this term from an unpublished essay by an unknown critic, and what is perhaps most immediately striking about this, for he is ordinarily a supremely confident critic, is Zukofsky's explicit recourse to another's views. The reason for this can best be understood, I believe, if we note that meaning there obtains a distinct and special sense. Defined in a way that binds meaning to a context of performative utterance, the new term can enter the equation with music and diction in a way that the term idea could not. Meaning is thus appropriately consequent, in Zukofsky's sequence of topics, to diction.

The only diction which is dead today is that of poets who, as some one has said of Matthew Arnold, have put on singing robes to lose themselves in the universal. Anent this matter, a paragraph from Roger Kaigh's *Paper* (still unpublished—the state of criticism in America is very low, as perhaps elsewhere) is not appropriate.

"The bias of paper, to this day, most radically affect logicians and philosophers. Logicians will admit that a word has more than one meaning, but each must be definite and thus distinct. Infinite shades of meaning cannot be recognized, for the instrument of formal logic depends upon static or categorical meanings, that is, definitions, for its operation. Otherwise the logician detects the fallacy of four terms. But categories which appear distinct upon paper derive an infinity of variations in speech. 'Yes' and 'No' are categorically distinct upon paper, but either may mean anything from emphatic 'Yes' to emphatic 'No' when spoken. For the context, gesture, intonation and pronunciation give words a stamp of meaning which a written form will lack."[4]

(It will be seen subsequently that Zukofsky had direct knowledge of the vicissitudes encountered in attempts to get 'Paper' into print.) Here Kaigh's argument that words in their written forms take on the character of logical categories is wittily introduced following reference to the universal. But Kaigh's point about the dialogic and performative aspects of language is then taken up by Zukofsky in a comment rather less permissive than his remark about the "only diction which is dead today" might lead us to expect.

> The diction employed by Pound, Eliot, Williams, M. Moore and Cummings has always tended towards the most definite connotation [*sic*] and to a varied play of connotation. The devices of emphasizing cadence by arrangement of line and typography have always been those which would clarify and render the meaning of the spoken word specific.[5]

Cadence, indicated by the arrangement of written forms (arrangements which can be understood to include diction rendered as lexical items written in series, as well as their typographical disposition as words on the page), produces that stamp of meaning acquired in the context of utterance. What Kaigh's distinction between words written and words spoken in relation to fine shades of meaning contributes to Zukofsky's critical discrimination of poetic values is the final term in the equation designating the congruence of poetic properties: music, diction, meaning. There is a case to be made, I think, that Kaigh's nominalist objections to the general categories of logicians and philosophers allowed Zukofsky to think through and synthesise Pound's tripartite division of poetic properties by bringing meaning into relation with formal features of poetic performance, and hence to detach it somewhat from denotation. "The things these poets deal with are of their world and time, but they are *modern* only because their words are *energies which make for meaning*." (My emphasis.)[6]

I find it striking that Zukofsky chose not to edit out reference to Kaigh when he incorporated this essay in *Prepositions*. In his retention of this passage in the collection of his miscellaneous critical writings in which much is revised, or omitted altogether, we might detect, as well as a gesture of indebtedness down the years, a recognition of the extent to which at this point in the essay Kaigh's thinking overlaps and facilitates his own. It has long seemed to me unfortunate, so tantalising is the glimpse given by Zukofsky, that the full reach and force of Kaigh's argument in 'Paper' were lost to us.

THE WRITTEN RECORD

The two other essays included with 'The Written Record...' in Basil Bunting, *Three Essays*, are 'Some Limitations of English' and 'The Lion and the Lizard'. Bunting worked on the first of these in the latter part of 1930, and published it (with Zukofsky's assistance) in *The Lion and Crown* 1,1 (1932).[7] The second is published for the first time, from a manuscript copy in the Zukofsky papers at the Harry Ransom Humanities Research Center, University of Texas at Austin; it appears that Bunting sent it to Zukofsky in 1935 when he was turning out old papers. To these is added (and perhaps just as well), "by way of an appendix", the much later piece 'The Poet's Point of View', first published in 1966.

'The Written Record...' is also published for the first time, from a manuscript copy in the Mountjoy Collection, Durham University Library. The title is supplied from the opening words of the manuscript, which is cited thus in the 1991 handlist of the Mountjoy Collection and in Peter Makin, *Bunting: The Shaping of his Verse*.[8] Makin's account of the essay confines itself, by and large, to its attack on Aristotelain logic, which he coopts for the purposes of his own attack on what he regards (not unjustly) as the relativism of contemporary critical theory and literary criticism. (His account of the essay comes in Part IV of his book, 'Theory'.) But his citations are too few and too brief to convey the characteristic tone of the essay, which for this reader at least was distinctly evocative of something imperfectly remembered. Paper is its primary referent: the phrases "paper age", "paper art", "paper records" occur in regular proximity. It attributes the concepts of permanence, universals, and intrinsic value to the ubiquity of paper. I am surely not the only reader to have had the experience of *déjà lu* on reading this essay, not because the themes are familiar (which they are) but because the motif *paper* carried a specific resonance. Having tracked that to its source in Zukofsky's essay it was a matter of minutes to establish its correlation. The paragraph from 'Paper' quoted by Zukofsky occurs in the final section of 'The Written Record...'. This was surely enough to confirm that the manuscript published as 'The Written Record...' is a surveying copy of 'Paper'. Reference in Part IV of 'The Written Record...' to Australian aborigines' belief in spirit-causation, as will be seen below, reinforced this identification. But was "Roger Kaigh", as cited by Zukofsky, the pseudonym of Basil Bunting? This question, in the first flush of excitement of discovery, did not immediately suggest itself, but on subsequent reflection its importance became obvious.

MS 14: Mountjoy Collection

The Mountjoy Collection at Durham University Library was acquired by purchase from Bunting's widow in 1988. It comprises 56 separate items, which the handlist assigns to five distinct groups: manuscripts and notebooks by Bunting; translations by others of poems by Bunting; correspondence; association manuscripts; and printed miscellanea. The first and fourth groups (Nos 1-20, and 34-54) are of interest in the present context. The material in the other groups, including correspondence from Zukofsky, is recent, i.e. datable to the 1960s or later. The first group, which includes the manuscript known as 'The Written Record...', consists also, for the most part, of recent material. (The other exceptions are some translations from the Persian from the late 1940s, undated transcriptions of Persian poetry from 19th Century editions, and *The Pious Cat*, a translation begun in the late 1930s and completed in 1977.) Most of the fourth group (Nos. 38-54) consists of manuscripts by Louis Zukofsky datable to the

1930s and early 1940s. It is, in fact, a major collection of manuscript material by Zukofsky, including versions of 'A-8' and 'A-9', *Arise, Arise*, material published in *It Was*, and the unpublished *A Workers Anthology*. As a collection it bears witness to the close association of Zukofsky and Bunting.

MS 14, known as 'The Written Record...', is untitled and unsigned. It comprises 11 typed leaves, the first two of which indicate that the text, although complete as it stands, has been revised by cutting from the head, and that the extant manuscript is the remainder of its original. The first leaf is an oblong slip of paper, and provides the first paragraph of the published text. The second leaf was originally numbered 2, but this has been altered in autograph to Roman I. (The rest of the manuscript is regularly paginated from 3 to 10, with an additional unpaginated leaf of notes.) The first eight lines of the second leaf, and most of the ninth, have been cancelled in autograph. This completes the cancellation of a passage suppressed by the removal of a leaf from the original manuscript, which would have been the first leaf of a text presumably paginated from 1 to 10—from which the paper slip which now constitutes the first leaf was probably cut. Lines 8 to 11 of the second leaf were originally an independent paragraph, but autograph editorial markings connect its uncancelled portion to the following paragraph to provide the second paragraph of the published text, a peculiarity of which is that it thus ignores the autograph Roman numeral at the head of this leaf, but follows the sectional division of the text thereafter. (The numbering of sections in the manuscript later skips from II to IV in error, and this has been corrected editorially.) Removal of the original first leaf of the manuscript may, or may not, also have suppressed indications of author and title; these might just as well, or might not, have been given on a separate cover sheet. As the manuscript now stands, however, it appears makeshift as well as anonymous. The first paragraph, present as a slip attached to the remnant of the original manuscript, might have the character of radical afterthought. Indeed, were it not for the opening conjunction of the second paragraph (which, however, originally linked its sentence to a different antecedent) I might be inclined to read this paragraph not as the essay's opening paragraph but as its summary, and insert the autograph Roman numeral after it as the original section number. Be that as it may, the new first leaf, as well perhaps as effacing identifying evidence, is indicative of a drastic revisionary motive not apparent elsewhere in the manuscript. Its closing reference to "two contemporary individuals" might even be the mark of another authorial hand.

Attribution of 'The Written Record...' to Bunting was on the basis of association. It bears no signature, but was discovered with a collection of papers which had belonged to him. The Mountjoy handlist cites the opinion of Peter Quartermain that it was written c. 1932-35; Makin, on internal evidence, is inclined to attribute it to "several years before 1930".[9] (We have seen that Zukofsky cites it in an essay published in 1931.) But on the basis of these dates two surely quite striking considerations might arise. The first is that, in relation to manuscripts in the collection by Bunting, MS 14 is exceptional because it is early. The second, by the same token, is that it might more plausibly be linked by date and association with the Zukofsky manuscripts. (I have not been able to obtain information about the arrangement of the collection when it was acquired). Indeed, it might be argued that the Mountjoy Collection divides as two categories of material: a carefully retained group of manuscripts with a Zukofsky provenance (I will deal below with the problem of transmission) but not including correspondence; and a miscellaneous accumulation of various later pieces.

Attribution to Bunting has been, I suspect, the expression of a pardonable wish on the part of Bunting scholars. This can be discerned, for example, in Makin's confident attribution based on the survival of the manuscript among Bunting's scant literary remains, but this is surely the confidence of a conviction derived from the pathos of the history he ascribes to the material object itself.

> When [Bunting] died, this single typescript was one of the carefully weeded bundle of documents that constituted the entirety of the "literary papers" in his possession: it had survived, that is, America, Italy, Scotland, Persia, and Italy, and had evaded that voracious engine, Bunting's wastebasket, for more than fifty-five years. I am certain that Bunting would have repudiated any imputation of systematic thought; yet it was left undestroyed, by a man to whom destroying, not preserving, was natural.[10]

We may relish, but not too much, the irony of Bunting's repudiation when we take account of what more can be learned of the history of 'Paper'.

Louis Zukofsky spent the summer of 1930, en route to the University of Wisconsin, in Berkeley. He announced his impending departure from New York in a letter to Ezra Pound: "Will spend my summer in Kaigh's attic and try to do my own work for a change—."[11] The correspondence with Pound continued over the summer, and Zukofsky reported from Berkeley on the progress of his own work, and plans made for it.

> Also decided (host and I) on a prospective wish-fulfilment. Should like i.e. publish his essay 'Paper' and my Hen Adams, E.P.—His Cantos, Chas. Rez. & Am. Po. 1920-1930 under title *Four Essays and Paper*. Have already written the foreword:
> "The essay Paper by Roger Kaigh is presented as the work of an Arunta, a native of central Australia, who used an Anglo-American name for reasons of his own. The author of the other four essays in this volume has, to the best of his knowledge, the only copy available, and it is printed here because it would have been manifestly impossible to take cognizance of its thought consonant with points of aesthetic criticism in the other essays, unless their author divulged the relation"—You have seen 'Paper' and are asked not to divulge its authorship.[12]

The projected book *Four Essays and Paper* is yet another of those projects of modernism not realised, but notable because Zukofsky's summary account of its contents both indicates a formal association between his four essays and states a "relation" between his own "aesthetic criticism" and a separately postulated "thought". The relation is implied not to possess formal status, not to be one of practice to theory, for example; its character requires to be demonstrated by juxtaposition so that the reader of 'Paper' might "take cognizance of its thought consonant with" Zukofsky's criticism: the elliptical syntax limits the relation to consonance and contiguity. Nevertheless, the relation is one which Zukofsky's readers might well wish had been made more fully open to inspection than has hitherto been the case.

Barry Ahearn, the editor of the Pound/Zukofsky correspondence, notes of 'Paper': "This essay seems not to have survived, nor has the 'foreword' Zukofsky mentions."[13] It has in fact survived, and under not unlikely circumstances. For the rest, forewords and such by Zukofsky are marked by brevity, and I suppose the "already written" foreword to be the paragraph in inverted commas quoted above.

The States, A Quarterly

At this point it is appropriate to interpolate an account of earlier references to 'Paper' retrieved from archival sources. I have not been able to trace the manuscript seen by Pound, or contemporary references to it in Pound's correspondence. References do, however, occur in Zukofsky's correspondence with Pound during 1929, and his letters indicate the significance he attached to the essay and also, I suggest, the application he made of its "thought" to his own work.

At the beginning of 1929 Zukofsky was preoccupied with plans for a quarterly, along the lines of Pound's *Exile*, to be called *The States*. A letterhead was printed, with addresses in New York and Philadelphia. Zukofsky was one of four editors, the others being a Philadelphia printer named Kay, who was to produce the magazine, Tibor Serly, and another—unnamed—who may possibly have been the author of 'Paper'. Zukofsky reported to Pound on the contents intended for the first number: these were to include, as well as poems by William Carlos Williams, Charles Reznikoff, and George Oppen, a "Critical Opus by Roger Kay on the concepts connected with Paper, Aristotelian logick, the relation of ideas to the structure of language, T.S. Eliot (by the way, or in summary), etc."[14]

Later in the year, after this scheme had fallen through, Zukofsky sent Pound copies of some of the intended contents, including 'Paper'.[15] At the same time, he discussed his forthcoming application for a Guggenheim Fellowship. The scheme of work he proposed was to complete '*A*' and write "a volume of criticism indicating a literary criticism of the vitalization of words, such as '*A*' might be founded on." This 'literary criticism of the vitalization of words' involved the separate treatment of specific cases (Donne, Henry Adams, Laforgue, Corbière, Rimbaud, Pound) but '*A*' would also treat some of its "subject matter" as poetry.[16] Zukofsky's term "vitalization" (which he posited as the outcome of "method") represents, I suggest, that accomplishment of precise verbal meaning described in the paragraph from 'Paper' he quoted in 'American Poetry 1920-1930', an essay which might be read as an account of method.

Recapitulation may be appropriate at this point in order to hold difficulties in focus. 'Paper' by Roger Kaigh has been identified, but the identity of Kaigh remains to be established. However, it is certain that "Roger Kaigh" was not the pseudonym of Basil Bunting, since references to Kaigh and 'Paper' occur in Zukofsky's letters to Pound well before his first meeting with Bunting.

Barry Ahearn identifies "Roger Kaigh", without explanation, as one Irving Kaplan.[17] Evidence for this identification will be found in Zukofsky's unpublished correspondence with Pound, and although I regard it as conclusive it is, nevertheless, somewhat peculiar. In a personal communication Ahearn has drawn my attention to a 1931 letter in which Zukofsky advises Pound to write to Kaigh for specific information on the American labour movement, to supplement the bibliography he had already provided, and then gives Irving Kaplan's name and address. In this letter the names are connected appositionally, and identification is based inferentially on the fact that Pound is not told to write care of Kaplan.[18] In addition to this, I draw attention to the earlier letter with which, presumably, Zukofsky enclosed the copy of 'Paper' sent to Pound.

> If you like 'Paper' write the author about it—Mr Irving Kaplan (sometime Roger Kaigh), 2611 Pacific Avenue, San Francisco, Cal.[19]

Independent confirmation of the identity of Kaigh and Kaplan is provided by Zukofsky's friend Jerry Reisman, also in a personal communication, although he tells me that he knows nothing about 'Paper'.[20]

The peculiarity of Zukofsky's references to Kaplan is that both are associated with the wish that Pound write to Kaigh. This is probably no more than a proper compunction not to confuse the Post Office, or embarrass Kaplan, but it is striking nevertheless. Elsewhere in Zukofsky's letters to Pound the name Kaigh is always used, with and without inverted commas: it serves as both the name of a person and a pseudonym. On the one hand, Kaigh has a local habitation as well as a name, not to mention a wife and an attic. He is the author of an essay which Pound knows in manuscript. But Pound is also made privy to the fiction that "Roger Kaigh" is the pseudonym of an Arunta aboriginal, and is asked not to divulge the author's identity. Here matters become complicated (more so, indeed, than is yet apparent), for Pound is also being asked not to divulge that "Roger Kaigh" is the person Zukofsky refers to as Kaigh. For Pound, that is to say, the Anglo-American name Roger Kaigh signifies both a person (Zukofsky's host for the summer and the author of 'Paper') and a device of polemic indirection. At the lower level of complication he is asked to conceal his knowledge that the author of 'Paper' is not, as alleged, an Arunta; at the higher level of complication, however, he is being asked to conceal his implied understanding that "Roger Kaigh" is not a pseudonym but the name of a real person. Pound was not actually being misled, for he had previously been told that Kaplan was "sometime Roger Kaigh", but in the meantime textually Kaplan was again Kaigh. The complication is significant at least to the extent that it is indicative of the degree of equivocation and uncertainty concerning authorship of 'Paper' at the time of its circulation (which may not have been wider than Zukofsky, Pound, and Bunting.) The scholars who attributed it to Bunting were, as much as anything, victims of this old confusion.

At this stage we need to pause. Do we not discern, except when Zukofsky points Pound in Kaplan's direction, two Roger Kaighs: the Kaigh who is Kaplan, and the "Roger Kaigh" who is the pseudonymous author of 'Paper'? This question might be put another way. When Zukofsky refers to his Berkeley friend as Kaigh is he also referring to the author of 'Paper', or is he not, by referring suppositionally to its author as "Kaigh", disguising its authorship twice over? This will sound complicated, but it has exactly the same degree of complication as the allegation that "Roger Kaigh" is the pseudonym of an Arunta, except that the Arunta is a fiction and Kaplan was not. Nevertheless, if Kaplan was not the author of 'Paper', but its authorship was dissimulated by pseudonymous use of a name associated with him, the fiction of his authorship—as "Kaigh"—would be promulgated. The fiction (however secretly kept) that he was the author of 'Paper' would not, however, be the same as the fact that he was not. I hope that this will not be taken for idle ingenuity. Two Kaighs remain logically distinguishable in Zukofsky's representations to Pound of his friend Kaplan and of 'Paper' and its authorship and, although I have no reason to doubt that they were one and the same, were their identity doubted, the implication would be that Zukofsky himself wrote 'Paper', and went to exceptional lengths to disguise the fact. But such doubt would open the way to questioning his presence in San Francisco in 1930 (which his correspondence with Pound would then appear to be at pains to substantiate.) Nevertheless, I have already indicated possible grounds for inferring that Bunting, at least, thought that Zukofsky wrote 'Paper'. But on what evidence? There is no reason to suppose that what was not clearly revealed to Pound would have been clearly revealed to Bunting, and whereas it is feasible to suppose that Bunting guessed at a truth behind the fictions surrounding authorship of 'paper', we cannot assume that he guessed right.

WHO WAS IRVING KAPLAN?

To recapitulate yet again, identification of Irving Kaplan as Roger Kaigh does not guarantee that he was the author of 'Paper'. It will be helpful, for the time being, to dismiss the name "Roger Kaigh" since it cannot be of further assistance in determining authorship. (It should be recalled, however, that reasons for supposing Zukofsky's authorship—and there is no direct evidence that this was ever supposed—are a consequence of confusions arising from the use of "Roger Kaigh" as both a personal name and a pseudonym.) But so far Irving Kaplan has been almost more of a cypher than "Roger Kaigh". What is there to know of him?

Zukofsky's widow recalled his friendship with Kaplan, which began when both were students at Columbia, in an interview with Carroll F. Terrell. Her evidence casts no light on the authorship of 'Paper', but it establishes Kaplan as an historical subject in his own right, and illuminates his relationship with Zukofsky.

> [Zukofsky] worked for awhile [*sic*] for the National Industrial Conference Board. That was the job he got through a close friend at Columbia known as Kappy. His real name was Kaplan, Irving Kaplan. Everybody called him Kappy. He was a statistician on Wall Street. Louie continued to see him for quite a number of years until they moved to Washington when Kappy got a job working for somebody important in the Roosevelt administration.[21]

Between New York and Washington, as has been seen, Kaplan spent some years in San Francisco. He was there in 1929, and at this time Zukofsky described him to Pound as an expert in corporation taxation. He was still there in 1932, when Zukofsky visited him again, in the company of Jerry Reisman, during the Spring and early Summer. At this time, according to Reisman, Kaplan was employed by the Pacific Gas and Electric Company. Reisman also met Kaplan several times thereafter in

New York, at Zukofsky's apartment, but had no contact with him after the mid-1930s. He describes Zukofsky and Kaplan as engaging in frequent political discussions which developed into intense arguments because Kaplan, unlike Zukofsky, favoured personal activism. Kaplan had "a good sense of humour and enjoyed kidding around. He was friendly, happy and good company."[22]

At this point, were it not for his habit of finding jobs for old Columbia friends, we might lose sight of Kaplan except for two items, or possibly three, listed in the Library of Congress Catalogue. He was the author of two papers, *The Research Program of the National Research Project* (1937) for the Washington Chapter of the National Statistical Association, and (with David Weintraub) *The National Research Project on Reemployment Opportunities and Recent Changes in Industrial Techniques* (1938). Perhaps he was also the Irving Kaplan (born 1904, the same year as Zukofsky) listed as co-author, with Charles Jack Lippey, of *Professional Cartooning* (Newark, 1939).

Kaplan was Associate Director of the National Research Project on Reemployment Opportunities and Recent Changes in Industrial Techniques of the Works Progress Administration, under David Weintraub. In October 1937 he helped Whittaker Chambers, another Columbia friend, get a job with the Project, and in the fullness of time this came to be seen as yet another episode in the systematic Communist infiltration of the Federal government. In the post-war decade Kaplan was a victim of the witch-hunts designed to purge American public life. He was implicated by the testimony of both Elizabeth Bentley ("the blonde spy queen") and Whittaker Chambers. According to Bentley he was a member of two spy rings, through one of which he passed information (he was then employed in the War Production Board); through the other he paid his Party dues. Bentley, who had operated as a courier between Washington and New York, informed to the FBI in August 1945. In the Bureau's report to the White House in November Kaplan was named as one of her contacts. She worked under the direction of the Bureau until 1947, and began to give public testimony before the House Committee on Un-American Activities in 1948. Chambers was then brought into the proceedings, and his testimony also implicated Kaplan. Like most of the others named by Bentley, Kaplan pleaded the Fifth Amendment, but such use of constitutional privilege against self-incrimination was deemed to be a sign of guilt. In the 1950s, when the State Department began to screen American citizens working for the United Nations, those with a history of such pleas were weeded out with the connivance of the Secretary General. Kaplan, who worked for the United Nations on a temporary contract, was dismissed in 1952, a dismissal upheld, with several others, by an Administrative Tribunal of the General Assembly in 1953.

This brings us no further forward with the question of the authorship of 'Paper', nor does it, I think, cast light on the author's use of a pseudonym, but it extends our understanding of Kaplan as an intellectual of a particular generation and type, and brings him closer to us. David Caute's comment on another dismissed member of the UN's personnel can be adapted to fit his case: his life experience "illuminates the whole radical predicament; not merely [his] fate, but the succession of impulses that led a person of progressive outlook to invest New Deal idealism in the war against Nazi Germany until, encountering and evading the mud barriers of the Cold War, this same idealism flowed outward into new international agencies, where peaceful coexistence and the war against poverty might be fought."[23]

It would be difficult to extrapolate from the arguments of 'Paper'—the insistence, for example, that logic and totemism are both systems for giving reasons—a strong disposition towards the politics with which Kaplan has now been identified, although the attempt might be made. But as a statistician, on the other hand, his intellectual discipline might well be thought to incline him to value particulars and distrust universals, and this is precisely the cast of mind we find throughout 'Paper'. And of course, in raising the question of the possibility of Zukofsky's authorship (there is no reason to enquire any further afield that I can see) I was raising a conceptual phantom. This was necessary since the complex identification of "Kaigh" left a logical cranny into which the possibility of other authorship might creep. But the probability remains that the two Kaighs were one and the same, and that Kaplan wrote 'Paper'. What persuades me of this rather more forcefully, however, is a combination of two sorts of reason. The first is that Kaplan is no longer a cypher. Although not much is known about him it is enough to establish his close friendship with Zukofsky through two decades. The second is that there are good reasons not to think that Zukofsky wrote 'Paper', and to accept his identification of Kaplan as its author. 1.) There is no reason to suppose that Zukofsky wished to mislead Pound, by forcing 'Paper' on his attention while disclaiming authorship. 2.) Had Zukofsky, as an "aesthetic critic", considered that the genre of 'Paper' was one with which he should not be associated, the reservation would apply to the essay as a whole. Zukofsky had no need to disown the contribution to the arguments of 'American Poetry 1920-1930' made by the propositions contained in the paragraph quoted from 'Paper'. On this score probability leads to the conclusion that 'Paper' is independent of Zukofsky's own critical writing, and that there is no reason to doubt the relation subsequently ascribed to them. 3.) Finally, the argument and style of 'Paper' do not suggest Zukofsky. It is speculative and assertive rather than categorical and demonstrative; despite what it asserts, moreover, its argument is discursively connected in a way that Zukofsky's arguments tend not to be. Its sense of humour displays an urbane awareness of paradox; Zukofsky's humour (not specially noticeable in his criticism) is marked more by a sense of the incongruous. But I need not elaborate my assertion. Hereafter Irving Kaplan will be referred to as the author of 'Paper'.

Foul Paper, Perfect Copy

The cancelled matter remaining at the head of the first full leaf of the Durham manuscript is an insufficient basis on which to draw conclusions about motives for the revision of 'Paper'. It is easily legible and begins some way into a quotation attributed to a "sage", whom I have been unable to identify or have identified, and I suppose that if the rest of the cancelled matter could be recovered (i.e. by discovery of an intact manuscript) it might, as well as identifying the sage, cast some light on those motives.[24]

Pound, unlike Bunting, kept papers, and since Zukofsky sent him a copy of 'Paper' it seemed the one most likely, of any copies, to have survived—unless, indeed, it was the one that passed into Bunting's hands. Such optimism has proved unfounded insofar as I have been unable to locate a copy of 'Paper' in either of the major Pound archives. However, I have located a second manuscript of 'Paper' among—a sufficiently obvious place—the Zukofsky papers at the Harry Ransom Humanities Research Center. This is typewritten manuscript of 28 leaves, and is a fair and perfect copy of the revised text of 'Paper' contained in the mutilated Durham manuscript: the text is continuous, and it supplies corrections of the sort Richard Caddel was obliged to make when editing the Durham manuscript. The Texas manuscript will, therefore, have been prepared from another, corrected manuscript of the original version of 'Paper', while the Durham manuscript, in its light, appears to have been a duplicate copy of the original quickly doctored to provide an imperfect copy of the revised version: an economy measure.

Quite what light is thus shed on the Durham manuscript's transmission to Bunting is unclear. However, the Texas manuscript, in addition to being titled and bearing the pseudonym "Roger Kaigh", has three other significant features. The text is dated 1922-1923 at its conclusion, where the pseudonym "Roger Kaigh" is repeated. A note on the title leaf repeats the gist of Zukofsky's proposed foreword to *Four Essays and Paper*, namely that the author is an Arunta and that Zukofsky has the only copy. A final leaf gives an address for "Roger Kaigh" in the care of Louis Zukofsky at 39-62 65th Street, Woodside, Long Island. This dates the manuscript to the Summer of 1937 when Zukofsky had 'Paper' retyped following Pound's suggestion that if it had still not been printed it might be submitted to *Globe*. Pound was recommending *Globe* as a source of income, and this may imply that he thought that 'Paper' was Zukofsky's, but Zukofsky's reply refers to it as Kaigh's.[25] Nothing came of this, but it is striking that Zukofsky was sufficiently interested in Pound's suggestion to have 'Paper' retyped; he also proposed to send *Globe* his 1936 essay 'Modern Times', a manuscript copy of which is also in the Mountjoy Collection.

Except on this occasion all references to 'Paper' are Zukofsky's, and all occur during 1929 and 1930; in the earliest of these its author is already identified by a pseudonym, but the fiction of Arunta authorship appears later. It arises (as will be seen below) from the ethnological background to the arguments of 'Paper', but has no ostensible purpose (except as a gag) except in its relation to a connection with Zukofsky's four essays (mostly written in late 1929 and early 1930), which was both actual and intended to be explicit. Just what this purpose was may be guessed, but I incline to suppose that it was discovered during Zukofsky's 1930 visit to Kaplan, and that revision of 'Paper' was undertaken then with a view to sustaining this exotic new cultural identity for its author. Such supposition is self-consistent and not inconsistent with any evidence, but is not independently corroborated.

'PAPER' AND BUNTING

'Paper' was part of the intellectual currency of Zukofsky and Pound in 1929 and 1930, although we don't know what value Pound ascribed to it. During this period Bunting was close to Pound at Rapallo, and met Zukofsky for the first time, in New York. We might assume the existence of no more than three manuscript copies of the original 'Paper': how, and under what auspices, did one come into Bunting's possession, and how had it acquired the modifications which bring it substantively in line with the revised version? It is unlikely that he obtained it from Pound, for in letters to him referring to 'Some Limitations of English' he makes no reference to 'Paper', and I infer that he was unaware that Pound had seen it. There is no evidence that I am aware of that contact occurred between Bunting and Kaplan. On balance I incline to the view that Bunting received the manuscript from Zukofsky. It is not clear when this would have occurred, and Bunting's surviving letters to Zukofsky are silent on this point. Zukofsky met Bunting between 11 and 19 July, 1930, before his trip to Berkeley, and they remained in contact during the rest of Bunting's American visit (he was back in Rapallo in March 1931), including a meeting in Wisconsin when Bunting was visiting his parents-in-law at Eau Claire.[26] It seems unlikely that Zukofsky would have thrust 'Paper' on Bunting at a first meeting and, in any case, if 'Paper' was revised thereafter, when Zukofsky was in Berkeley, the manuscript in Bunting's possession would preclude that possibility. As regards Zukofsky's motive for giving a copy of 'Paper' to Bunting, its relation to his own work has been noted, and he would have been aware that Bunting shared some of its points of reference. It is noteworthy that the manuscript in Bunting's possession is devoid of indications of authorship, including the Arunta fiction. (I forbear to speculate how the silence of textual anonymity might have been breached when the manuscript was put in Bunting's hands.)

These considerations are significant if Bunting wrote 'Some Limitations of English' with 'Paper' in mind. Before 21 November, 1930, he had sent the essay to *Hound and Horn* and *The Criterion*, and there was opportunity for him to have obtained 'Paper' before that.[27] He had met Zukofsky again in Wisconsin, and corresponded with him. Opportunity on its own is not enough to constitute proof, however, and there would have been equal if not greater opportunity for Zukofsky to show Bunting 'Paper' after 'Some Limitations of English' was written. (It is possible, indeed, that Bunting acquired his copy later, following the Globe episode, on his second visit to America in 1938.) Makin suggests that 'The Written Record...' (i.e. 'Paper') "leads to the more sophisticated thought of...'Some Limitations of English'", but such a notion is inapplicable if they are by different hands.[28] Nor are they, indeed, to be differentiated in terms of degrees of sophistication, since they are written from different points of view and address different issues. Nevertheless the case may be advanced hypothetically that 'Some Limitations of English' was written with 'Paper' in mind, and this can best be done by considering how the essays differ in their treatment of the same idea: the relation of language to thought.

'Paper' is centrally concerned with the illusions of permanence and authority induced by a written or "paper" culture, in which words become terms susceptible to final definition, and abstractions acquire the status of universals. Aristotle, who "decided that the search for these phantoms [i.e. universals] was the most glorious thing in a moral life", formalised the system of logic whereby propositions about the universe might be regulated.[29] In Section IV of the essay it is argued that formal logic is presumptive and circular; moreover, regarded as a belief system, it is comparable to the Australian aborigines' belief in spirit-causation: both are designed to supply reasons for systemic failure in practical cases. Indeed, "logic is the art of giving reasons". In Section V it is argued that there are homologies between habits of thought and habits of speech, and that in Aristotle "the relation of logical forms to grammatical forms...was directly determined". This raises the problem of the determination of thought by language: "How final, or even reasonable, would Aristotle's logic or metaphysics, Kant's categories of the understanding or his logical table of judgements, appear in a language of another origin?" Referring these questions to an unspecified native American language of the North-West coast, it is suggested that were its speakers "given to naïve speculations on the basis of their 'transcendental' categories of understanding, they would find, instead of our time-worn and unsolved problem of unreality, a simple and final distinction in terms of their grammatical concepts or habits of speech—as we find the distinction of 'substance' and 'attribute' or 'negative' and 'affirmative' simple and final. But these latter classifications, so simple to us, may be involved speculative matters to them."[30]

These arguments all serve the essay's distinction between definition and meaning: "context, gesture, intonation and pronunciation give words a stamp of meaning which a written form will lack". Here, precisely, is where Zukofsky found the argument of 'Paper' relevant to his concerns for the vitalization of words; its extension as a critique of western intellectual and institutional culture (a critique, as it were, from within: 'the revolt of paper against itself') is not noted, nor was this Bunting's concern. (Elsewhere they both, of course, indicate other grounds for a more extensive social critique.) Zukofsky uses 'Paper' to suggest how writing may obtain for itself some of the virtues of speech. Bunting, in his essay, is concerned with the limitations of language in general and, as his title indicates, of English in particular, and regards these limitations as both cognitive and expressive. He thus admits to his essay many of the topics dealt with in 'Paper', but deals with them cursorily in the first of its two sections, under the heading 'These Platitudes'. If he had read 'Paper' he refused to let its excited insistence affect his *sang-froid*.

'Some Limitations of English', when read against 'Paper', reveals difference of emphasis. In preliminary remarks about style, contradicting Buffon, Bunting detaches style from the man and attaches it to thought: it is "skill in the use of language to convey thought", and later he appeals to Wittgenstein to indicate "the limits of language in general as a medium of thought". This bracketing of writing between thought and language situates additional preliminary remarks on the limitations of language: unlike mathematics it affords neither precision nor accuracy. These are not the same as either definition or meaning in 'Paper': for Bunting the poet's empirical judgements are approximate and, like the farmer's, based on direct experience and precedent.

For Bunting, therefore, there is no necessary opposition between speech and writing (and its superstructure of cultural practices), and something more like resistance between language and thought. Thus he approaches the determination of thought by language in his own way. While he observes that "we owe most of our industrial machinery...to the tongue we speak, as well as the whole system of chemistry which enables us to invent and manufacture high explosives with which to persuade speakers of less analytical languages to acquiesce in our notions", this barbed irony is parenthetical, as is the suggestion that "some savage languages are more in harmony [with] the recent development of physical philosophy", so that "speakers of such a language [may] be the leaders of thought in an age in which synthesis rather than analysis is the prime process of thought". But Bunting is neither triumphant nor dismayed to discover that the languages of different cultures may imply different metaphysics and cosmographies, since "one realises that the corner of the known universe expressible in any language is small". He is rather more struck by the fact that "John lives in a world which here and there coincides with l'univers de Jean", and that it is "possible to perceive facts and relations in French which do not exist in English, and vice versa".

Hence for Bunting it is axiomatic that languages condition thought differently, including the perception of facts and relations, and that for the writer this occurs on a more intimate scale than is implied in 'Paper' by the grand contrast of world views and cultures, in which Kaplan follows Lévy-Bruhl. The second section of Bunting's essay, headed 'Ergo', is then specifically addressed to how the English writer may "understand the limitations of the language" and "overcome them". This is not the occasion to dwell on the localism already implicit in Bunting's view of the writer's relation to language, or his practical suggestions (which might be constructively compared with Zukofsky's.) But it needs to be noted that his suggestions are intended to overcome limitations discovered in the analytical tendency of English: writers should "try to bring a more synthetic element into it." Under the heading 'These Platitudes' he had indicated that the analytical bent of modern languages "falsifies reality and causes us to live in a world of self-constructed fantoms", and here his views, and choice of word, are remarkably close to 'Paper'. But he does not endorse the view that meaning is most fully realised and vivid in speech. Proximity and difference of views can perhaps best be illustrated by quotation of two extended passages from Bunting.

> Our accidence is almost wholly resolved into autonomous abstract notions. We retain a genitive which, however, tends towards the condition of an adjective, and a few tense modifications of the verb. The rest of the modifications of meaning in a set of related ideas are now expressed by pronouns auxiliaries and prepositions utterly abstract words which standing by themselves have a meaning only for the most inveterate logician and yet which refuse to coalesce with their principals to make a more concrete word which would be valid to people less given to splitting ideas, chipping off *I* from *am*, etc.

Bunting here is hankering after the integrity of the Latin verb, and he has things to say about the advantages an inflected language has for the arrangement of words. In 'Paper' the verb "to be" is duplicitous because of its use both as a copulative and to mean "to exist"; Bunting prefers the inflected forms of the verb of a dead language only available in writing. If Bunting knew 'Paper' this is surely shrewdly oblique, but still more so, perhaps, is the second of these passages.

> Impersonal utterance is increasingly difficult. Demonstratives imply the existence of a localized speaker and if they are used at all freely the poet is apt to find that what he designed for a universal has become a particular, what was to apply to the world at large or men in general has become attached to his own personal self and in so doing has lost indeed not a larger validity but the appearance of it. What was to have come home forcefully to all readers has turned into gossip.

But if this applied to 'Paper' it will be seen, the approved "universal" notwithstanding, that this is not contradiction but modification. 'Paper' has nothing to say about the person or personal meaning: its concept of speech refers not to an action but to a transaction. From his different direction, Bunting's "designed universal" remains purposive. Bunting appears to share with 'Paper' the understanding that it is the quality of utterance rather than logical proof that carries conviction. For, as 'Paper' has it, in another appeal to the performative character of spoken language, "arguments are decided 'ad hominem'. They are settled by their length and loudness; by a wry face, a laugh or a shrug of the shoulders". This is meaning performed as dialogue. But Bunting's sense of localised discourse (any language dealing only with its own 'corner of the known universe') also surely implies a notion of linguistic community as inherently dialogic. It is possible to conclude on the distinction that whereas in 'Paper' the universal is understood to derive from abstraction for Bunting it is a projection of the concrete.

This is a considerable distinction, needless to say, but whether or not Bunting saw 'Paper' before he wrote 'Some Limitations of English', or set out silently to moderate what he may have regarded as over-emphatic, comparison reveals that both essays cover similar ground and share similar views. Both, for example, regard thought as relative to language, and consider that the language in which they are written has an inbuilt tendency to deplete experience, to make the lived world a phantom. But they do not have a common purpose, and whereas in 'Paper' the writer's position is that of an intellectual, critical of his own class, Bunting's contemplation of the future, for writing at least, is tempered by a vision of the past. Just as our language has "lost the benefit of a whole view, a unified conception, concentration, intensity", so this is "comparable to the breakup of craftsmanship with its complex of deft motions".

It is worth emphasizing that similarities as well as differences between the essays arise from the writers' independent thought and argument, and do not simply reflect a common point of reference, but it will probably be helpful, in order to establish such a distinction, to indicate what that point of reference was, and to suggest why Bunting was dismissive of what was, for Kaplan, immensely exciting. Bunting was an attentive reader of *The Criterion*, and there, even if from nowhere else, would have acquired a knowledge of contemporary anthropology and its cultural readings of the "primitive".[31] Indeed it was precisely the "primitive" or archaic aspect of W.H. Auden's *Paid on Both Sides: A Charade* that seems to have drawn his attention.[32] It can be supposed, therefore, that he recognised the

intellectual background of 'Paper' at once, and found it commonplace—
which, indeed, by 1930 it arguably was. Literary appropriations of such
material, moreover, were becoming two a penny. But Kaplan was writing
in the early 1920s, when this anthropological work was more novel, and
although his contemporary sources appear completely assimilated their
outcome in his essay is so much his own work that it is misleading to
regard them even as background. He worked back, unless I am mistaken,
to their primary sources.

Kaplan's immediate source for information about both Australian
aborigines and North-West Coast native Americans would be Lucien
Lévy-Bruhl, *Les fonctions mentales dans les sociétés inférieures* (1910),
which he must have read in French.[33] Here, as well as the ethnographic
data Lévy-Bruhl compiled from fieldwork reports, he would have come
across two important arguments. The first is embedded in a critique of
the English school of anthropology, which by its theoretical dependence
on the concept of animism implicitly subscribed, Lévy-Bruhl argued, to
a universal theory of mind. The second, which underpins his book as a
whole, was that the concept of collective representation allowed a common
and comprehensive, but pre-logical system of mental representation to
be identified among "primitive" peoples. In 'Paper', of course, Kaplan
stands Lévy-Bruhl's relation of the pre-logical and the logical on its head.
Moreover, he was not content to rely on Lévy-Bruhl's ethnography: there
are details in his account of Australian aborigines' ceremonies, and the
grammatical structure of a native American language, which he would not
have found there. Kaplan, that is to say, consulted Lévy-Bruhl's sources
for additional data.[34] Is it fanciful to claim that the suggestion that "Roger
Kaigh" was the pseudonym of an Arunta originates in Kaplan's reading of
Spencer's and Gillen's account of their fieldwork with the Arunta tribe?[35]

In 'Some Limitations of English' Bunting refers parenthetically to
Lévy-Bruhl on the subject of "savage languages". For him these were no
more than a starting point, as his account to Pound of his essay indicates.

> It implies that Kaffir has advantages English hasn't as a medium
> for precise thought. It traces idealism to our syntax. It states that
> there can be no radical improvement in human affairs without
> first an overhauling of the language—carried out of course by
> poets in poetry.[36]

In summary this is perhaps closer to 'Paper' than to the essay Bunting
wrote, although its emphases are in place. But it is possible to feel that
Kaplan was able to find rather more in Lévy-Bruhl than Bunting. For

surely, in this final quotation—from Lévy-Bruhl—is the seed of that part of his argument which Zukofsky was so taken by.

> The Coroados of Brazil complete and perfect the meaning of their sentences by their accent, the speed or slowness of the pronunciation, and certain signs made with hand or mouth, or other gestures.[37]

For Kaplan, of course, these performative aspects of meaning are not exclusively "savage".

If a dialogue can be established between these two essays then it is not necessarily important to establish that Bunting wrote in response; yet if he did not he must have read 'Paper', when it came into his possession, as an essay addressing his own topics. Circumstantial reasons for supposing that he thought it to be Zukofsky's have been indicated above, and it remains to mention a public riposte by Bunting to Zukofsky. That is the 'Open Letter to Louis Zukofsky' of 1932, in which he takes issue with Zukofsky's Preface to An 'Objectivists' Anthology. Here he argues with Zukofsky out of respect, and challenges him where he deviates from the excellence of his normal practice. This critical attitude might be motive and method for 'Some Limitations of English', as well as suggestive of its occasion. For the poet who wrote "Criticism, especially my own, is painful to me" it is difficult to suppose an occasion more compelling than 'Paper'.[38]

NOTES

1. Basil Bunting, *Three Essays*, edited and introduced by Richard Caddel, Basil Bunting Poetry Centre: Durham 1994.

2. Louis Zukofsky, 'American Poetry 1920-1930', *The Symposium* 2 (1931), 72, 73.

3. Ibid., 77, 78.

4. Ibid., 78-9.

5. Ibid., 78-9. I draw attention to the phrase 'definite connotation' as a probable error in the printed text' Zukofsky subsequently amended it to read 'precise intension' (*Prepositions*, Rapp and Carroll: London 1967, 139).

6. Ibid., 79.

7. Basil Bunting, letter to Ezra Pound, 21 November, 1930 (Yale). Bunting informed Pound that he had already sent the essay to *Hound and Horn* and T.S. Eliot.

8. Peter Makin, *Bunting: The Shaping of his Verse*, Clarendon Press: Oxford 1992.

9. Ibid., 290 (n. 70).

10. Ibid., 290.

11. *Pound/Zukofsky: Selected Letters of Ezra Pound and Louis Zukofsky*, edited by Barry Ahearn, Faber and Faber: London 1987, 35. (Letter dated 18 June, 1930.)

12. Ibid., 41. (Letter dated 8 September, 1930.)

13. Ibid., 42n.

14. Louis Zukofsky, letters to Ezra Pound, 28 January and 3 March, 1929 (Yale). It will be noted that Kaigh is here spelled Kay. This may be dittography, but may also indicate a family connection with the printer (it is not known what Zukofsky's connection with him was.) The suspicion that the fourth editor was 'Roger Kaigh' is aroused by Zukofsky's description of him as 'a guy who wishes to die in obscurity, tho' he has sent you material under a pseud. which you replied to with a favorable note.' Furthermore, if Kay was Zukofsky's familiar name for Kaplan at this time, it may identify Kaplan as the Kay mentioned in 'A'-2, 5, and 6. These references are more extensive in the versions published in *An 'Objectivists' Anthology* (1932), where Kay's gender is explicitly male, than in *'A' 1-12* (1959) and later editions. (Zukofsky revised these sections of 'A' in 1942.)

15. Louis Zukofsky, letter to Ezra Pound, 8 September, 1929 (Yale).

16. Ibid.

17 *Pound/Zukofsky*, 35n.

18 Barry Ahearn, personal communication, 30 April, 1995. The letter cited is dated 2 March 1931 (Yale).

19 Letter of 8 September, 1929, cited above.

20 Jerry Reisman, personal communication, 29 May, 1995.

21 Carroll F. Terrell, 'Louis Zukofsky: An Eccentric Profile', in Terrell (ed.), *Louis Zukofsky: Man and Poet*, National Poetry Foundation: Orono, Maine [1979], 49-50.

22 Jerry Reisman, personal communication, 12 July, 1995.

23 David Caute, *The Great Fear: The Anti-Communist Purge under Truman and Eisenhower*, Simon and Shuster: NY 1978, 329. My summary of the allegations against Kaplan, their background, and consequences, is based, additionally, on the following: The Earl Jowitt, *The Strange Case of Alger Hiss*, Hodder and Stoughton: London 1953; Earl Latham, *The Communist Conspiracy in Washington: From the New Deal to McCarthy*, Harvard University Press: Cambridge, Mass. 1966; Herbert L. Packer, *Ex-Communist Witness*, Stanford University Press: Stanford, Ca. 1962; Allen Weinstein, *Perjury: The Hiss Chambers Case*, Viking Press: NY 1978. Mention should also be made of James Burnham, *The Web of Subversion: Underground Networks in the U.S. Government*, The John Day Company: NY 1954, for its account in Chapter 7, 'The Reception Halls', of the National Research Project, David Weintraub, and Irving Kaplan. Burnham states that Kaplan was born in Poland in 1900 or 1901, and attended the City College of New York and Fordham Law School as well as Columbia. His book is a popular account of Comunist disloyalty, subversion and espionage, one purpose of which was to alert Americans to the continuing internal threat to national security and interest. The book is more complex than that, however, for Burnham did not cease to write as a political philosopher, and was clearly not at ease with the figurative language to which he had recourse to narrate the actions of individuals as directed and concerted. 'Many of the jobs have all sorts of potentialities for an imagination that might think in terms of webs, cells, networks, intelligence, and that sort of thing.' (Third 'Americanist Library' edition, Western Islands: Boston & Los Angeles 1965, 117.) This is telling because these are the terms in which Burnham thinks, of course, not those of a different imagination bent on subverting those jobs to serve its ulterior purposes. Elsewhere Burnham's 'web dwellers' are portrayed more as adept boondogglers and log-rollers, careerist networkers on fat salaries, which he specifies with glee. One suspects that this appeal to popular indignation was in part a diversion from the difficulty of moving discursively from the theory of what Communists were for (to serve the interests of a foreign power) to what Communists did (like pleading the Fifth Amendment), since such a task would have required an account of his

own intellectual history in relation to the topics of class and revolution. It was precisely such a history, from the early Twenties down to the Fifties, that his subjects had to be denied. Indeed, Burnham came close to arguing that legal provision needed to be made to define who was, and was not, Communist, since Communists could not be relied on to do so. If Kaplan read Burnham's book he might well have reflected, in view of its terminological difficulties and circular logic, that it furnished fresh illustrations for the arguments of 'Paper'.

24 The truncated quotation reads as follows. ['...] ingenious word-twisting of esthetic souls. I am not afraid to say that, at the present day, we do not understand a single line of the Iliad, of the Divine Comedy, in the sense primitively attaching to it. To live is to change, and the posthumous life of our written-down thoughts is not free from the rule: they only continue to exist on condition that they become more and more different from what they were when they issued from our minds. Whatsoever in future may be admired in us, will have become altogether alien from us.' This is described as stating a bald truth which the paper age dismissed as subjectivism (a concept which belongs to the middle of the 19th Century), but the sage who spoke out against the spirit of the age remains to be identified.

25 Ira Nadel informs me that Zukofsky lived at the Woodside address from July to September 1937. This is confirmed by unpublished correspondence in the Pound papers at Yale, which Barry Ahearn has drawn to my attention: Pound wrote to Zukofsky about *Globe* on 24 July, 1937; Zukofsky's reply is dated 7 August. *Globe* was a travel magazine published in St. Paul, Minnesota, for which Pound may have supposed that an essay mentioning aborigines' ideas about spirit-causation provided suitable copy.

26 Bunting left Zukofsky a note on 11 July (information from Peter Quartermain); on 19 July Zukofsky informed Pound that they had met (information from Barry Ahearn). Bunting mentioned his visit to Wisconsin in a letter to Pound dated 27 October (Yale); Victoria Forde (*The Poetry of Basil Bunting*, Bloodaxe Books: Newcastle upon Tyne 1991, 28) mentions that Bunting saw Zukofsky while on a visit to his parents-in-law, and I suppose this to be the occasion she refers to. Bunting's letter to Pound of 21 November, cited above, mentions that he has been in correspondence with Zukofsky, but letters from this period have not survived with his others to Zukofsky at the Harry Ransom Humanities Research Center.

27 See note 7, above.

28 *Bunting: The Shaping of his Verse*, 290-91.

29 Here and throughout the ensuing discussion of 'Paper' and 'Some Limitations of English', I quote from *Three Essays* (where, of course, 'Paper' appears as 'The Written Record...'). Since both essays are short and quoted material is easy to locate no page references will be given.

30 Kaplan here refers, I think, to speakers of the Klamath language (see note 34, below.)

31 See Robert Crawford, *The Savage and the City in the Works of T.S. Eliot*, Clarendon Press: Oxford 1987, 177-78 and 191-92, for an account of the attention given to anthropology by T.S. Eliot as editor of *The Criterion*.

32 See his remarks in 'English Poetry Today', *Poetry* XXXIX, V (Feb. 1932), 270-271.

33 The first of Lévy-Bruhl's books to be published in English was *La mentalité primitive* (1922), translated as *Primitive Mentality*, George Allen & Unwin: London 1923. *Les fonctions mentales dans les sociétés inférieures* appeared later, translated as *How Natives Think*, George Allen & Unwin: London 1926.

34 For example, Kaplan would have found the *reason given* in explanation for failure of the Arunta rain ceremony in Baldwin Spencer and F.J. Gillen, *The Native Tribes of Central Australia*, Macmillan: London 1899. 'In the case of many of the totems it is just when there is promise of the approach of a good season that it is customary to hold the ceremony. While this is so, it sometimes happens that the members of a totem, such as, for example, the rain or water totem, will hold their *Intichiuma* when there has been a long drought and water is badly wanted; if rain follows within a reasonable time, then of course it is due to the influence of the *Intichiuma*; if it does not, then the non-success is at once attributed to the evil and counter influence of some, usually distant, group of men.' *op.cit.* 170. Lévy-Bruhl draws extensively on the work of Spencer and Gillen, but because the Intichiuma ceremonies interest him for what they reveal about 'primitive' mentality as a system of collective representation he is not interested in the efficiency of the ceremonies in achieving a specific outcome (indeed, the question could not arise), nor is he interested in the psychology of individuals or groups engaged in a particular performance of a ceremony. Hence he ignores data which for Kaplan was important. I suppose that Kaplan also read Emile Durkheim, *The Elementary Forms of the Religious Life*, George Allen & Unwin: London 1915. Durkheim's book, first published in French in 1912, is based almost exclusively on Australian data. In its account of the Arunta form of the Ichthiuma ceremony Kaplan would have come across, on facing pages, his references to ceremonies at Lake Eyre (332) and explanations of ritual failure (333). But Durkheim's account is interpretive and syncretic, and he is not greatly interested in the purposes of the ceremonies he aggregates or their particular detail, and, in fact, the Lake Eyre ceremony he refers to was to ensure the reproduction of the carpet snake. Durkheim is concerned to make the point that 'it never enters [the native's] mind that a favourable result could be obtained by any other means': for him the results intended are exotic and, in any case, as natural events they are understood as the outcome of the operations of scientific law; as a sociologist what interests him is the social cohesion achieved by irrational belief. Kaplan, on the other

hand, sees logic as the art of giving reasons and, without Durkhiem's (or Lévy-Bruhl's) evolutionist and positivist prejudices, he finds the Aruntas' capacity to rationalise significant of more than their ignorance of natural causation. Thus if Kaplan checked the source, quoted above, for Durkheim's remarks about the explanation of unfavourable results he would have found an account of the matter specifically with reference to rain-making, the example of aboriginal expertise instanced in 'Paper'. My point is not so much that Kaplan used Lévy-Bruhl's and Durkheim's material critically as that he consulted their sources. Explanation, rain-making, and Lake Eyre could not, I think, have been brought together as they are in 'Paper' if he had not done so. Similarly, Kaplan's comments on the structure of his North-West Coast native American language go into more detail (for example, concerning indistinction of nominal and verbal forms, and the verbal form of negation) than he would have found in Lévy-Bruhl. I suspect that he referred to A.S. Gatschet, *The Klamath Indians of southwestern Oregon*, Government Printing Office: Washington 1890 (cited by Levy-Bruhl) and as well, perhaps his 'Real, true, and genuine in Indian languages', *American Anthropologist* (n.s.) 1 (Jan. 1899). I have not been able to consult either of these.

[35] The work of Spencer and Gillon was extensively illustrated with photographs, and has great immediacy; this was not lost on T.S. Eliot, who thought that it was 'not necessary, perhaps not even desirable…to peruse all the works of Miss Harrison, Cooke, Rendel Harris, Lévy-Bruhl or Durkheim. But one ought, surely, to have read at least one book such as those of Spencer and Gillen on the Australians…' ('War-paint and Feathers' [1919], cited in Crawford, *The Savage and the City*, 98.) Baldwin Spencer revised some of his work with F.J. Gillen as *The Arunta, A Study of a Stone Age People*, 2 vols, Macmillan and Co.: London 1927, and this may have revived Kaplan's interest, or reminded Zukofsky of it, and suggested identification of the author of 'Paper' as an Arunta. It would not have been a sufficient source, however, for references in 'Paper' to aborigines, and does not suggest that the date given in the Texas manuscript might be misleading.

[36] Letter of 21 November, 1930, cited above.

[37] *How Natives Think*, 164.

[38] Basil Bunting, 'An Open Letter to Louis Zukofsky', *Sulfur* 14 (1985), 8. (Initial publication, in Italian translation, as 'Lettera aperta a Louis Zukofsky', in *Il Mare*, 1 October 1932.)

Writing by Numbers: A Preview

A review of *False Memory* by Tony Lopez
(The Figures, Great Barrington, MA, 1996)

Crozier's review of the first part of *False Memory* appeared in *Jacket* Eleven in April 2000 under the subtitle 'Writing by Numbers: A Preview'. As a note at the end of the review made clear the second half of Tony Lopez's poem had recently been published as *Data Shadow* by Reality Street Editions.

Some of *False Memory* has already been seen, but Lopez's poem remains to be seen full scale: one hundred fourteen-line stanzas deployed, on the decimal system, in discrete proportionate sections, six out of ten being given here. Of these the first and second, 'Corneal Erosion' and 'Studies in Classic American Literature', were published in *Negative Equity and other poems* (Equipage, 1995), where they bracket four other, free-standing poems, amongst which the title poem is exceptional by its foreclosed brevity. Four stanzas of the third section, 'Assembly Point D', made a fugitive appearance as a Short Run Press item. *False Memory* continues a history of work in circulation while in progress, now complete in MS and in search of a publisher; this is by way of a reader's report on what of it is currently available in this edition.

In any of these sixty stanzas language emits the toxic glow of an intertextuality for which a functioning media awareness is its sufficient context. Much of it has been heard before, or heard already after being read, with or without accompanying visuals. What stands between *False Memory* and print journalism is that Lopez has no story to tell or opinion to editorialise; if anything he's beguiled by the tectonics of number systems. The even number series of the poem's exposure as parts of work in progress requires the shifting point of the decimal fraction to be given its values (2, 0.4 6 sections), and this ratio, however fortuitous, is more or less the parodic inversion of how for the poem as a whole the relation between higher and lower units, the decimal system coordinating the whole to its subordinate sections, does not include the sum of its parts. Quite different properties of cardinal numbers are implied by the poem's stanza, even if qua sonnet its antecedents reach no farther back than Ted Berrigan's fourteen-line accumulations. These number systems have in common the integer of the line of verse, but are thereafter incommensurable; discontinuous number systems exclude the possibility of dialectic, there's no talking to them, and to preclude synthesis at this structural level turns out to be crucial to Lopez's project. This systemic stand-off of arbitrary limits sustains the effort to attain them; at this size it is not quite compulsive repetition, and as an instrument for producing verses its effect is prodigious rather than profligate though I might review my opinion if he were to let rip on another 12,600 lines.

I suppose that the decisions on which the poem's schema was based were more simple and pragmatic than description may suggest, though not the less significant in their consequences. For this is a work conceived of as massively flawed, without prospect either of resolution or the complete exposition of variables, only of termination: there could be no stopping, short of exhaustion. The flaw does not occur in either the stanza or the system on which it is deployed, for both are flawless abstractions rigorously conceived to be embodied almost anyhow, but the mutual constraint of their separate embodiment is felt throughout the writing, in effects of tension and compression, both locally and in the aggregate.

I suppose also that little or no adjustment of details or passages was required as the writing proceeded (the manner of publication may bear this out), and that despite explicit specification of the finished article work on it could be brought to a finished state as it was carried out. Whatever the case, the writing has not, it appears self-evident, been undertaken to realise a preliminary concept of the poem itself, which requires some notion of corresponding perfections of idea and execution—indeed, the more completely the poem is apprehended as meeting its specification with so much the less urgency will be felt the driven purpose of its writing which, while demonstrating skill and resourceful artifice both of a high order, is yet more striking for its persistence in rehearsing damaged and painful matter.

Section titles in *False Memory* replicate concepts contingent on public discourses which in their globalisation cross-contaminate while keeping open a place for local colour. Here they are knowingly not to be taken lightly or on trust, though not because they're not the things of which they're replicas. Inauthenticity is not what hurts in this case, indeed Lopez's replicas must by design be intended to outlast their originals. For while the operations of the originals sustain a topical immediacy, a democracy of received ideas, in the medium term their character is to be received as dated mendacities, conceptual replication scarcely speeding up the process from participation to the onset of dismayed recall, let alone the active pleasures of memory.

From the start, therefore, this writing anticipates the post-modern as a future condition of the person; and since participation in public discourse is an experience of its virtual reality to replicate any of its items is never the perpetration of an unmitigated irony, inverted commas measuring off distance, adding reference as if value. Knowingness is painful, the hurt acknowledgement of complicit discourse, fifth column of an invasive other, the wonted system of a known agent, though hardly a foreign body, doesn't amount to diagnosis. Hence no prognosis, let alone cure. Therapeutically it's like with like, and a lot more of the same, not turning round hostile weaponry even in small doses.

Participation in the misfortune of others has been stoic, charitable, the debt to be paid by any sinner, but we can no longer bear such a universal figure of ourselves and incline instead, as occasion serves, to gloat, feel bitter or, as here, undergo the abjection not of the sinner but of the other in us. This is the condition of language in *False Memory* and the significance retrieved by its title: the utterances of and about the way we live now of accredited others, professional, corporate, &c, &c, are encouraged to refract and mingle episodically in a garrulous, monologic continuum. Lopez's writing, more than ever, engages with dystopian anxiety the grievous fictions of contemporaneity: it is beset and irked by its inexhaustible material on every occasion, but by its denial to Lopez of his own voice, so fully has he read himself into and written himself out of it, genuine horror is forestalled. And if there could be a better life for one and all how, from personal wishes, can it be imagined for others?

This is the ostensible double-bind of poetry with a conscience, compromised by utterance in the very act yet compelled in default of responsible utterance to impute of itself, we are told, its intrinsic value. Lopez eludes this *mise en abîme* by implied acknowledgement of what is alleged to be both mutually entailed and excluding, for on the one hand utterances are kept sedulously incomplete and attributed by type, and on the other hand the writing, by sheer productive efficiency, disclaims any but added value. Such deference draws attention away from the demonstration, nonetheless, of a situation in which incompatibles manage to co-exist, but it is not thereby misconceived, for while the poem is so contrived as to disconcert any reading, it delights in being read. Such reader friendliness is scaled to a short attention span, and is neither too much nor too little, and if the problematic proposed of this kind of writing remains uncontroverted its mordant humour has been relieved by a lightness of touch both wary and assured.

Lopez will be old enough to recall the slogan "the private is public"; *False Memory* is premised on the reverse proposition, which more resembles common knowledge, the more forceful for that without being echoed from the rooftops. Supposing language to have been privatised, that it is alien, but that it can be impeded from speaking of and for us, the poet must then make the best of a bad job and become its consumer, connoisseur of false consciousness. In its wary assurance this might seem to fit Lopez's writing, but falls short of acknowledging the ambition evinced by it, out of the ordinary and instructive. Lopez situates his writing in relation to current discussions of the very possibility of poetic language, but does so fully intending that the poetic require the public; whatever the condition in which he finds it.

There is a necessary ambivalence here, however minimal the concept of the public as the domain of the poetic, in view of the closures and appropriations of public discourse accepted to underpin the method of composition, but such ambivalence is a genuine attainment requiring the recalcitrance of ambition in the face of obdurate theory. It doesn't amount to a politics, since the public and its opposite are not commutative terms battling for priority, but it is a demonstrative critique of the cultural pessimism of that homologising rhetoric bent on seeing the whole in the part but never, in its misery, vice-versa. In the face of pseudo-dialectical stasis Lopez's ambivalence can be salutary.

Obituaries

Crozier wrote two obituaries for *The Guardian*. The first, for Douglas Oliver, was published on May 6, 2000, and was headed "A poet articulating ethical values in a world of injustice and joy".

At the time of his death from cancer at the age of 62, the poet Douglas Oliver was at the height of his powers, and on the threshold of a new stage of work after retirement from teaching at the British Institute in Paris.

Until 10 years ago, his writing was known mainly to a select and exacting readership of fellow poets, as was inevitable since he chose to publish with specialist imprints run by poets. This was a deliberate choice, and a significant career move for a poet whose first appearances in print were in *Encounter* and the *London Magazine*.

His first book, *Oppo Hectic* (1969), registered this change of allegiance by acknowledging, alongside the names of those respected magazines, others with names such as *The Anona Winn* and *Resuscitator*. A volume of collected poems, *Kind* (1987), did much to consolidate his reputation, both with his initial readership and with a younger generation of poets.

Yet success at this level of public activity was not something Oliver was proud of; what was important was the fostering of a probity of literary relationship between poets, editors and publishers, and the development of a social space for poetry. This had enabled him to write as he wished— to sustain long-term projects (for instance, *The Diagram Poems*, published 1979 but begun in the early 70s) with an attentive audience for work-in-progress.

As the focus of his concern for ethical value and spirit shifted from the private and personal to the more inclusively human, social and political, Oliver insisted on his writing as a mode of public address, not seeking a wider audience from ambitious motives but the broadest possible spectrum of the public. He was pleased to perform at Poetry Slams, while living in New York in the early 1990s, submitting his poems for approval to a popular audience to be scored competitively. His career began moving in a new direction.

Even before Howard Brenton's outburst in *The Guardian* in 1992, acclaiming *Penniless Politics* (1991) as setting the literary agenda for the next two decades, and invoking both *Paradise Lost* and *The Waste Land*, Oliver had taken the step, necessary in order to reach a broader public, of publishing with a trade paperback house. *Three Variations On The Theme of Harm* (1990) would be the best introduction to the range and diversity of his imagination and technique (had Paladin kept it in print), for it brought together new poems, his first novel, *The Harmless Building* (1973), and the long poem *The Infant And The Pearl* (1985).

More successful were Bloodaxe's republication of *Penniless Politics* (1994) and the *Penguin Modern Poets* (No 10, 1996), in which Oliver appeared. Just days before he died, Bloodaxe published *A Salvo For Africa*, in which, in opposition to the tendency of wealthy countries to regard Africa as no more than "a hopeless sink into which aid money disappeared", he pits his own imagination against that collective "failure to imagine" in an effort to redress it. This book of reckless and driven optimism is sure to be seen as a summation, both political testament and poetic legacy. But there will be readers seeking a more inclusive view of his achievement, for whom earlier work, including poems in the lyric vein that he never abandoned, remains undiminished by later work with a more public stance.

Restlessness characterised the Oliver I knew: he moved from Cambridge to Paris, to Coventry, to Brightlingsea, back to Paris, to New York, to Paris again, where he finally seemed to settle. Born in Southampton, he went late to the University of Essex, having left school at 16, before becoming a journalist on local newspapers in Cambridge and Coventry (the latter stint yielding a deadpan interview with Philip Larkin, hilarious for insiders who knew that a poet was asking the questions), and at Agence France-Presse.

He has been acclaimed as a political poet on the basis of a utopian vision of human community, yet his journalist's feel for actuality led him to posit hope as utopian, and secreted somewhere was a Calvinist instinct of terror and guilt. He was, at bottom, an old-fashioned antinomian, led to seek the manifestations of spirit wherever they spontaneously occurred, in voodoo ritual or the ceremony of the Orthodox church—and, above all, in persons. But I doubt that he ever saw in himself the greatness and generosity of spirit that move his writing and, expended on friends and strangers alike, made them quicken in recognition and wish for the best in themselves.

He leaves two daughters from his first marriage. His second wife, Alice Notley, whom he married in 1988, survives him.

Crozier's obituary for Barry MacSweeney appeared on May 18, 2000, under the heading "Tyneside poet who lived out the myth of exemplary failure".

Barry MacSweeney, who has died aged 51, had a varied and brilliant poetic career. He was unabashed in his pursuit of poetry as a high and illustrious vocation, never treating his calling lightly, although he damaged his own life and some others. There was no element of posture in his make-up; his fantasy went into his poetry, where life encountered art to be articulated as a series of imagined voices.

MacSweeney was born in Newcastle-upon-Tyne and educated at Rutherford Grammar School. After O-levels he joined the *Newcastle Evening Chronicle*, went on Harlow Technical College's journalism course and subsequently worked on Westminster Press local newspapers. This included a long stint on the *Kentish Times*, and he was finally deputy editor of the *South Shields Gazette*, to which he contributed the column *Mouth Of The Tyne*. He contracted the journalist's industrial illness, alcohol dependency, the struggle with this losing him (temporarily) his ability to write poetry, his job and eventually, despite support from the Royal Literary Fund and the Society of Authors while in detox at Farm Place, his life.

Newcastle in the mid-1960s was a good place for a young poet: Basil Bunting was at the *Chronicle*, receiving overdue recognition as England's major modernist poet; his protégé Tom Pickard ran an eclectic series of readings at the Morden Tower, on the circuit for any visiting American poets; Jon Silkin moved from Leeds, bringing with him the long-established magazine *Stand*. This ambience, including a thriving youth culture, was self-consciously local, either to the city or the region and the north-east—both the moorland landscape around Allendale and its derelict industrial sites and communities inadequately redeveloped—remained a constant frame of reference for MacSweeney.

He was not inward-looking, however, and made contact with a network of young poets grouped around *The English Intelligencer*, and the milieu of little magazines and small presses that then opened up to him, where his own imprint Blacksuede Boot Press had a distinguished part to play in the rediscovery of the 1940s poet Nicholas Moore.

He also came to the attention of Michael Dempsey, editor of Hutchinson's New Authors imprint, who published his first book, *The Boy From The Green Cabaret Tells Of His Mother* (1968). This was an ill-conceived attempt to launch MacSweeney as a 1960s counter-culture personality, with maximum publicity: he was mentioned in *Vogue* and nominated for Oxford University's chair of poetry. None of this can have done MacSweeney much good, but I doubt that it did him any harm, for he was a poet of quite different mettle.

His notion of the artist was formed around a myth of exemplary failure and belated recognition: Rimbaud was an early model for this, others included Chatterton, Shelley, Van Gogh, Jim Morrison and Robert Johnson. Such identifications were the basis for a poetics of direct utterance in which MacSweeney's voice mixed with others to inveigh, to celebrate or entreat. More than he detested the destruction of communities witnessed in the last two decades, he loathed its impact on individual lives, whose vulnerability he already understood. Posited against social and personal crisis were exalted recollections of a natural world of plants, creatures and the elements. What carried this through as poetry was verbal flair raised to the highest level, enabling him to manoeuvre from tact to excess, from the elevated to the plain, with the confidence of an adept.

MacSweeney was prolific, publishing more than two dozen titles between 1968 and 1999. Particularly notable were *The Last Bud* (1969), *Brother Wolf* (1972), *Odes* (1978) and the selection included in *The Tempers Of Hazard* (1993) which, to his distress, was pulped by Paladin in the year of publication. *Pearl* (1995), a work of redemptive pathos, evoking the figure of a childhood sweetheart as a presence in nature, on the confines of social existence, was reprinted with *The Book Of Demons* (Bloodaxe, 1997), his most substantial recent collection, where he projects himself as maimed and abject, hapless yet percipient victim of the demon drink, in writing that is both comic and terrifying.

It would be unfortunate if this final self-identification became his own myth, for although here he foresaw, correctly as it happened, the manner of his own death

> One day choke on it, tongue
>   jammed backwards down
> throat's clogged highway

the poet he might have survived to become, discovering fresh instigations to rage or rapture in old age, remains far from unthinkable.

He married twice.

The Young Pound

Ezra Pound, *Collected Early Poems*, Faber & Faber, £12.00

This review of the Faber edition of Ezra Pound's *Collected Early Poems*, edited by Michael John King, appeared in *PN Review* 6 Vol. 5/No. 2, January/February 1979.

More "stale creampuffs"? The various self-derogatory remarks uttered by Pound during the last years of his life were accorded an often unscrupulous welcome, whereas his less overt but more consistent acts of self-criticism in the collection of his work have met with a different kind of attention. It is to be borne in mind that a good fifth of the confections reprinted in *A Lume Spento and Other Early Poems* in 1965 had survived in the canon of his shorter poems established by Pound in the 1926 *Personae*; a circumstance which should not, however, be interpreted as the poet's self-indulgence, but rather as a matter of economy in presentation. *The Collected Early Poems* now makes available the contents of the six early books from which Pound made cuts in 1926, together with a number of poems from other printed sources, and from manuscript (principally the 'San Trovaso Notebook' of 1908). The "early" of the title can therefore be taken to refer to a period which terminates at an important watershed in Pound's career, somewhere between the publication of *Ripostes* (1912) and *Cathay* (1915). But because this volume does not supersede the *Collected Shorter Poems* (the title under which the 1926 *Personae* has been issued since 1968), to which the reader must still refer for *Cathay, Lustra, Hugh Selwyn Mauberley*, and so on, it must be admitted that were it not for the *Cantos* there would be little justification for this elaborate reissue of so much rejected material. It is because the *Cantos* are as a whole little read and less understood that the publisher's enterprise in uncovering for us the full extent of the foundations of Pound's career is to be welcomed. Little is revealed that might specifically augment his poetic reputation, and no fresh evidence is brought to light to modify the received account of Pound's early eclecticism and metrical ingenuity; but, by adding to the available record some 150 poems belonging to a period represented in the *Collected Shorter Poems* by a mere sixty, the general aspect of Pound's beginnings is substantially modified. Pound was an honest and intelligent editor of his early work; what was impossible to convey editorially, however, was the persistent and uncertain effort entailed by his early writing. Whereas the 1926 selection suggests a series of fairly rapid stylistic and thematic evolutions, the mass of the poems appears to be a dense network of recurrent preoccupations. Figures and motifs are repeated and reworked in a way that suggests that some quasi-symbolist value attaches to them, in excess of their immediate figurative occasion: there is, for example, the subject of an apparitional face, glimpsed or sought among the crowd, as in this poem from *Canzoni* (1911).

Und Drang (VIb)

I have gone seeking for you in the twilight,
Here in the flurry of Fifth Avenue,
Here where they pass between their teas and teas.
Is it such madness? though you could not be
Ever in all that crowd, no gown
Of all their subtle sorts could be your gown.

Yet I am fed with faces, is there one
That even in the half-light mindeth me.

The face remembered and invoked here belongs to that type of visionary lady whose aetherial passage is the subject of poems such as 'Ballatetta' and 'A Virginal'. But the figure in this poem is a distinct anticipation of the faces of 'In a Station of the Metro', and also point back to the concluding poem of *Personae* (1909), which Pound printed in italics as if in epilogue.

Piccadilly

Beautiful, tragical faces,
Ye that were whole, and are so sunken;
And, O ye vile, ye that might have been loved,
That are so sodden and drunken,
           Who hath forgotten you?

O wistful, fragile faces, few out of many!

The gross, the coarse, the brazen,
God knows I cannot pity them, perhaps, as I should do,
But, oh, ye delicate, wistful faces,
           Who hath forgotten you?

The Young Pound

But not all the figures that preoccupied Pound present such a continuous sequence of development. Whereas that of the face contains its value, iconically, other figures take on more dramatic means of articulation, and reveal Pound in the process of changing his mind about their significance. In 'Fifine Answers' (*A Lume Spento*, 1908) for example, Pound celebrates the imprudent freedom of the gipsy dancer's life in terms analogous to those employed, we infer, by that "Good 'Hedgthorn'" whom he accuses of sentimentality in 'To a Friend Writing of Cabaret Dancers' in *Lustra*.

This kind of development, critical rather than rhetorical, is noteworthy because it charts the movement of Pound's poetic intentions towards a more open encounter with the empirical bases of experience, away from an almost total reliance upon a theoretical model of experience compounded from the various literary models (such as Browning) he had at his disposal. To understand the dynamics of this sequence of events it is better not to regard it as the substitution of one kind of material for another, but rather as an endeavour to match and adjust two different orders of experience. This is put very well in the essay on Cavalcanti where Pound writes of "the dogma that there is some proportion between the fine thing held in the mind, and the inferior thing ready for instant consumption". This sense of proportion is the very heart of Pound's work: it both exemplifies its fullest meaning, and underlies its stylistic and technical evolutions. What Pound sought was an exact but vital, rather than rigorous, definition of experience, and he found in the inferior thing an instrument for the expression of the equations of psychology and language that he envisaged. 'In a Station of the Metro' is the instance of the most compact and theoretical expression of such a definition.

But Imagism and Vorticism, which for Pound were aspects of the same principle, stand on the further side of that first important watershed in Pound's career, and represent a conceptual rather than a technical attainment, dependent upon the solution of problems of poetic syntax and rhythm with which Pound had first to struggle. Four main characteristics appear predominant from the *Collected Early Poems*. (1) Although Pound's subjects reveal a strong interest in the psychology of experience, he very rarely dealt with his own empirical experiences. (2) He entertained a high notion of the potency of literary experience, and applied such experiences to his own work as a consistent range of influences. (3) He almost invariably used a model of discourse based upon the first person. (4) His work possesses what might be described as an affective doctrinal content, an amalgam of transcendentalism and neo-platonism presented as ecstatic perception.

In his introduction to Pound's *Selected Poems* T.S. Eliot stated categorically that Pound owed nothing to Whitman, and in the limited sense of the technical derivation of Pound's *vers libre* he is no doubt correct. But the whole question of Whitman's paternity of free verse is a notorious red herring which Eliot has used to obscure the question of other ways in which Pound might owe something to Whitman and the New England tradition. The undercurrent of affective doctrine running through Pound's work from the start has an immediate antecedent in a line of feeling promoted by Emerson in essays such as 'Nature' and 'The Over-Soul'. Pound used an Emersonian vocabulary in the note he added to the typescript of 'Malrin', while still at Crawfordsville, Indiana: the poem, he explained, "arises from a perception how the all-soul of mankind is one and joineth itself wholly at some time and returneth to God as a bride. And he the great hero of the new things spiritual is whoso waiteth for all the rest aiding as he may, yet daring to be last." What Pound must have recognized, however, from the examples available to him, was that Emersonian doctrine was an inadequate basis for a poetic. The emphasis it placed upon personal experience was insufficiently correlated to a range of constraining information, since language itself tended to be seen as a reflex of the self. When Pound did try to write in Whitmanesque cadences the result was a tedious, attitudinizing pastiche. Yet Pound was true to his native tradition in the way he started out with an interest in personal feeling, although in his case the interest was often of a rather special kind, the temper of which is exemplified in the draft of an essay on poetry in the 'San Trovaso Notebook', which begins: "All art begins in the physical discontent (or torture) of loneliness and partiality. It is…to fill this lack that man first spun shapes out of the void." From this, the very note of transcendental estrangement, he goes on to speak of the "essences of beauty" that have "grouped themselves into form", and glosses the perception of form as "not the perception of matter but of space matter does or might fill".

The immediate direction in which the young Pound was led by such habits of thought involved the projection of various poetic identities for himself, by which he became the possessor of esoteric knowledge and mythic experience, and guardian of an occult poetic tradition stemming from Greece and Provence. The poems are profligate of figures for the relationship of the singular sensitivity to the spirit of the whole, such as raindrops, wind-borne seeds, flames, travellers, exiles. 'Histrion' (*A Quinzaine for this Yule*, 1908) is a prime example of this kind of thing.

The speaker presents himself as a medium through whose plastic identity an esoteric mystery is perpetuated. But this passage through the self of the souls of great men is really nothing more than a reworking of transcendental notions about the relation of the individual identity to others. And indeed, when Pound annotated 'Guillaume de Lorris Belated, A Vision of Italy' with reference to Richard of St Victor's definition of contemplation, the passage in question employs a distinctly Emersonian vocabulary.

>   ...I saw
> How all things are but symbols of all things,
> And each of many, do we know
> But the equation governing.

Reference to the section on Language in 'Nature' might have been more appropriate. It seems obvious that a number of issues raised by Pound's early work are clarified if this background is borne in mind. It would appear, for instance, that his employment of the apparatus of masks and personae is not merely derivative, but a carefully adjusted strategy. (One might say that a third or fourth generation Transcendentalist poet would inevitably, if he had his wits about him, turn to Browning and Yeats rather than Whitman.) The use of "decadent" figures and sentiments, on the other hand, can be seen to be of largely incidental significance. The tendency to think of the self and feelings in spatial terms was, again, an Emersonian trait.

Pound's position in the London poetry world between 1908 and 1912 was altogether curious. His behaviour, socially as well as poetically, was dated in comparison with that of contemporaries like Hueffer, Storer, and Flint. But, when it came to the point, he rather than they was able to construct a poetic based upon the "living tongue" precisely because his transcendentalism made it impossible for him to adapt efficiently to the manner of the 1890s. Pound's London contemporaries had rejected their immediate predecessors for obvious reasons. The poets of the Rhymers' Club were condemned to be marginal and lightweight because their dream, however fine, was no more than the lyrical mode of the normal terms of discourse current in the world on which they turned their backs. (American transcendentalism, on the other hand, had allowed itself to be recuperated by bourgeois society when it mistook the individual mind for a universal; a conceptual rather than a formal error.) Pound's sense of experience was altogether too diffuse and inward to allow him to become an adept handler of the lyric syntactic closures of first person experience. Instead he tended to wander off into redundant paraphrase and parallel but loosely coordinated grammatical structures of a thoroughly Whitmanesque order. But what often appears clumsy and inept in the early poems, deficient in syntactical control and psychological concreteness, was potentially fruitful. For what Pound needed to discover was an alternative to the normal discourse which the poets of the 1890s shared with the world they, and Pound, rejected; specifically, Pound needed to invent a discourse of primary experience which would not be based upon the first person. The free-floating, loosely attached clauses of his early work were the prototypes of the absolute verbal equations for experience, free of discursive location, that constituted Pound's initial achievement. The concluding lines of 'The Flame' (printed in *Canzoni* as section VIII of 'Und Drang') are typical.

> If I have merged my soul, or utterly
> Am solved and bound in, through aught here on earth,
> There canst thou find me, O thou anxious thou,
> Who call'st about my gates for some lost me;
> I say my soul flowed back, became translucent.
> Search not my lips, O love, let go my hands,
> This thing that moves as man is no more mortal.
> If thou hast seen my shade sans character,
> If thou hast seen the mirror of all moments,
> That glass of all things that o'ershadow it,
> Call not that mirror me, for I have slipped
> Your grasp, I have eluded.

If the translucent soul corresponds to the fine, esoteric thing held in the mind, then lines eight, nine, and ten (each of which is a variant of the central figure of an earlier poem, 'On His Own Face in a Glass') approximate in different ways to the inferior thing to which, in the esoteric Pound, they can only imperfectly correspond.

But the transition from lines such as these to 'Petals on a wet, black bough' called for more than the exercise of an editorial blue pencil. Pound's inferior things are subordinate here to a grammatical self which loads them with personal allusiveness; they are imperfect equations, symbols for an ineffable, interior self, and as such incapable of sustaining the autonomous status accorded to the "image" by Pound's later theory. What Pound seems to have gone on to recognize was that the syntactic authority of the self might be transferred, by a process of exteriorization, to rhythm. By dispensing in such a way with the conventions of normal discourse he could release himself from the psychological strain, very apparent in 'The Flame', of resisting at all points the pressure of what he thought of as inferior social values. Detached from their social definitions, the inferior things might be free to co-exist on the same plane, so to speak, as whatever other items of information a poem contained. Poetic discourse could then proceed according to the specific values of its various parts, rather than at the direction of some privileged agency operating within the poem by grammatical proxy or, as was the case with Pound, through the intermediary of mask or persona.

The nature of poetic rhythm thus conceived is unlike that of rhythm with a metrical base, which is essentially a forward moving vehicle, governed by expectation. It is required, instead, to function as an instrument of arrest, control, and coordination. Pound possessed the model for a rhythm endowed with such properties in his basic notion of form as "space matter does or might fill". Form in this sense does not inhere in things as such, but is an impalpable demarcation within the mind between the abstract and the inert. (Thus it was possible for Pound to think of forms interpenetrating, and of form potential in matter, awaiting release by the mind.) Such a spatialized rhythm can have an actual character in the typographical disposition of a text, but this is strictly secondary to its fundamentally mental structure; it is primarily perceived as a mental topology of language, whereas metrical rhythm is governed by the perception of number.

Pound came to believe that a verbal rhythm of this sort could be an absolute expression of experience, but this somewhat theoretical account of the bases for such a belief runs ahead of the matter. A few poems in *Ripostes* exemplify the way in which the rhythmic coordination of syllables and phrases can bind language into a shape in which experience is made concrete, from inferior things, yet is not yoked to a discursive context of meaning. The achievement of 'Doria' and 'The Return' depends upon a scrupulous perception of the specific qualities of individual syllables, and the way in which they combine in sequence, and while it might be suggested that much of Pound's early practice enabled him to acquire such skill, it is the canzoni, which he carefully expunged from the canon of 1926, that show Pound systematically developing his mastery of the syllable. Pound thought that these poems constituted something of a special case, and admitted that they said "nothing in particular", and for this reason, perhaps, found himself able, within a metrical structure, to make a fine discrimination between syllables, and the speed of different phrases, so that groups of syllables knot together, separate, and recombine, as in the following stanza from 'Canzon: The Spear'.

> That fair far spear of light now lays
> Its long gold shaft upon the waters.
> Ah! might I pass upon its rays
> To where it gleams beyond the waters,
> Or might my troubled heart be fed
> Upon the frail clear light there shed,
> Then were my pain at last allay'd.

It was by way of the coordination of individual syllables at this level of attention that Pound arrived at the just proportioning of feeling and language, the expression of primary experience outside the terms of first person discourse, that he sought.

It is a comparatively easy thing to supply the imagist poems that Pound went on to write with a few adjunct parts of speech and so make them over to the model of a more amenable discourse. But to turn 'In a Station of the Metro' into a simile or a personal statement is to import into the poem an additional content which it was Pound's whole purpose to reject. It is not possible to doctor the *Cantos* in this way but, faced with such an extended piece of writing in which the conventions of normal discourse are systematically dispensed with, the parallel recuperative strategy is to treat it as an accumulation of details. To do so is sheer folly. What the *Collected Early Poems* show is a mind searching for, and on the verge of discovering, a model of its form. In the *Cantos* that mind gives us the record of its passage through the world of inferior things, which memory treasured. Noble, pathetic, and deranged by turns, what is recorded was, to say the least, an act of immense worldly abnegation.

John Ashbery—Rhetorical Strategies

David Shapiro, *John Ashbery, An Introduction to the Poetry*.
Columbia University Press, New York 190pp $16.20

Published in *The Literary Review* (ed. Anne Smith) No. 9,
9th to 22nd February 1980.

Most introductions to a poet's work follow in the wake of previous critical studies, intent on tidying up the variety of attention and opinion to be met with among his established readership, and refocusing it in a synoptic view of the text. It is a non-partisan, disinterested sort of chore. David Shapiro, however, has written the first full-length study of Ashbery's work, and his account of his subject illustrates both the privileges and the limitations of the insider's point of view; not only is he himself a poet of a somewhat Ashberyesque persuasion, he has also been able to draw much of the evidence to support his arguments from personal interviews with the poet. One of the virtues of Shapiro's book, therefore, since within his writing Ashbery is a figure of extreme reticence, is that it shows us Ashbery's work as Ashbery probably wishes it to be seen.

The revaluation of the neo-Dadaist elements in Ashbery's writing is also welcome, for it rescues him from that eulogistic misappropriation of certain features of his rhetoric by means of which Harold Bloom was able to place him within a tradition of visionary self-transformation. Whatever tradition John Ashbery may belong to, his civility, his affectionate retention of superseded manners are the converse of an ambitious spiritual transcendence. He is more plausibly a descendant of the New York Cooper than of the New England Emerson.

Shapiro gives Ashbery's work his wholehearted endorsement as a major poetic text of the present by means of such key terms as "reflexivity" and "meaninglessness", which serve both to describe the procedures of Ashbery's writing and secure its vital relation to its period. This is an honest attempt to confront what for many readers are insuperable difficulties in Ashbery's work, and as John Unterecker remarks in his otherwise otiose foreword, (in which he perversely advances his own view of Ashbery as a type of experiential realist,) Shapiro is not so much concerned with exposition of the meaning of Ashbery's text as with the sensibility that gives rise to it and its general cultural context. It is thus possible for him to deal quite summarily with much of the work that brought Ashbery adulatory reviews in the early seventies, while treating as canonical the more refractory intermediate work of *The Tennis Court Oath*.

Allowing for the necessity of upstaging Bloom (who sees that book as an outrageous yet negligible aberration on Ashbery's part), Shapiro's selective attentions in relation to Ashbery's work as a whole do imply a definite aesthetic *parti pris*. He argues that critical priority attaches to the very existence of Ashbery's poems, and this is probably less commonplace than it might seem, for given the range of qualities found to be definitive of Ashbery's writing, (parodistic, disruptive, and opaque, in addition to reflexive and meaningless, all relative rather than inherent qualities,) from a certain angle the very existence of an Ashbery poem is an occasion for surprise. If Ashbery did not exist it would not be necessary to invent him, although Shapiro doesn't have the nerve to say so. It is here that privilege reverses into limitation.

Shapiro's most direct perceptions here tend to be far too knowing, and he is fundamentally uncertain as to how to apply them. He is too pat with analogies drawn from other contemporary art forms, a procedure which invokes the spirit of tolerance rather than understanding, and gives us very little sense of what it is actually like to read an Ashbery poem—to become closed in a discourse of such purposeless and deliberate rhetoric.

While he is right not to treat the qualities he discovers in the writing as clues to motive, recognising that aesthetic effects are not ends in themselves, he is not equally right to treat them as a thematic collocation. Shapiro tends to see, operating at large in Ashbery's work, such fundamental preoccupations as false notions of causality, and the contingency of an arbitrary universe: disunity is the central theme, and the aesthetic integration of such problematic material the primary exegetical function, to be undertaken in metaphrastic readings of some of Ashbery's longer poems.

Shapiro's readings do repay our attention, but they are limited by their premises; he does not come to grips with the poems' large-scale rhetorical accomplishment, their expansive display of confidence in their actual existence, and reads too much into the disruption and ellipsis of Ashbery's local rhetorical strategies. Ashbery's writing has more than enough equanimity not to be perturbed by visions of a corrupt modernity, and the manner of his appropriation of its discursive modes does not permit him to be censorious.

As it turns out, Shapiro is at his best writing about Ashbery's earliest poems, and balances accounts of sources and procedures in tactful and persuasive analysis: it is unfortunate that this chapter, rather than serving as the starting point for the study is preceded by two chapters in which Ashbery's difficulty is misleadingly premised and elaborated, his rhetorical strategies misconceived as aesthetic properties. For in the aggregate Ashbery's rhetorical strategies, the local features of which Shapiro describes with accuracy, while failing to observe the opportunism with which they are borrowed from all periods, including the poet's own, properly lead beyond the poems to their author.

Ashbery's poems ought, perhaps, to be seen as the products of an almost complete introversion, the autonomous activity of the mind aloof from all but the barest recollections of the sensorium, a poetic self refined to the exclusive task of textual production. The nostalgia that Shapiro discovers in Ashbery's poetry, early and late, would then be one of its most authentic accomplishments, as though the initial freedom of the mind at liberty faced the inevitable encroachments of textual necessity, and that impeccable freedom was found at last displaced among the objects of memory.

American Photography

Weston J. Naef, *The Collection of Alfred Stieglitz, Fifty Pioneers of Modern Photography* (New York: The Metropolitan Museum of Art / The Viking Press, 1978, $30.00. Pp. xiv, 530)

Harry W. Lawton and George Knox (eds.), *The Valiant Knights of Daguerre, Selected Critical Essays on Photography and Profiles of Photographic Pioneers by Sadakichi Hartmann* (Berkeley, Los Angeles and London: Univ. of California Press, 1978, £15.00 / $25.00. Pp. xvi, 364)

Walker Evans First and Last (London: Secker & Warburg, 1978, £14.95. Pp. vi, 204)

This review was published in the *Journal of American Studies*, 14.3, December 1980.

Aesthetic exploitation of the machine is characteristic of American art (it was more than historical accident that brought Duchamp to New York for the successful realization of his career), and the aesthetics of photography, the mechanical art par excellence, has been the work of American pioneers since the end of the 19th Century. Photography should occupy a recognized position in American Studies, and these three books constitute as good an introduction as any to its complexities for a newcomer to the field. Each book is of value for itself, each deals with primary materials of photographic scholarship, yet taken together they also illustrate something of the confused state of photographic studies, for each exemplifies a different treatment of materials, the differences having less to do with adequacy or appropriateness of scholarship than with critical intention towards and conception of the very character of the object of study. Each, considered in the context of the other two, begs the questions, Why do we study photographs? What materials do we require in such a study? What editorial criteria should apply to the publication of historical material?

Alfred Stieglitz and Sadakichi Hartmann, contemporaries and, on occasion, collaborators, were arguably the chief American proponents of photography as fine art, Stieglitz not only by virtue of his own photographs, but also as a publisher and exhibition organizer, and Hartmann as critic and theorist. Stieglitz was also, in the earlier stages of his career, an important collector of photographs, both by gift and purchase, and the greater part of his collection is now in the Metropolitan Museum of Art. Mr Naef's book is a work of great scholarly accomplishment, almost worth its price for the bibliography alone; its value is out of all proportion to the kind of utility the catalogue of a museum collection might normally be expected to afford. Not only does Mr Naef's book-length Introduction provide a fresh and exceptionally thorough account of Pictorialist and Secessionist photography, largely superseding earlier work by Robert Doty (*Photo-Secession*, Rochester, N.Y., 1960), it might also reasonably be claimed to be the single indispensable text for the study of Stieglitz's own work by virtue of the account it provides of the contexts in which his early photographs were made. Yet one crucial dimension is absent. Although the Stieglitz collection, which the catalogue illustrates in full, provides the occasion for an exemplary historical narrative, it contains no work by Stieglitz himself apart from studies of the nude made in collaboration with Clarence White, seen here in the context of White's other work in the collection. Mr Naef's brief being to catalogue and illustrate the collection, it is proper that he should stick to it, but there arises in consequence a possible imbalance between the two parts of the book, so that it needs to be used with a degree of circumspection. The collection cannot serve as an index to the style it illustrates, for not only is work by Stieglitz absent, it also includes neither the work of P. H. Emerson, the prototype of English pictorialism, nor, at the other end of the style's period, work by photographers such as Kertesz whose mature styles developed out of pictorialism. Mr Naef is not unaware of this discrepancy, and not the least interesting aspect of his Introduction is its analysis of the relationship of Stieglitz's collecting activities to other, more central, issues in his career: such questions as value (how to price a photographic print), coherence (what had a place in the collection), and quality (which photographers to represent in depth) all have a bearing on Stieglitz's attempts to professionalize photography, to define his own position in photographic history, and to establish appropriate aesthetic criteria for making and viewing photographs. Stieglitz's collection is, in fact, sufficiently arbitrary (he excluded the work of immediate predecessors), idiosyncratic (it includes works using techniques he abjured), and personally haphazard not to be eloquent on its own behalf, and its publication benefits from just such a commentary as Mr Naef's Introduction provides.

While the Stieglitz collection is undoubtedly an important historical document it is equally a major archival resource, and it might be suggested that the publication of photographic archives unduly complicates the writing of photographic history. Why not, in effect, dismember the archive, treating it as a source of prints by major photographers such as Steichen and Coburn, and forget the work of such marginal figures as Anne W. Brigman and Harry C. Rubincam? The reason why not, in this case, is that as document rather than archive the collection ultimately reflects back on a figure of such major importance as Stieglitz. Mr Naef has managed to combine the roles of archivist and historian with immense tact, and has given us an essential book. The abundant writings on photography produced between 1898 and 1915 by Sadakichi Hartmann, much primarily occasional, some the product of critical reflection, scattered among a variety of journals and newspapers, present a not dissimilar occasion for the exercise of editorial tact and judgement. Is it possible to portray Hartmann the neglected historical figure, bohemian aesthete and journeyman critic, while at the same time assembling a cohesive body of writing by which to assess his practical and theoretical contribution to the history of photographic criticism? Are Hartmann's writings original documents, or do they rather uncover (as the editors argue, in the case of the Salon Club, they do) neglected areas of history? Too many of the essays collected in *The Valiant Knights of Daguerre* (a title which represents Hartmann at his worst) merely show how Hartmann squandered his talents in flattering attention to the provincial photographic club-world which doubtless constituted his primary readership; for Hartmann this kind of involvement may have been justified both as an educative ploy and as a means of scouting for new talent, and it accords with the democratic, Whitmanesque, strain in his outlook, but from the point of view of modern scholarship such material might find a more appropriate place in a study of the photographic sub-culture of the period. It is arguable, however, that Hartmann's relationship to the photographic community at large, the overall shapelessness of what he wrote, its frequent reactive impulse, all of which govern the coherence of his critical achievement, were as much determined by his problematic position vis-à-vis the metropolitan and cosmopolitan ambience generated around Stieglitz as by a need to write for money. It is noteworthy that Hartmann's important contributions to *Camera Work* belong to the opening and closing phases of the magazine's history; also that the absence of any reference to him in Mr Naef's book does not represent a glaring omission.

While Hartmann is credible as a critic of the Secession he is less so in his endorsement of what he wished to see as its possible alternative, and as a mirror of his times he reflected much that was merely peripheral; it is hard not to feel in this respect he has been less than well served by his editors. Yet despite the dispersal of critical focus, the involvement in photography's political in-fighting, it is possible to discover from Hartmann's more considered writing a developing theory of photographic aesthetics, and a gradual working out of contradictions latent in the positions taken in his early criticism. Hartmann was always an advocate of the 'straight' photograph, and decried the use of studio props, and manipulations of the medium, by which a fine art status was sought by many photographers; but his arguments from the intrinsic qualities of the medium (the blurred tonal outline especially), and their suitability for the depiction of modern subjects, enclosed an aesthetic of the impression, of the pictorial as pre-existent in the natural or urban scene. His contempt for the strong tonal contrasts of primitive photography provided an aesthetic rationale for a previously edited sense of what made up "the pictorial beauties of life and nature," and misty or twilight atmospheres were valued agents for unifying the diverse features of a depicted scene in the cause of pictorial effect. Yet this attachment to unified picturesque effect provided the motive for most photographic manipulators. The route by which Hartmann subsequently came to envisage a way out of this contradiction, without abandoning his formal commitment to straight photography, although it stopped short of a recognition that photography might assume a documentary motive, anticipated new approaches to pictorial composition that would express the purposiveness of objects (in this he seems to look forward to some of Paul Strand's work), and involved a particular esteem for the street photography of Coburn and Stieglitz.

It is possible to trace in Hartmann a development, impelled perhaps by the individualist prejudice which caused him to look askance at an imitable style, from a provincial taste for the picturesque towards a recognition that straight photography was not a replication of how the eye sees, and that the photograph might constitute a new type of image, segmenting rather than synthesizing the world. Hartmann's strength as a writer on photography does not lie in a comprehensive theory (he had none), nor in the breadth of his views, but rather in his willingness to re-examine a limited number of ideas in the light of fresh evidence; he also can help us to see pictorial photography in the context of the more general visual aesthetic of its period. His editors' critical apparatus, on the other hand, is more often a hindrance than a help: exact information as to which illustrations they have supplied, and which originally accompanied Hartmann's writings, is a major omission (did Hartmann really illustrate his brief remarks on the squalid picturesque with photographs by Jacob Riis?); the bibliography of Hartmann's writings involves a departure from the standard chronology, and is instead organized alphabetically, with an internal alphabetic sub-division according to the various names (including variant spellings) under which he wrote, all of which makes it both unnecessarily complicated and virtually impossible to use.

It is not at all clear whether the name of Walker Evans, who died in 1975, should be taken to establish authorship of *First and Last* or read as part of the book's title. If the motives of Hartmann's editors are incompletely resolved, in this case the editorial role is startlingly self-effacing. The photographs are handsomely reproduced, without captions, by the duotone process; there is a list of subjects, with dates, negative dimensions and, in some cases, details of ownership, at the back; the only other text (leaving aside for the time being what is printed on the dust jacket) is an anonymous Publisher's Note which, without doing so directly, presumably credits those responsible for the selection of Evans's work. This is not the first attempt to epitomize Evans's career, and judged simply as a picture book it is effective both as an illustration of the diversity of Evans's subject matter and as a demonstration of the direct sensuous pleasure photographs can provide. But the tone of pious self-effacement before a monument of pure art seems inauthentic. What about the photographs remaining of the 20,000 from which these 219 were so laboriously chosen? Does editorial labour, not to mention privileged intimacy with the complete oeuvre, confer value and authority? Are these Evans's best photographs? Do they constitute the best survey of his work as a whole? Don't these photographs, in fact, communicate more fully, when seen collectively, than they do when seen as a choice of individual images?

Evans has the historical distinction of being the first photographer to break with the Stieglitz tradition of the exhibitable fine print. Throughout his career the usual presentation of his work was through publication, in either a magazine or a book, often in conjunction with a collaborative prose text. Evans established for himself a convention, related to developments in camera technology, not of the individual image but the series of images, and it would be wrong-headed to argue that this was merely his expedient adaptation to economic circumstances. Evans is the master of the documentary segment, but there is a returning tension between his images and the margins which excise them from the continuum of the real world, while a similar tension is often generated within his images, both in depth, plane surfacing behind plane, and laterally, where two planes converge at the corners of objects. Evans's aesthetic consistency is bound up with the consistency of his attention to particular subject matter, and his work requires to be seen in the context of the terms in which it was made—the motif, or location, examined in depth—and equally in terms of the way he presented it in publication. This argument might be taken further to suggest that seen on its own an Evans photograph is in danger of becoming an item of dated social reportage, and that his language is only fully articulate when relations are established between individual images. *First and Last* does lend itself to being read in this way, and it is undeniable that the book's format underwrites the sheer presence of Evans's images, but it is still at best no more than an addition to existing literature. The dust jacket blurb makes much of the claim that Evans's work has hitherto been largely misunderstood, but even were it to be conceded that his work has been in pawn to a 1930s cultural ethos of "social consciousness and political commitment," by withholding any indication of the situations in which the photographs were made and published those responsible for this book do not so much create the occasion on which Evans's work is allowed for the first time to speak for itself as impose on the actual qualities of the work an inappropriate notion of the self-adequate image. There is, in fact, an aura of commerce about the book, not so much by virtue of its affinity with the coffee-table genre (the price is actually quite modest for what it provides), as by an implicit sub-text which fosters the kind of immaculate and exclusive prestige on which the art market thrives.

Carl Rakosi in the "Objectivists' Epoch"

Crozier made three contributions to Michael Heller's *Carl Rakosi: Man and Poet* (University of Maine 1993). The first, reproduced here, gives an account of Rakosi's early work and reflects an interest which lead in turn to Crozier's edition of Carl Rakosi's *Poems 1923-1941*, Sun & Moon Press 1995. Crozier's two other contributions to the volume were 'Remembering Carl Rakosi: A Conjectural Reconstruction of 'The Beasts" and 'A Handlist of Carl Rakosi's Early Poems, 1923-1941'.

To insist briefly, and however pedantically, on literal respect for the plural noun and its inverted commas is to signify appropriate regard for an historical emphasis already implicit, under the cover of contemporaneity, in the date annexed to the collective identification which appears above the roster of contributors' names on the cover of Louis Zukofsky's guest-edited number of *Poetry*: "Objectivists" 1931. Once historical perspective has been assured, however, it is both reasonable and convenient, despite Zukofsky's own scrupulous exclusion of any such usage, to cite Objectivism as a determinate historical category, without thereby requiring of the term that it endorse the notion of an essential Objectivist poetic. On this question we should agree with Zukofsky. Zukofsky's editorialising in his number of *Poetry*, and in the subsequent *An "Objectivists" Anthology*, has been taken to sanction, inevitably, attempts to formulate of Objectivism some theoretical essence, but interpreters should be forewarned by Zukofsky's preliminary statement of principles, in which his definition of "An Objective", when its use is extended to poetry, emphatically concludes of the "objectively perfect" that it is "inextricably the direction of historical and contemporary particulars."[1] Zukofsky may have dabbled in revolutionary teleology, but History, however its direction is written, even by Marxists, and especially when it deals in particulars, will not disclose an essence. One particular of Zukofsky's Objectivism was its activism: grounded in literary history, it was equally an attempt to influence its future direction. Equally part of the history of Objectivism is Zukofsky's subsequent withdrawal from such public engagement, in his case into a family-centred quietism.

By the position it occupies in both the "Objectivists" number of *Poetry* and *An "Objectivists" Anthology* Carl Rakosi's early poetry (by "early" I mean no more than to distinguish it from the poetry he has written since 1965) is historically situated in relation to Objectivism and is also, but more importantly, inextricably particular to its history. This account of Rakosi's poetry between the years 1924 and 1941 proposes, as its subsidiary motive, to contribute to the writing of that history, and will be appropriately schematic, since as a preliminary account its concern must include narrative and chronology. The dates indicate a period which begins with Rakosi's first magazine publications, and ends with the publication of his *Selected Poems*, but they also bracket, approximately enough, Objectivism's historical epoch, which it is convenient to think of as spanning the decades on either side of the public announcement of the existence of "Objectivists" in 1931. 1931 and 1932 (the year of publication of the *Anthology*) effectively mark a watershed in the history of Objectivism, at which it divides into two distinct phases. In addition to defining a poetic "Objective" in terms of historical particulars (given greater emphasis in the *Anthology* by editorial concern with epic complexity), Zukofsky was insistent in his role as guest editor of *Poetry* on locating a position within recent developments in American poetry. In 'Program: "Objectivists" 1931' he drew attention to his essay 'American Poetry, 1920-1930', from which he reprinted his list of "absolutely necessary" works by Pound, Williams, Moore, Eliot, Cummings, Stevens, McAlmon, Reznikoff, and (citing *Exile* numbers 3 and 4) Rakosi and himself. The older generation of poets, and the younger generation of "Objectivists", both write "in accordance with the principles" set out definitionally at the head of his 'Program'. The mandatory list is Poundian rhetorically and, in the way Zukofsky works through his list in 'American Poetry, 1920-1930', so are the principles. "One proceeds with useful principle (Ezra Pound's *Pavannes* and *Divisions*, or *Instigations*, or *How to Read*, or all three). 'Emotion is an organizer of forms' (Pound). The image is at the basis of poetic form. In the last ten years Pound has not concerned himself merely with isolation of the image—a cross-breeding between single words which are absolute symbols for things and textures—...but with the poetic locus produced by the passage from one image to another". This is less clear than we might like it to be, but despite the loose equation of emotion, form, and image, Zukofsky quickly gets down to details ("the passage from one image to another") and here, and in his subsequent analyses of the treatment of the image by other of the poets on his list, we might conclude that he assigns "principle" an instrumental value. It does not, in other words, provide a standard of judgement. We should understand that Zukofsky's editorial judgement was exercised after systematic exclusion of poets not sharing like principles. Within the field of common principle he is prepared to judge and differentiate: "one may study the progress of individual work rather than its use in an evolution of poetry [...] literary mechanisms for expressing the movement of individual brains".[2]

From within the historical perspective provided by Zukofsky it might appear that Objectivism was the continuation of Imagism under another name; indeed this has been suggested more than once, but this will not do. Although Zukofsky's essay was acknowledgedly 'A Sequel to M. Taupin's Book, 1910-1920', there was tactical advantage to be gained from dating a relevant literary history no further back than 1920, and thus stopping short of Imagism's major epoch.[3] The legacy of Imagism was already in dispute when Zukofsky wrote, its principles the subject of conflicting concepts and interpretations. We might contrast Zukofsky's understanding of passage as locus with Allen Tate's limiting view of Imagism in his Preface to Hart Crane's *White Buildings* (1927). For Tate "single vision" and "central imagination" are signs of the superiority of Crane's poems to "the decorative and fragmentary world" of Imagism, whereas for Zukofsky Crane's poems are disabled by "indefinite language" and "verbal indecision".[4] Tate's analysis of Imagism, incidental as it was to quite other concepts of poetic discourse, need not detain us for the time being. The historical situation of Objectivism towards Imagism was problematic, and it is unhelpful to see it in terms of an "evolution", to use Zukofsky's word; arguments along such lines are about legitimacy and not much else. The more usual sense of who the Objectivists were is of greater service, for Objectivism is then seen in terms of specific claims made about an historical generation—the young American poets to whom Pound persuaded Harriet Monroe to devote a special number of *Poetry* under a young poet's editorial hand—and what we then need to take into account is the character of a rising and successor generation. But since we are not dealing with a natural genealogy the figure, however suggestive it may be, needs to be understood in terms of relations of perception, appropriation, and convergence through which is constructed that sense of necessity asserted by Zukofsky; and no matter how inevitably that might be felt at the moment of juncture between one generation and the next, there remains an ineradicable generational difference, and this seems to me to go a long way towards defining what Objectivism was historically. What divided the poets on Zukofsky's "absolutely necessary" list and the younger contributors to the "Objectivists" number of *Poetry* was social identity and experience. The principal "Objectivists" of 1931 were Jewish, they were susceptible to left wing politics, and if they did not all join the Communist Party the influence of its politics made itself felt in what they

Carl Rakosi in the "Objectivists' Epoch"

wrote. Zukofsky would go so far as to describe 'A' as "an epic of the class struggle".[5] Their literary careers slowed down or came to a temporary halt by the 1940s. The sense that any development represented by Objectivism was precocious, even premature, contributes to our understanding of its history, and the later careers of its protagonists. What is suggested, then, is that historically Objectivism is situated in relation to a general literary situation and a moment at which poets of different generations could be identified in terms of shared principles, and that its history consists of the literary trajectories of a few poets, who are then the exemplary Objectivists, around that moment. In this light Rakosi's career is both particular to and typical of that history.

Rakosi's career before the "Objectivists" moment of 1931 needs to be read in terms of the literary situation as it presented itself to writers of his generation. What then becomes apparent is that although it was a generation with something of a common frame of reference—Imagism, for example—its cohesion was superficial, and concealed a potential for rupture which developed, in due course, along lines marked, as much as anything, by social difference. Rakosi belonged, that is to say, to a generation of American poets who, at the start of their careers in the 1920s, took initial direction from the expression of contemporary experience and sensibility made possible by the innovations of the first generation of modernists. Tate made precisely this point about Crane: "From Pound and Eliot he got his first conception of what it is, in the complete sense, to be contemporary." Unlike some other members of his generation (Tate himself, for example, and more especially Yvor Winters) Rakosi did not ally his poetry to the formulation and propagation of a new literary-critical canon, and thus make a theoretically entailed connection between writing in the present and the literature of the past on behalf of a stabilising cultural order of the sort Eliot seemed to adumbrate in 'Tradition and the Individual Talent.' His writing identifies him, instead, with poets more concerned to investigate the formal uses to which the data of contemporary life might lend themselves. Like Rakosi, these poets were mostly from immigrant families and, cut off from cultural traditions which American experience tended, in any case, to negate, their attention to formal compositions that could be understood as the specific, unprecedented resolution of their experience was expedient and necessary. It was also their special distinction. As members of immigrant families they were immune to nostalgia for the American past, and as Americans in the process of assimilation it is not surprising that they were less concerned with their perception of the immediacies of experience than with the discourses in which that experience was constituted. We need always to remind ourselves that America in the 1920s was not the London of 1913, and that the world of lived experience, as well as poetry, had been modernised, and continued to be modernised and rationalised at an accelerating rate.

These "Objectivists", as they became, are to be seen as initiators of the first revolt against institutionalised modernism by virtue of their rejection of the impersonal theories of discourse implicit in the notion of poetic values sustained by tradition. (It should be noted that Eliot used "tradition" as a stalking horse while in pursuit of other game. When Tate says that Crane's poetry is "in the grand manner" it is its traditionalism that wins his approval.) Their work may also be seen as an attempt, not altogether well timed, to incorporate and extend the innovations of the first generation of modernists at a moment when that generation was losing momentum and cohesion. Such a revolt, however, was inauspicious at the start of a decade in which the main opposition to the academic modernism of what became the "new criticism" came from left wing demands for a literature of solidarity and social commitment. Objectivism represents, then, a particular development of early modernism, rather than its straightforward evolution, still directly responsive to the instigations of the previous generation by virtue of an understanding of poetic form as a resolution of responses to contemporary experience and its characteristic discourses, rather than a conceptual order able to accommodate and so regulate an awkward and perhaps undesirable novelty. This development took place (perhaps only could have taken place: Rakosi and Zukofsky both were refugees from university teaching posts) outside the new establishment of literary power relations, brought into existence by the alliance with modernism of an increasingly professionalised literary criticism. This alliance, the main site of modernist affiliation for poets of Rakosi's generation, was built up around an analysis of modernism of the sort suggested by Tate's remarks about Hart Crane. Its concepts and related values are evident in Winters's review of *An 'Objectivists' Anthology*, in which he reproached the Objectivists for their lack of "rational intelligence", and read them as "sensory impressionists of the usual sort".[6] For Winters, as for Tate, the agency of form was conceptual; it represents (for Winters it could only do so by conventions of metre; for Tate it was signified by an intuited imaginative centre) the mind's rational control of disorderly sensation and feeling. Inevitably, therefore, they would find in Imagism and Objectivism no signs of unifying intelligence. Their realism precluded anything approaching Zukofsky's understanding of words as "absolute symbols", and its implication that form is actualised in the local and sequential relations between particular words. What is striking about Winters's theory of form, in particular, is that rational intelligence is represented symbolically, by metrical verse; its textual domain, that is to say, is the aesthetic, which acts as a corrective to the confused emotions and muddled thought of modern life. Despite the attention his criticism gives to the local vitality of poetic language, its denotation and connotation are for Winters cognitively weak. It is as though he recognised the place of modernism's energy and expression but can only assign such qualities affective status. What is outside the poet's mind, including the instrumentality of language, is a source of brute sensation and vagrant mood; it is without organisation or unity. One does not, however, have to be a phenomenologist not to suppose the mind capable of representing only its own coherence, nor idly complaisant in acknowledging the discourses that constitute the greater part of daily life. No doubt much of the twentieth century deserves our contempt, but contemptuous dismissal is a luxury as well as a cliché.

It is not that Rakosi and the other Objectivists stood outside the literary situation of their generation; Tate and Winters were, in their own way, outsider figures; indeed, the figure might apply to the whole generation "*entre les deux guerres*". The point is, rather, that the Objectivists were successfully outflanked: we can see this being done very neatly in the pages of *Hound and Horn*—at first friendly to Pound and his young men, its literary policy was eventually dominated by the opinions of Winters.[7] None of this any longer matters, but it is against just this background of generational identity and rupture that the contour of Rakosi's career shows up most clearly.

As a student at the University of Wisconsin between 1921 and 1924 Rakosi was one of a brilliant group of student writers: Kenneth Fearing, Leon Serabian Herald, and Margery Latimer.[8] Their brilliance was to rebel against local standards of taste, represented by *The Wisconsin Literary Magazine* and the faculty poet, William Ellery Leonard, and to gravitate instead towards modernism. They felt the lure of New York, of *The Dial* and *The Little Review*. Their group was able to sustain its cohesion by mutual interest and encouragement throughout most of the decade, though in Rakosi's case this was a matter of letters and the occasional visit. We might expect the pattern of his life between 1924 and 1935, finding work in different regions and cities, settling for no more than a year or two, to have left its trace in his poetry, but just where it does so we cannot aim to know. But the pattern reveals, as well, some of the personal dynamics of Rakosi's situation: unlike the others of his group, Rakosi did not try to support himself by writing; he looked for a career that would provide financial support but in the process, since jobs were not hard to find, he was able to see the country; most of all, perhaps, the need for financial security equated with a need to distance himself from the family setting. Rakosi's adoption of a new name for legal purposes, quite typical of children of immigrant families, speaks not only of a social identity defined outside the relationship of family but also of a distinction between the citizen and the poet. To what extent, in Rakosi's case (as compared to Williams, say, or Stevens), the demands of work and writing were in conflict is an idle speculation, but the knowledge that Rakosi's writing was the site of a genuine personal conflict—that he sought financial security in order to write, but that professional involvement was a distraction—will help to clarify its history. It provides the context, for example, for Latimer's constant encouragement to publish; her suggestions about where to send work correspond to his list of publications: *The Little Review*, *New Masses*, *Exile*, *The American Caravan*. The break in their correspondence between 1928 and 1931 correlates with a period in which Rakosi did not publish; when he resumed publication in 1931, at Zukofsky's instigation, he told Zukofsky that he had not been writing. Indeed, in a letter to Pound at this time Rakosi claimed to have written nothing between 1925 and 1931. This is hard to believe. In any case the chronology of publication is not a secure guide to the chronology of the writing. The second group of poems Rakosi published in *Poetry* (November, 1931) he described as early work, and there are grounds for supposing that among the poems published in *Pagany* in 1931 and 1932 are some that dated from the period in which he was submitting work to *Exile*. My own conclusion is that Rakosi's writing between 1924 and 1941 falls into three phases: the first up to 1927 or 1928; another from perhaps late 1930 to 1932 or 1933; and a third, with a moment of intensity around the time of the Munich agreement in 1938, represented by the previously unpublished poems in *Selected Poems*. It seems of significance, in relation to the personal dynamics of Rakosi's situation as a writer, that he was anxious to collect his work in book form (in 1932, and again—successfully—in 1940) at moments in his professional life when he thought its pressures would make it difficult for him to continue writing. He may also, of course, have reckoned that a book might provide the impetus to continue.[9]

An aspect of Rakosi's precocious brilliance was the rapid development of his writing away from an aestheticism which in the 1920s could still seem advanced, which in England, in particular, exerted a blighting effect throughout the decade. In this respect Rakosi compares favourably with, say, his near contemporary Fitzgerald. In Rakosi's case this development was achieved by projecting on to the motifs of aestheticism a sardonic self-consciousness, signified less by an antithetical persona than by a confident verbalism, flamboyant rather than grotesque, through which grotesquely appear various contemporary scenes and personages. Rakosi's earliest published works already bear traces of this as social wit projected on to personal feeling, with excursions into a lurid and subversive diction. They allude to aestheticism's conventional refinements of sensitivity, but for all the symptomatic references to Whistler, or the highlights glimpsed on a woman's hair, and genuflection to the intensities of the sonnet form, these poems neither depend on such stock devices and effects, nor re-enact the decadent poet's anxious celebration of the crises of sacred and profane love. In one sense Rakosi was no more than working over ground on which Eliot had preceded him, but whereas Prufrock was given to reveal the absurdity of the modern courtly lover, guiltily aware of his fleshly bachelor existence, the equivalent figures in Rakosi's poems are unequivocally youthful and jauntily resistant rather than absurd. The difference is telling, but of no more than incidental significance; these poems don't command the ability of Eliot's rhetoric to represent two positions simultaneously. But although in Rakosi's version the female may have the propensity to immobilize the male, to bore him to sleep, he retains the prerogative of action, if only of aesthetic, action, to "compose the shifting forms to beauty."[10] Such last-ditch refinements of a late-Victorian problematic could be, at the most, no more than a starting point. "Beauty" was already a flawed touchstone, and the spectacle of a young poet digging himself out of the sexual politics of a situation in which the female could only be imagined in terms of an outdated and literary convention (as Fitzgerald imagined his female characters), however compensatingly grotesque she might then appear, reveals not much more than his ambiguous commitment to a literary discourse the main attraction of which, we might suppose, was its continuing challenge to the celebratory populism represented by Sandburg and (at Wisconsin) Leonard. The energy of these very early poems is found not in their negotiations with aestheticism but in the way its formal proprieties are pulled indecorously out of shape by the solids with which Rakosi's agile invention furnished settings for personages who themselves remain no more than symbolist enigmas.

In these poems sex and courtship are not associated with desire. They are figured on the scale of world or cosmos, which on the human scale are projected, aesthetically enough, in terms of music. Part of Rakosi's development is the discovery of his proper subject in his figures (for which Imagism provided some precedent), and we can understand this as the composition of forms as purposive in itself. The solids of Rakosi's invention ("the lean of sagging flesh", "a sleep guitar on sober braids") approach the intelligible quality of forms which brought together can represent the copresence of the compositional intelligence. We can see the development worked out in 'Sittingroom by Patinka' in which, although the female figure has obvious poetic antecedents, the concern is not with her portrait but the interior she inhabits.[11] The distinction is crucial: the lady is figured inside a discourse in which, as a conspicuous consumer, her furnishings take on the salient role. I quote the first of the poem's four stanzas:

> I found Miss Levi in a plush repose,
> counting the curves pitched in her portly mirrors
> by seven bored and pygmy globes. Her floors
> were tourmaline supporting topaz standards.
> Moist for the mouthing of mild platitudes,
> here evenings passed Venetian glasses and
> oak planes through green transitions. Walnut backs
> diffused her satin cases. She seemed faint,
> ecstatic in her parlour sunsets, stamping
> her wronged head on an old medallion.

The visual imagination is still, surely, not far from Beardsley, with a glance at Pound, perhaps, in the last two lines. But Rakosi has been listening to the cadences of Stevens, and there are other poems in which his influence is thematised to the point of homage. Rakosi is not quite shaping his lines around the movement and cadence of the phrase, but in abandoning rhyme for a modified blank verse he shows an assurance of touch by which those lines which are not end stopped do not butt against their metrical confinement but turn on a grammatical figure of unfolding statement. Sexual drama is directed into its setting, description of which uses active verbs in such a way that its details figure as more than grammatical subjects and take on a quasi-erotic life of their own. The rhetorical self-possession of the language, and the busy décor, merge in a series of deliquescent twilights. With Tate in mind we might find it helpful to revive the question of manner in order to distinguish it from style: style in this poem has aplomb rather

Carl Rakosi in the "Objectivists' Epoch"

than grandeur and is integral to the poem's theme since it is the figure of the composing intelligence, which is concerned less with the human sexual drama than with its inflection within its particular cultural setting. Sex and courtship are dissevered by consumption. The writing wilfully tends away from any representation of a self which is able to maintain a moral distance from what the language supposedly attributed to it denotes. Point of view and its associated antitheses are situated within the poetic discourse rather than as its implied origin.

Much as I can admire this poem I draw attention to it in order to indicate the route by which Rakosi arrived at his more characteristic writing, which is not defined by the consciousness of sex which the young Rakosi recognised in himself. In 'Scriptural Program' the sexual problematic is again resited, using a parodic version of scriptural cadence and imagery to provide a fictive context for an encounter which is this time more conventionally erotic.[12] The male protagonist is here more explicitly dramatized, and "Miss Levi" metamorphosed, perhaps as "my Jewess" who "brings me the Holy Land". Structural correspondence between lines and phrases gives the poem an open-ended range of particular allusion but its rhetoric is simplified accordingly to a series of binary oppositions. But Rakosi's poems had already, by their juxtaposition with aestheticism of their own subversive rhetoric, been required to compress much within a narrow compass. Despite its explicit Hebraism, therefore, this poem seems less a development than the exhaustion of Rakosi's initial situation as a poet. In the next poems to be published he abolished the aesthetic dilemma by resiting it so radically, in the vulgar certainties, that is to say, of contemporary existence, that carefully negotiated discursive transitions are no longer required as a means of purchase on debased literary convention. To borrow an apposite phrase from Pound, Rakosi now addressed the "drear horror of American life" in a variety of its public forms: cinema, advertising, success, and—on the margin of public and private life— vaudeville.[13] In 'Vitagraph', 'Characters', 'Wanted', 'Superproduction', and 'Revue' the personages are not enigmas but the stereotypes of a grotesque national identity parade. With the exception of 'Vitagraph', in which deadpan narrative is matched closely to its subject like the captions of a silent Western, these poems do not feed directly on the language of their originals, so that our attention is eventually drawn to their originals' actuality rather than (as in Cummings for example) their mere vulgarity.[14]

CHARACTERS

One of our brassy beefeaters
in grandstand on the continent
bares biceps to the gaping millions,
sinks shaft in market, pockets wheat
holds cornucopia of cash.
Cheers heard before his private front
as he lands place with notables.
We call this tribute in a nutshell,
a miracle of entertainment.

Speaking of beaus sartorial,
perplexed young girl hands laugh to lovewise.
I am a lovely, irresistible girl
of seventeen, with wondrous witching orbs.
Why do I blaze in my intangibles
like any mandolin romantic,
you, stable as the sterling?

Character and plot are presented in language at once more summary and more agile than is natural to them; indeed it is this language which provides the critical gaze by which they are exposed to our fascinated recognition. But although the poem's language has the function of making strange things that are already all too familiar, point of view is attributed to the stereotypes of grotesque normality. Satiric intelligence is here invested in style, which is perceived as an increasingly fine margin of difference around a text in which character, action, and setting are closely adjusted. If the writing seems deliberately to assist the gaudiness of its own style it does so to sustain a necessary consistency, for gaudiness is an effect of opacity and density produced by a method of off-centre denotation. Our recognition of what is given as unfamiliar is an outcome not of decoding a set of metonymic exchanges but of sudden adjustment to an unwanted orientation of the things represented, a reorientation towards the discourse within which such things are normally inscribed. In addition to this, the consistency sustained by style provides cover for denotations which are not so much off-centre as camouflaged, and which brought into the open disclose a subversive sub-text. We might consider the precise inflection of "stable as the sterling", for instance, in a poem published the year after Churchill put sterling back on the gold standard.

Carl Rakosi in the "Objectivists' Epoch"

With these poems Rakosi established himself as a modern poet. There are two aspects to what I mean by this. First, his language observes no necessary distinction in writing between literal and figurative construction; it is consistently figural, even when its grammar is declarative. (Certain formal qualities in his writing are incidentally a consequence of this, notably textual integration rhythmically and rhetorically, which are primary to the aesthetics of modernism.) Second, meaning is continually negotiated across the figural composition, given in it but also to be interpreted; no position is represented from which it is supposed authoritatively to derive. If we also identify Rakosi as a stylist we might feel inclined to trace this back to the finely ironic sensibility of aestheticism, and we might not be entirely wrong, but the derivation will no longer provide any useful purchase. His adeptness of phrase, and confident management of tone and cadence, are skills of a high order, and they are indeed characteristic, but their contribution to style does not define it. We recognise in Rakosi's style a various figure, sensuous and intelligent, which contributes to meaning; as a figure of language its theoretical antecedents are in Pound's logopoeia. For a writer to use style in this way is, necessarily, attended by risk, notably of that verbal gusto, an excess of skill, which makes style its own derivative, but some of Rakosi's revisions, substantially of whole lines and stanzas, show him alert to this. But, as a primary locus of Rakosi's writing, style in the sense I use here seems to have provided productive impetus. Pound's selection of poems for Rakosi's first appearance in *Exile* endorsed those in which style takes on structures of cultural discourse embedded deeply (indeed, still embedded) in modern America, but these need to be set beside others in which Rakosi calls into play discourses from early American history, the culture of Europe, as well as those of courtship and sex, now freed from the sexual politics of aestheticism. Such discourses were all, in one way or another, personal to Rakosi as immigrant, European born, and attracted to women. In addition we can see emerging a set of topics more local still to his individual existence, in which multiform life is seen in relation to the absolutes of a void metaphysics; his writing becomes both speculative and learned, possessed of a vocabulary, amenable to the turnings of his style, which implies knowledge not only of the contemporary scene but of mineralogy, chemistry, marine biology, music, photography, and ancient history.

It was at the point this represents in his development, more or less, that Rakosi received significant recognition when Zukofsky recruited him as an "Objectivist". When Zukofsky approached him in late 1930 Rakosi had lived in Texas some two years, working as a university English instructor, teaching high school, and involved in settlement work. From the ardently admiring tone of Margery Latimer's first letter to him after their correspondence was resumed in 1931 it appears that the account Rakosi gave of his life since 1928 was of unstinted effort to put his life on a secure professional footing; but at the same time we should recognise that Rakosi was still playing the field, and was undecided, or simply not economically in a position to decide between social work, education, medicine, or the law. Zukofsky's schedule for the February, 1931 number of *Poetry* was tight, but Rakosi was in a position to send enough poems to allow Zukofsky to make his own selection and offer to place others with magazines such as *Pagany*. Zukofsky's response to Rakosi's poems was too fulsome to bear repeating, but he was as well a fastidious editor, and Rakosi's contributions to both the "Objectivists" number of *Poetry*, where he occupied the lead position, and *An "Objectivists" Anthology*, carry the imprint of Zukofsky's hand. For Poetry he chose poems (and, I suspect, decided their sequence) which deal with the mind's own isolation, and its intervening presence in the world in which it is constituted. It is traditional to posit nominalism against the realism implied by the views of Tate and Winters, and the term has been used with some cogency (by Zukofsky among others) to characterise the language of modern poetry. But Rakosi's is scarcely ever a poetry of perception; in his writing ideas and vocabulary are immitigably actual, the form of mental activity situated in the lived world. The effect of this can be to people the world of poetic discourse with imaginary figures which nonetheless are not fictions, and it was poems of this type that Zukofsky preferred.

UNSWERVING MARINE

This is in the wind:
that an old seaman

                    paces the planks again
as his weedy hull parts

                    the saltseries inaudibly.
What ho! She carries full sails
And the chant of the grog-quaffers

                    in an important manner.
But there is no port
and the wind is distracted

                    from her simple stern

like the mind.
Continuously the undefined plane

                     emerges

in the form of a ship,
her nose speeding in the brine-ellipsis,
routing the shads and alewives

               from her shaping way.

And the wind
and the mind sustain her

             and there is really

no step upon the gangway,
nothing but the saltdeposits

          of the open.

Rakosi's fascination with ships and voyages once led him to embark as mess boy on a freighter (though he never left port), and is evident in many of his poems. In this one, ship and sailors achieve ghostly permanence as epiphenomena of mind and wind, but in his contemplation of the mind's relation to nature Rakosi goes beyond Stevens in 'The Idea of Order at Key West' because he argues from neither the expressive power of nature nor the transcendent power of the mind. Whereas in Stevens these notions are opposed and can only meet around the symbolist fiction of the singer, Rakosi's wind and mind own an equivalence which speaks of the mind's capacity to invent materially from the physical properties of nature. Rakosi's ship and sailors behave like any others, whereas Stevens's singer must remain *sui generis*. The mind's engagement with the intelligible qualities of nature, from which transaction comes material and intellectual culture, might serve as the privileged figure in Rakosi's poetics. It is also thematically diverse, to be encountered in an account of building carpentry, in references to exact machine processes, and to scientific measurement of different sorts. Specifically under the aspect of craftsmanship we might like to trace it back to the hours Rakosi spent watching his father, a skilled watchmaker, at work in his shop. But beside this must be set the mind's contemplation of itself in isolation, when its action sets nature at a distance, and its affinity is with nature conceived in terms of its furthest reaches into time and space. The relation is then inverse, away from home and sex; the mind in nature is abstract, polar, a voyage without destination. 'Unswerving Marine' is the third in the group of four poems by Rakosi in the "Objectivists" number of *Poetry*, and within the group as a whole there is a sequence of feeling which starts in withdrawn self-sufficiency ("And I, my lover, / skirt the cottages, / the eternal hearths and gloom, / to animate the ideal / with internal passion") and ends at a figure of metaphysical solitude ("Tumblers in the nebula, / is not every man / his own host?").

The extent to which, when he began to publish again in 1931, Rakosi was drawing on capital is uncertain, but publication, and correspondence with Zukofsky, were a spur to writing. 'A Journey Away', Rakosi's main contribution to *An "Objectivists" Anthology* appears to have been produced under Zukofsky's exacting tutelage and hortation—or, to see matters in less kind a light, it received the impression of Zukofsky's faith in his ability as a rewrite artist.[15] Zukofsky informed Rakosi that in the *Anthology* he wished to display the essential Rakosi, not his variousness, but that he proposed to do so in relation to its major category of "epic", "a chain of facts which exists".[16] To this end he assembled the poems he had chosen in the order in which they were to appear, assigning them numbers rather than titles, so that in sequence they would represent a contemporary journey. If Rakosi were to demur Zukofsky thought that the resultant composition might be equally suited to the third, collaborative section of the *Anthology*, in which he printed his rewrite of Rexroth's 'Prolegomena to a Theodicy', which Rexroth declined to acknowledge as his own. It's hard not to think of the version of 'A Journey Away' published in *Hound and Horn*, shorter by two sections, and the sections differently ordered, as Rakosi's recovery of his own text. It's hard also not to believe that the interest Zukofsky took in Rakosi's writing was not altogether benign in its effect. Around this time there are references in Rakosi's correspondence to a poem several pages in length on which he was making gradual progress, and I assume that this refers to 'The Beasts' and the poems eventually derived from it. If I am right to take these poems as the fragments of an abandoned work— abandoned for whatever reason—it would then seem that the account I am advancing of Rakosi's writing and its situation will need to recognise two quite different issues. The first is that the "Objectivists" quickly lost whatever advantages were to be gained by announcing their group identity. Whatever the individual benefits of collectivity, as a group they were unable to consolidate their position; indeed the *Anthology* already looks like a retrenchment, and we might suppose that the historic status of Objectivism has been achieved only by the subsequent careers of its protagonists. It is against this background that we should see Rakosi having to compete for space and accept substantial abridgement in order to publish 'The Beasts' in *Poetry*. The second is that the work Rakosi abandoned was a poem

Carl Rakosi in the "Objectivists' Epoch"

of far-reaching and complex ambition, in which were drawn together an apprehension of the role of the mind within evolutionary time, the dilemmas of personality, and the variety of forms within the social and economic structures of the modern city.

> Contested between two responsibilities
> like a gizzard thrown to two dogs,
> judging between two faiths,
> I saw the city

In this figure of bitter division we might discover the site of the integration the poem first sought.

The absence of this poem, as it originally existed, from the available canon of Rakosi's work can only be matter for regret, as is the non-appearance of the book which Rakosi intended to publish at this time. But despite such regrets we cannot avoid noticing that by the time Rakosi was negotiating with *Poetry* about how much of 'The Beasts' might be retained he had begun writing poems in a new manner which could not sustain the same level of ambition. Zukofsky thought that 'The Beasts' was too tender in its account of a world in crisis, and bearing in mind his phrase about "the direction of historic and contemporary particulars" we might take him perhaps to mean that Rakosi's account of the crisis of capitalism was not ideological enough to become objectively perfect. On the other hand, the poems in Rakosi's new manner, 'Good Prose', for example, and 'Sappho', are written in accordance with Zukofsky's exposition of the relation between quantity and clarity of image in the lyric as practised by Williams.[17] These poems are elegant and witty vignettes, but I can't help feeling that their elegance is stylish in a way that Rakosi's previous writing was not.

At this point I should insert a word or two of caution, lest the account I am attempting of Rakosi's career and development mislead readers. Between 1931 and 1934 Rakosi published about twice the number of poems that he published between 1923 and 1928. They are all, I believe, work of genuine distinction, and confirm the many-sidedness of Rakosi's talent that was acknowledged by Zukofsky; but in this essay I have not attempted to give a complete account of that many-sidedness, neither have I ventured to assess the actual weight of what Rakosi achieved. I will, however, state the opinion that it is an achievement in which we may recognise a poet of major stature, and that this is a judgement that can stand without any account taken of Objectivism, although it is, of course, one which materially affects our sense of what Objectivism amounted to.

There is not much left to chronicle. The magazines in which Rakosi published, with the exception of *Poetry*, were short-lived and peripheral: *The Lion and Crown*, *The New Act*, *The Windsor Quarterly*. They do not have a place in the roster of seminal little magazines, but they deserve to be studied, and not only as signs of the dispersal of Objectivism. Two poems were published in a series of brochures issued by the Modern Editions Press.[18] By 1933 Rakosi had aligned himself with the Communists; his involvement with social work was career oriented, and under his legal name he began to publish papers—still of interest—in this field.[19] He married, became a father, published a book, and wrote no more poetry for a quarter of a century. But such a summary is too rapid to convey the time scale over which this development took place. We should think of Rakosi throughout the second half of the 1930s as a writer on the left, and we should remember that during these years, when he was living in New York, Rakosi was, for the first time since his years as a student at Madison, situated physically in a literary milieu, of a sort. He was a signatory to the manifesto of support for the Spanish Republic issued by the League of American Writers in 1938, and heard W.H. Auden ("like a young Byron") address its Congress.[20] He wrote poems of political protest, addressed to the average American citizen. In his papers at the University of Wisconsin are drafts of poems of profound personal anguish and political outrage prompted by the German occupation of the Sudetenland and the Munich agreement, but the phrases in which he expresses his anguish are too fraught with emotion to connect with those which express contempt and defiance. In the *Selected Poems* too much is sacrificed for the sake of local clarity and didactic content, with one telling exception, in which Rakosi joined together two of his poems about ships.[21]

SHIPS

One o'clock. A rainy night.
The sea air darkens on the wheelhouse.
The binnacle glows.
　　"Ho there, ho!"
The whole hull of *The Frisco Cross*,
a twin-screw tanker, lights up.
　　"Who are you?"

A dry face. The chronometer tilts.
"All lights burning brightly, sir."

A little river steamer from the tariff frontiers,
twelve cabins and a white light on the masthead,
with its house flag and a freeboard of 6", boys
running with mates' receipts and bills of lading,
carries kilderkin imperial kegs and stingo firkins.

But the great turbo-electric ocean liner, fire-insured,
has circulating ice water swift for the belly,
and anchor hooks and foreign mail.

What tells here results from the decision to prefix to a poem which somewhat didactically contrasts two classes of shipping another which evokes the romance of navigation on the open sea; the telling difference is surely something like tenderness of regard even for the luxury liner. Such tenderness, it seems to me, reaches forward to the poems that Rakosi would come back to write.

Notes

1 Louis Zukofsky, 'Program: "Objectivists" 1931', *Poetry* 37, v (February, 1931).

2 Louis Zukofsky, 'American Poetry, 1920-1930', *Symposium* 2 (1931).

3 i.e. René Taupin, *L'influence du Symbolisme français sur la Poésie americaine*, Paris 1929.

4 Allen Tate, 'Foreword', *White Buildings: Poems by Hart Crane*, New York 1926 [1927]; Zukofsky, 'American Poetry, 1920-1930'.

5 Notes on contributors, New Directions in Prose and Poetry, Norfolk, Conn. 1938

6 Yvor Winters, *Hound and Horn* 6.1 (October-December) 1932.

7 For a detailed account of Yvor Winters's association with Lincoln Kirstein and *Hound and Horn*, see Leonard Greenbaum, *The Hound and Horn: The History of a Literary Quarterly*, The Hague 1966

8 Leon Serabian Herald published a book of poems, *This Waking Hour*, NY 1925; his 'Autobiography' was serialised in *The Dial*. Kenneth Fearing is deservedly well known to devotees of detective fiction; his satiric verse, more mordant and

sarcastic than Rakosi's, is still read. Margery Latimer, who died in 1932, is being rediscovered—rightly—by feminist literary historians. One of her novels, *This is My Body*, NY 1930, is based on the personalities of the group. Rakosi appears in it as Schevel Pukalski.

9 Various statements and conjectures in this paragraph and elsewhere are based on conversation and correspondence with Rakosi, and on unpublished material in his papers in the University Libraries, University of Wisconsin—Madison, letters from Margery Latimer in the Jean Toomer Archive, and Rakosi's correspondence with Pound in the Ezra Pound Archive, The Beinecke Rare Book and Manuscript Library, Yale University Library.

10 Carl Rakosi, 'Creation', *Palms* 2.4 (1924).

11 Carl Rakosi, 'Sittingroom by Patinka', *The Little Review* (Spring 1925).

12 Carl Rakosi, 'Scriptural Program', *Two Worlds* (June 1926).

13 Ezra Pound, 'Prolegomena', *The Exile* 2 (Autumn 1927).

14 Carl Rakosi, 'Vitagraph', *The New Masses* 4 (August 1926); 'Characters' etc., *The Exile* 2.

15 Zukofsky's habit of rewriting other poets' work was not without its theoretical justification: 'rehabilitating the good to its rightful structure is always possible with writing in which something was seen, a quantity heard, an emotion apprehended, to begin with.' 'American Poetry, 1920-1930'.

16 René Taupin's definition of 'epic' is prefixed to the first section of *An 'Objectivists' Anthology*, ed. Louis Zukofsky, Le Beausset, Var, and New York 1932.

17 Zukofsky's remarks on quantity will be found (again) in 'American Poetry, 1920-1930'. Carl Rakosi, 'Good Prose', *The New Act* (June 1933); 'Sappho', *The Windsor Quarterly* (Summer 1933).

18 Carl Rakosi, *Two Poems*, NY [1933]. Other brochures in the series were by Horace Gregory, Paul Bowles, and Laurence Vail.

19 See, for instance, Callman Rawley, 'A Glimpse of the Unattached Woman Transient in New Orleans', *The Family* 15.3 (May 1934). The paper juxtaposes the writer's sympathetically excited imagination of his subject ('large hordes of very young girls [...] overrunning transient centers throughout the country') and the 'much less dramatic' facts.

20 *Writers Take Sides: Letters about the war in Spain from 418 American writers*, New York 1938. (I am indebted to Eric Homberger for drawing my attention to this document.)

21 Carl Rakosi, *Selected Poems*, Norfolk, Conn. [1941]. The poems joined together were the final section of 'A Journey Away' (both versions), and 'Happy New Year', *The Windsor Quarterly* (Spring 1933).

Carl Rakosi in the "Objectivists' Epoch"

(Fourth) International Modernism: The Case of Harry Roskolenko; or, Apocalyptic Transports of an Objectivist

This essay arose from a talk given as part of an international three-day conference organised by Steve Clark and Mark Ford at the University of London, July 1998. This is its first publication.

In 1939 a brief notice of Harry Roskolenko's first book, in a Welsh little magazine, described him as "one of the most interesting young American Trotskyist poets".[1] Other poets in this special category would have included Sherry Mangan and John Wheelwright, but I'm not aware that their work had any currency outside the USA at the time. In Australia a few years later Roskolenko, "the American poet in the US Forces", was among those taken in by the Ern Malley hoax, intended by its perpetrators to debunk "the whole literary fashion as we know it from the work of Dylan Thomas, Henry Treece and others".[2] The term "Fourth International Modernism", in other words, is not intended as a *jeu d'esprit* merely. Indeed, the overlapping parentheses of the essay title are meant to suggest that the correlation of politics and poetry in the case of Roskolenko (1907–1980) is not straightforward. He was not one of those "New York Intellectuals" for whom the dialogue between Trotskyism and Modernism, centred on *Partisan Review* in the late 1930s, established a post-war career. Indeed, by the time the Fourth (or Trotskyist) International was founded in the summer of 1938 Roskolenko was already breaking with its American affiliate, the Socialist Workers Party, in a one-man secession from the life of political organisation and revolutionary activism. Nevertheless, the term's components, part-juxtaposed and part-superimposed, are capable of evoking earlier and rather different phases (after Trotskyism had given up on the Communist parties, following the Nazi revolution in Germany, and before Modernism had been historicised) that serve to place him initially. At the same time in their similarity and difference they constitute a figure for what in Roskolenko most engages attention, the way his case presents a context juxtaposing poetic avant-gardes so unlike that I can think of no occasion of their being thought of together: the American "Objectivists" of Louis Zukofsky, and the British "New Apocalypse" of J.F. Hendry and Henry Treece. My "Fourth International Modernist" is then a question-begging hybrid, the uncanny offspring of this unlikely juxtaposition—so

163

much so, indeed, that when an initial version of this essay was presented as a conference paper mention of the Ern Malley hoax seemed to set off an anxious frisson in the room lest Roskolenko (himself a man of many aliases) turned out to be pure invention.[3]

Considered as avant garde interventions in the immediate field of contemporary poetry both "Objectivism" and the "New Apocalypse" were short-lived (say, 1930-34 and 1938-43 respectively) and their protagonists' long-term careers have tended to be retrospectively associated with closed chapters of history.[4] I identified them as specifically American and British in order to indicate their immediate cultural environments, since these inevitably have a bearing on the historical perspectives within which they will be seen (or not seen). However, to differentiate them thus is not to assign their unlikeness to differences of national identity; indeed, their speculative conjunction in the case of Roskolenko should warn against this. There may be no narrative in which both occur, despite their historical proximity, because narratives of 20th century poetry typically assume the perspective of a national culture, but their unlikeness needs to be posited elsewhere, in other assumptions, involving large-scale distinctions of literary ethos, whereby a canonical construction of modernism is still set over against romanticism, so that if "Objectivism" is to be seen as a phase of modernism indigenous to America, the "New Apocalypse", *per contra*, will be seen to fold into the New Romanticism that sprang up in Britain during its wartime isolation (isolation from continental Europe, be it noted, but not from the USA or the Empire and Dominions).

But what of Harry Roskolenko, a figure so spectral as to remain at risk of being taken for a figment of the imagination? Here I am only concerned with the first decade of his long and varied writing career. This period comprises his earliest published work, both as a "revolutionary" or "proletarian" writer and as a poet who wrote in accordance with Louis Zukofsky's "Objectivist" principles; his publication in journals such as *Pagany* and *Caravel*, situating him within an international avant garde; his work with the Federal Writers Project in New York, leading to the publication of his first book *Sequence on Violence* (1938); and his publication of *An Exile's Anthology* (1940, co-edited with Helen Neville, also from the New York Federal Writers Project), which included work by both American and British poets. It also comprises his experience as a militant in the political and labour struggles of American Trotskyism, brought to an end over the perennial issue dividing Trotskyists from former-Trotskyists, the class character of the Soviet state, and the imperative to defend the legacy of the October revolution, notwithstanding its Stalinist deformations, "as long as private property and the means of production and exchange are still nationalized".[5]

Like Zukofsky, Roskolenko was the son of Jewish immigrants on New York's Lower East Side. Unlike Zukosfsky, his formal education ended when he was 13. His education thereafter, however, was not exclusively in the school of survival and hard knocks, as itinerant labourer and merchant seaman. His sea voyages took him to some of the great European cities: London, Paris, Hamburg, where he spent several months ashore before being deported for his involvement in political street violence. His education was also that of the autodidact, gleaned from libraries, both the random collections of books on board ship, and the 42nd Street Public Library, a nest of lay intellectuals. For a month in 1930 he took classes unofficially at the University of Wisconsin, Madison, where, as chance would have it, Zukofsky was passing a year in exile from New York as an English Instructor, and compiling the 'Objectivists, 1931' issue of *Poetry*.

The impressions they formed of one another, recorded at the time by Zukofsky in letters to Ezra Pound, and more than 30 years later by Roskolenko, are more revealing of the mutual condescensions of class and cultural difference than active literary disagreement. In addition to courses on literature and economics, Roskolenko took a course "with a pale young man, a friend of Ezra Pound, and the pale young man meant poetry". Roskolenko recalled the names of his two other professors, William Ellery Leonard and Selig Perlman, but the reference to Zukofsky is coded, as though by the 1960s his name counted for nothing.

> He looked like the poet, his pallor almost gothic, his voice disappearing when he lectured—as he was really more ghost than man, though he had created a school of poetry called Objectivism. It was equally ghostly, dispossessed of body and blood, but possessed of obscurantism and Poundian undercurrents of scholarship, social credit, illusions of history, and the pale reflections that lived on and off literary quotations.[6]

The adequacy of this account of Zukofsky's "school" may be gauged from what I shall say about Roskolenko as an "Objectivist", but in one sense—not that intended by Roskolenko—Zukofsky did see himself as superintending a school *for* poets. "I shall, however, have the satisfaction of setting several proletarians on their writing arses—Roskolenkier—etc if they profit by my lessons" he wrote to Pound in April, 1931. Here Zukofsky distinguishes himself, as he does elsewhere, from exponents of "proletarian" writing: "to them…I'm the sediment of the bourgeoisie".[7]

At this date the fissure between modernist and socially committed writing, with its demand for realism and reportage, was still not deep, and Zukofsky could treat it with a degree of irony, while looking to the self-consciously proletarian *New Masses* as a reservoir of potential talent. A December 1931 letter to Pound mentions its management's inefficiency about providing him with the addresses of poets he wanted to consider for his issue of *Poetry*.

> Anyway, I'll have to launch this issue with what I've got. Mike shd. be pleased with my redemption of Comrade Roskolenkier—& you shd. see what I had to do to wade thru the stuff & then come out after putting it together (???) with—dignity. I mean certain lines in one poem naturally belong in another—signed L.Z.—But what will happen if I stop running my correspondence courses?[8]

Zukofsky did not hesitate to improve the work of his contemporaries. His *An 'Objectivists' Anthology* (1932) includes a section of 'Collaborations' in which his initials are appended to poems by Kenneth Rexroth, Jerry Reisman, R.B.N. Warriston, and William Carlos Williams, his collaborative role variously represented as abridgement, arrangement, and rewriting: a division of labour whereby the words are those of the putative author, but have been "put together" by L.Z. In Roskolenko's case it is not clear what the threat was to Zukofsky's dignity; it might have been the laboriousness of the task, or his abject, proletarian subject matter. Whatever the case, Zukofsky's temerity as an editor of others' work was governed by principle, and Roskolenko's poem 'Supper in an Alms-House', in the 'Objectivists, 1931' issue of *Poetry*, will serve to illustrate this.

The principles in accordance with which Zukofsky's contributors wrote are set out in a headnote to his 'Program' and derive from his extension of the noun "objective" to apply to poetry as "Desire for what is objectively perfect, inextricably the direction of historic and contemporary particulars."[9] This is not quite a statement of principles since the component concepts—the objectively perfect, and the particular—are juxtaposed, without a verb to articulate their mode of inextricable connection, and is better read as a demonstration of principle whereby concepts are particularised and distinguished. Zukofsky's 'Program' is

The Case of Harry Roskolenko

supplemented by his essay 'Sincerity and Objectification' in which sincerity is the quality of language when direct perception of experience is registered, and objectification the formal resolution as a poem of instances of such quality. The terms are not mutually entailed since objectification requires sincerity as necessarily prior to it; mapped on to Zukofsky's principles they gloss "inextricably" as signifying the priority of "historic and contemporary particulars". Objectification may be driven by the desire for perfection, yet this tendency is also—as we are to understand from "direction"— implicit in the verbal apprehension of the particularity of experience. Such principles sanction Zukofsky's collaborative editing as contributing to the objectification of the "minor units of sincerity" achieved by his not always willing collaborators.[10]

I suppose that Zukofsky detected in the work of the new, young proletarian writers traces of sincerity misdirected by tendentious propagandist aims. In considering Roskolenko's 'Supper in an Alms-House' both as a proletarian and a revolutionary poem and as written in accordance with "Objectivist" principles the question of what Zukofsky may have contributed cannot arise; speculation about an original, "uncontaminated" version would be pointless. The poem stands as an example of Roskolenko's writing at a specific stage in his career, marked by a specific literary association; equally, Zukofsky's principles, to the extent that they are demonstrable in this poem, represent his understanding of what constitutes excellence in poetry at a specific stage of development. We are to think of the poem as itself an "historic and contemporary particular".

SUPPER IN AN ALMS-HOUSE

On seven inches of sidewalk I stand.
I look into the street where autos move—
their wheels whir the comfortable away
and leave poison for my nose.

This land—at least this city—must be intelligent;
walking attires on men, constant new scenes.
Even an aged man will change his shirt and boil his cuffs,
his collars starched, his suspenders lifted to his neck;
or let the typist swish her coat together—firm—
a man collapses.

The moon is in the cellar with religion;
as the bottles pop they find a new law.

I shall bow to him in religion
for a bowl of string-bean soup.
His hair is combed, his vest garlanded.

Looking to the East where the sun once came today
even the rapture of the Lord I shall miss
as the soup finds its worship
. . . .
And the cannons do not aim at the sky.

'Supper in an Alms-House' provides a sweeping view of the America of the Depression, drawing together the famished subject, the "comfortable" other, and the "intelligence" undeniably at work in modern civilisation— marked by novelty and change (even the change of clothes), and the state and ideological apparatuses of armaments and religion. At the very centre of the poem "a man collapses", whether from excitement or hunger is not explicit, so that two discourses are in play in this figure, in one of which the allure of sex makes men go weak at the knees, while in the other the effects of starvation are an observed detail of daily life. Although the poem's subject matter includes a soup kitchen it is not exclusively concerned with the realistic detail of proletarian experience; as the title suggests, it is a comment on charitable relief embedded in civic ideology. The central figure of a man collapsing is axial to the poem, its ambivalence disseminated throughout the writing in less condensed figures such as the internal rhyme "autos" and "nose", the exchange of "bow" and "bowl", and the conversion of spiritual rapture to appeased hunger in an act of profane "worship" in which the onomatopoeic verbs "whir" and "swish" seem to echo. Not all of the detail is clear: sun and moon belong with the sky at which "the cannons do not aim"; the "moon... in a cellar" stands ambivalently with religion over against "a new law" in a context suggestive of a speakeasy. In both cases, however, the reader has the experience of negotiating an ambivalent exchange.

This ambivalence is produced by the poem's disjunctive isolation and setting out of successive items of detail, including comment. These are the "minor units of sincerity" that comprise the poem, not so much particulars denoted as the vivid accuracies of the language of their apprehension: "seven

The Case of Harry Roskolenko

inches of sidewalk", "the soup finds its worship". Disjunction, the rapid movement from one detail to another ("I stand. I look…"), avoiding a specious local closure of grammar and themed motif, can be understood as the technique of objectification whereby completion is the achieved quality of the poem. Zukofsky's term for this, "rested totality", can seem to connote some massive aesthetic inertia, but Roskolenko's poem seems to me, with its central fulcrum, to attain a balance and completeness of articulation of its moment of historical crisis.

It would be a mistake to see this poem as a one-off, ghosted by "L.Z.", and redeemed from proletarian squalor. The circumstances of its publication may sanction it as "Objectivist", but it does not thereby cease to be a proletarian or revolutionary poem, to use the jargon of the time. Indeed, such terms have their use in placing Zukofsky himself who also, like Roskolenko, published in the left-leaning little magazines springing up across the United States. They both appear in the first issue of *Left*, from Davenport, Iowa, which carried an editorial manifesto stating that "the valid, significant art of today and tomorrow finds its impetus, substance and sincerity in the emergence of the proletariat through the revolutionary movement."[11] Both also appear in the second issue of *Nativity: An American Quarterly*, from Columbus, Ohio, the editor of which wrote "Because the artist must express fecund things, and because he has found the bohemian rendezvous barren, he must, of necessity, turn to the proletariat. […] The poet who will speak validly of the proletariat, must speak from the proletariat".[12] Elsewhere, however, in the same issue, Zukofsky is to be found advocating the critical opinions of William Carlos Williams and Pound. Set aside the editorial slogans and these and similar little magazines in which Zukofsky published, such as *Morada* and *Front*, will stand revealed as part of a poetic ambience that includes the 'Objectivists, 1931' issue of *Poetry*, with a constantly overlapping personnel. Indeed, what then chiefly distinguishes Zukofsky's position as an editor—from that of the editors of Left, for example—is his openness to poets of the previous generation. From this point of view the terms "Objectivist" and proletarian and revolutionary are not, for the time being at least, mutually exclusive, but the latter are the more self-consciously avant garde. I don't think it is pressing the point too far to think of Roskolenko's other poems from this period as both proletarian, in so far as they refer to a certain range of experience and, in so far as they are attentive to detail, and embed comment in totalising juxtapositions (including audible details of words), as "Objectivist" correlations of sincerity and objectification. It should not be overlooked that proletarian poetry was not all of a piece. It can envisage an audience of revolutionary proletarians to be hectored, as in these lines from S. Funaroff's 'Poem…': "Arise! // Prepare in the dawnlight / a hod of red bricks for your shoulder! // March!" Here it is merely the colour of the bricks that distinguishes the built environment of socialist reconstruction, "the homes of days of the new sun!", from capitalism's "grey desolate cities", the new dawn rhetoric notwithstanding. By contrast proletarian tenacity and indominatability can be read between the lines of Roskolenko's 'In a Hospital': "WORKERS silently die", "silent in beds clinging to poverty / holding the habits of life—they die". The poem's proletarian credentials, despite its workers' lack of revolutionary fervour, were attested by its inclusion in an annual of revolutionary verse.[13]

Zukofsky, nevertheless, identified the cult of proletarian literature with the writers grouped round the communist *New Masses*—with whom he associated "Comrade" Roskolenko—who for their part dismissed the contemporaries he admired (not only Pound and Williams, but also E E Cummings and Marianne Moore) as "blind on the imminent problems of the day".[14] His reports to Pound on this aspect of the local literary scene are caustic and impatient, and he twice alludes to the counter arguments of Trotsky's *Literature and Revolution*: "no literature writes Trotsky [...] is proletarian".[15] Richard Johns, the editor of *Pagany*, which became increasingly open to proletarian writing, was more indulgent, and recalled being taken by Norman Macleod to meet Jack Conroy and Roskolenko at a "Sunday picnic for workers and their families held in the Bronx" in 1931.

> That Sunday in the Bronx was rewarding for Johns as he watched the sharp eyes of Macleod and Conroy study these one-day-off-from-poverty reivers. He knew that some of the feeling and expression used to describe these people and their condition would appear in the pages of *Pagany* between such extremes as Mina Loy and Kenneth Burke.

Roskolenko is described as "a young man who had been a sailor and an oiler on drawbridges, who had been gathered in under the revolutionary blanket of the proletarian writers", whose poetry, given such a background, was "an amazing manifestation [...] a rich individuality of sensitivity and feeling."[16]

From their different points of view both Zukofsky and Johns situate Roskolenko within a Communist-led proletarian literary movement. What

The Case of Harry Roskolenko

is missing from their accounts is the understanding that Roskolenko, far from being a loyal party member, had been a Trotskyist mole since 1929. Under instructions from the Trotskyist leadership he had joined "the official Communist Party, to bore from within as their secret agent; to spread, quietly and subtly, Leon Trotsky's opposition to Stalin's policies on world-wide political and economic questions".[17] In the light of such knowledge, the question arises whether his identity as a proletarian poet formed part of his cover. Certainly, by January 1933, writing to Johns from the office of the Trotskyist journal *Militant*, Roskolenko had come out.

> A couple of us are getting out a magazine, strictly if I can use that in a broad sense, PROLETARIAN. I don't believe in the theory prevalent in the Marxist circles about the possibility of building a literature PROLETARIAN, the vogue of the New Masses; if you are acquainted with the theories laid down by Trotsky, expressed in a book called LITERATURE and REVOLUTION, the fundament of Culture of the old regime is examined, also the path the new Culture will take.[18]

Roskolenko, like Zukofsky, seizes on Trotsky's argument that the notion of a proletarian culture was an irrelevance since the dictatorship of the proletariat was a transitional phase leading to the achievement of a classless society. Hence Roskolenko distinguishes between domains in which the epithet "proletarian" has relevance: on the one hand that of industrial activism, the domain of revolutionary politics sustained by *Militant*, and on the other that of culture, where the agency of class over time is less clear-cut. In Roskolenko's case this is more than a theoretical distinction on which to base a literary position, it is also a political position, distinguishing his own revolutionary politics as a Trotskyist from that of Communists. The two points are brought together in the contributor's note he later wrote for *The New Caravan*.

> I consider my work to be of a socially revolutionary nature but not proletarian poetry. Never having had a passion for Liberalism I am not a member of the Communist Party (this is biographical).[19]

Although its tone is far from being all of one piece, no hint remains of proletarian poetry in *Sequence on Violence*, which included none of the poems Roskolenko published prior to 1934.

Proletarian poetry was far from dead in 1938, the year of publication also of S. Funaroff's *The Spider and the Clock*, which included a statement 'Towards a Theory of Revolutionary Poetry'. Indeed, there is allusion in *Sequence on Violence* to the title of Isidor Schneider's aggressively proletarian *Comrade Mister* (1935). But if proletarian poetry is a subtext here, so also is a more refined type of Marxist poem, if I am right to catch an echo of the closing lines of W.H. Auden's *Spain* (1937) in Roskolenko's line "History does not call you Comrade or Mister".[20] The allusion is there, I think, because Auden's "History" is imagined as addressing the *defeated*, and a principal theme of Roskolenko's poems now is defeat: in Germany, in Spain, and the defeat of revolutionary optimism by Stalinism. This theme is explicitly recognised by Lewis Mumford in a statement included in the publishers' promotional leaflet: "Here is the war, the defeat, the frustration of our time... In Roskolenko's poems our disasters are confronted: our pains transmuted... He is a poet who has quietly mastered defeat."[21] Mumford takes his cue from titles of poems, 'Defeat by a Lake' and 'You Were Saying There Will be Disaster', but the point might well be put differently by saying that Roskolenko had discarded some illusions in order to confront a world increasingly mechanised and militarised, its reality disclosed not in the class struggle but by mass destruction and death. These lines from 'Union Square' surely register a specific disillusion.

> There is nothing urgent here—
> yet I saw one face blaze into the sun,
> antagonistic, the slogan of *eyes* and *hands* raised—
> the face a placard glowing: there is nothing here
> but monuments and rituals
> and people standing, reading papers.[22]

The exceptional, however, is not a sign of true vitality, for the soap-box orator is reduced by metonymic displacement to a placard bearing a slogan (in an earlier published version the face is "a banner"); revolutionary enthusiasm has become public ritual.[23]

Sequence on Violence was written in part under the auspices of the Federal Writers Project, which Roskolenko started to work for in 1935, on the "security" wage of 23 dollars a week, as a researcher for the various State and City guides the Project sponsored. Since the Project paid for and owned what the writers produced creative work was a problem: what if, by supporting its writers' creative work, the Project came to own the rights to a best-seller?[24] Nevertheless, there was a demand from writers on the Project for their creative work to receive recognition, although such recognition tended to come from outside the Project: the July 1938 number of *Poetry*, for example, was a 'Federal Poets' Number', with an additional 16 pages and featuring the work of 26 poets (including both Funaroff and Roskolenko). Eventually the Project established a Creative Section, "for the good of American Literature", paying a few of its writers, Roskolenko among them, to produce their own work.[25] For the directors of the Project, clearly, literary writing was only to be thought of in terms of individual creativity and the ownership (and possible exploitation) of intellectual property; a set of beliefs in tension with the notion of a cadre of publicly funded writers with shared literary commitments (to American Literature, for instance). Whatever Roskolenko's own theoretical views on literature, the identity of proletarian writer under such circumstances would in any case be untenable.

The concept of literary writing can provide a helpful entry to *Sequence on Violence* because it is so fuzzy as to require immediate interrogation: what sort of poetry is this if not proletarian poetry? An immediate answer to this question is that the poems bear the traces of Roskolenko's reading of his contemporaries. A number of satirical poems, for example, suggest a careful reading of Ezra Pound's *Lustra*. 'Union Square', with its recall of the apparitional faces of 'In a Station of the Metro' is one such. Another is 'A Spasm in the Tomb of Sleep': "Your deportment, my excellent friend / ranks with Suffenus—in the twenty second / poem of Mr Gregory's *Catullus*." The poem is addressed to "N.M.", whom I take to be Norman Macleod, another evolutionary poet.

> What a gay poet you are—
> notorious, but I expect, someday a slender knife
> or a necktie, or perhaps a gun
> will put an end to you;
> and suicide, it is said,
> is not for warriors, comrade![26]

The satire includes the double irony that his poems are insufficiently those of a class warrior, and (with Stalin's purges in mind) that "N.M." runs the risk of being liquidated by his political comrades. In learning from Pound, of course, Roskolenko was following Zukofsky's example, and it is not forcing the point, I think, to discern in these poems some of those local accuracies of language, and disjunctive arrangements of details, that allow 'Supper in an Alms-House' to be considered "Objectivist".

In contrast to this, and standing out also by its consistency against the variety of *Sequence on Violence*, is writing in a new and very different mode. Whereas an "Objectivist" poem deploys particulars of situation of milieu, so placing them via precisions of language that they become figured elements within a textual economy based on rapid movement of syntax, in this other sort of writing figuration tends towards the abstract and symbolic, within a more leisurely textual economy of word-combinations that generate metaphors as concepts. In the following comparison of passages from 'Death in Spring' and 'The Year' it is not assumed that the former has chronological priority, but the latter is offered as an example of Roskolenko's new mode.

> That wintry day we stood on a bare seacoast,
> watching waves icily tap the shore:
> you wondered how soon you'd sail, you hurled a boast!
> I smiled at your heroism grown by leaps to war:
> But today seeing the papers I have read—
> Your name listed among the International dead.[27]

Not until its final line is there confirmation that the poem belongs to a distinct sub-genre, the Spanish Civil War elegy, and that its title might easily have been 'Death in Spain'. But death here is final, and heroics are the cause of a death from which no comfort is drawn; the poem is atypical of its genre in not insisting that death shall not have been in vain, and this is because Roskolenko foresaw the future differently. There is a plain dignity of statement about the writing, as befits an elegy, but the attitude to revolutionary enthusiasm is that of 'Union Square', whereas 'The Year' suggests that the significance Spain bore for Roskolenko had more to do with the bombing of civilian populations, in Barcelona and Guernica, than with the self-sacrifice of volunteers in the International Brigade.

> On streets they trailed into hills
> a maddened mercury of gruesome moods;
> passed on wintry gales to bare seacoasts
> where bombs fell from aerial harvests,
> to blind the deaf, deafen the sightless:
> They rode on horses along the spray—
> dashed into the foaming sea
> on the steel atonal symphony.[28]

The Case of Harry Roskolenko

Imagination is unsituated and omniscient, impersonal and generalising: instead of the "bare seacoast" of 'Death in Spring', where two people stood together, there are "bare seacoasts" (and most of the other nouns are plural); to the same end, its first and second persons are dispersed as an inclusive third person plural. But what end do these changes serve, which I have suggested are representative of Roskolenko's new mode?

These are the closing lines of a poem of modern war in which cities are bombed, burned and abandoned to the rats. Roskolenko has imaginatively internalised the European experience of violence—specifically, perhaps, as available to movie newsreels—to project it as general and emblematic. This goes some way to explaining the textual economy of adjective-plus-noun word combinations, supported by pronouns without explicit reference, but does not explicate particular combinations. What are "aerial harvests", for instance, given that bombs are dropped from bombing aeroplanes? Perhaps a squadron of such planes is a perversion of the idea of harvest, the product of labour serving an unproductive purpose. Or perhaps, the idea of harvest again perverted, it signifies the "mowing down" from the air of buildings and people. Figurative use of "harvest" with ironic purpose—"harvest of death", "harvest of war"—is so commonplace, indeed, that such ironies have lost their edge. We should be cautious about applying an empirical test (can a fortress fly?) to apparently implausible word combinations before considering how they may be read in their immediate context. This means giving some thought to intention, and "aerial harvests", I suggest, is intended to draw together aspects of an event sometimes thought hard to connect: the release of an explosive device at high altitude and its ground level detonation.

The very same cognitive difficulty is intended, I believe, in 'Crossing the Latitudes', where in this passage the image of the rose, in a different type of word combination, draws attention to the political significance of the psychological problems machines can occasion. A particular aestheticized version of the bomber pilot's dissociation of cause and effect, which gained some notoriety at the time, is figured by the inclusion of "the rose" in a list of Fascist and Communist insignia.

> The Volga nervously meets the Rhine and Mediterranean,
> exchanging watery salutes from drying lands:
> the sacred twigs, signet, swinging sickle and the rose!
> A blustering corporal's raised hand!
> his open palm or clenched fist
> addressing the multitudes who wade the waters:

for no Noah's boat they bring to top the seas.
Yet to drown, to swim or walk with ease—
with the diver's suit of stratagem;
the dull leather and visor in a secret world
will not wet your infant soul
suckling between the seas and drying lands.

Allusion is made to the political emblems of Europe's totalitarian states—
the fasces, hammer and sickle and, implied in the "blustering corporal",
the swastika—since only by not using their proper names is it possible to
introduce the rose as another such symbol of atrocity. Within this context
"the rose" alludes to the aesthetic delight expressed by Mussolini's son
on observing the effect of fragmentation bombs on Abyssinian cavalry,
which he compared to the blooming or opening of a rose.[29] In this passage
disillusion and the intimation of disaster are brought into alignment also
(if not quite as cause and effect): Trotskyist beliefs about the character of
the Soviet Union as a workers' state are banished by its bracketing with
Germany and Italy, and there is no escape from the flood. (The image of
Noah's Ark is less incongruous than may appear in excerpt; the poem,
in keeping with its title, is organised around imagery of ships and ocean
voyages.)

   Taken as a whole the passage epitomises the variousness of the
writing in *Sequence on Violence*. It opens with standard topographical
personification to represent the totalitarian states, with reference in passing
to environmental side-effects of Soviet hydroelectric projects. It proceeds
by representing symbols that embody a myth of the state by means of
figures that deprive them of instant recognition, so that they are only
identifiable within the set they comprise rather than separately. Finally,
about mid-way, another line of figuration is generated, synthetically as it
were, from what precedes it. As the passage develops it foregrounds the
turn in Roskolenko's writing towards a mode of conceptual metaphor in
which reference tends to become effaced. This is a high-risk strategy, since
there can be no guarantee that a largely metaphorised textual economy
will have secreted within it any concepts whatsoever. That said, I don't
think that such reservations apply in this case, where in the closing lines
signification turns crucially on the force of negation, from which is to be
inferred that utterances even in such a metaphorised mode of discourse can
be propositionally true or false. So, here, faced with the problem of what
stance to adopt, in the face of the recognition of disaster that follows loss

The Case of Harry Roskolenko

of ideological certainty, no solution is offered. One can only start again from scratch and confront a personal dilemma.

Because this manner of writing has fallen so much into disrepute it's easy, perhaps, to overlook the fact that in the late 1930s a style based on a metaphorised textual economy—one in which, in particular, verbs are strongly figured—was emerging as right up to the minute. Indeed, it is precisely the style of the modernism that provoked the Ern Malley hoaxers: "the whole literary fashion as we know it from the works of Dylan Thomas, Henry Treece and others."[30] But if the turn Roskolenko's writing took was convergent with a new fashion, in his case its immediate genealogy points back to the different example of Hart Crane. Indeed, 'Crossing the Latitudes' solicits the reader to make the connection, as if the late poet's condensations of metaphor provided both example and sanction. It might be no more than thematic coincidence that the poem inscribes the titles of Crane's two books, *White Buildings* and *The Bridge*: "tall white buildings", "the watery bridge"; nor is *The Bridge* necessarily the textual source for the "minstrel lad from Cathay" invoked at the beginning of Roskolenko's poem. But where, if not from the 'Cutty Sark' section of *The Bridge*, has Roskolenko got his *Rose of Stamboul*?

> What has come to the '*Rose of Stamboul*':
> is her windy dance forgotten?
> Her sails were slithered, wind gone from the canvas![31]

Roskolenko's creative misreading confirms the derivation, for in Crane's poem 'Rose of Stamboul' is not the name of a ship at all. Like 'Cutty Sark' and 'Flying Cloud', but the 1923 Sigmund Romberg operetta.[32] Crane's invocations of the 'Rose of Stamboul' evoke a popular tune played on a nickel-in-the-slot pianola. As has already been seen, within a metaphorised textual economy "rose" is a less than stable signifier.

Throughout the 1930s there was increasing transatlantic exchange between poets and magazines. In New York the Gotham Book Mart ("Headquarters for Experimental Literature") was agent for British magazines such as *Contemporary Poetry and Prose* and *Seven*, and in London the Parton Street Bookshop stocked American publications. The mutual interest and exchange is evident in Julian Symons's remarking of Crane that "no modern poet except Dylan Thomas is, for me, more affecting, more able to twist words to the shape of the reader's tears".[33] Thomas, for his part, denied conjecture that Crane was a stylistic influence, claiming not to have heard of him before the suggestion was made.[34] Roskolenko's own stylistic derivation from Crane, in the light of such a comparison, suggests how the turn of his writing in *Sequence on Violence* lent his work a quality that made it recognisably so much of the moment—not the least to British readers. For by this time, of course, Thomas—the paragon of the new style by virtue of the fascination he exercised for admirers and detractors alike (Symons was clearly both of these)—already had his followers, among them the writers associated with the "New Apocalypse". Inadvertently, therefore, and at a distance, Roskolenko found himself in new literary company.

Correspondence with Henry Treece established a relationship of mutual esteem and support. Treece sent him Thomas's poems, which Roskolenko drew to the attention of Edmund Wilson, and they reviewed each other's books.[35] At one stage Hendry and Treece planned a second number of *The New Apocalypse* to feature American writers, to which Roskolenko was to have contributed.[36] I wouldn't want to make too much of this by labelling Roskolenko "Apocalyptic", even though the term became a byword for work in Thomas's vein, and Treece sought to enlarge its scope by eliding it with what was subsequently termed "New Romanticism". Nevertheless I think that some of what Hendry says in his account of "apocalyptic writing" can apply to Roskolenko, and in more than a descriptive way. When Hendry describes apocalyptic writing as "giving birth to images and prophecies of ruin" the cap surely fits.[37] But Hendry is also centrally concerned with an idea of myth as both individual and collective projection, proposing that the apocalyptic writer is one who observes the contemporary breakdown of collective myths while, in the process, seeking a valid myth of the self: "the decay of modern systems, whether political, philosophic, or scientific, has become pathological, and observers, in describing the sickness, are at the same time revealing the cure—the approach to the wholeness of man in place of abstractions."[38] Is it far-fetched to discern the double process Hendry describes at work in 'Crossing the Latitudes'? I think not. Roskolenko will have observed the decay of political belief in himself, and in the poem he prophesies the collapse of political systems, and projects a myth of the self as the "infant soul".

Roskolenko knew Europe from his years at sea, and his brand of revolutionary politics informed his imagination with a particular idea of Europe. A conscientious objector who changed his mind, there is no trace in him of the isolationism that sought to keep America out of coming

The Case of Harry Roskolenko

events in Europe. His engagement with the work of British contemporaries, with a basis in affinity of both style and imagination, need not therefore be surprising. Its practical outcome was the anthology of American and British poets, *The Exiles' Anthology* (1940), which appears to have eluded notice for reasons easily understood. Its principal interest is as a gathering of work by the British poets whose careers began in the late 1930s (and as such it may be considered precursor to another American anthology, Kenneth Rexroth's 1948 *The New British Poets*.) It makes an interesting pair to *The New Apocalypse*: both were prepared under peacetime conditions, and published in wartime. Indeed, the war is directly acknowledged by the editors.

> Poetry and War, bastard twins, appear in this anthology as the Janus-faced hallucinations of contemporary political and aesthetic activity.[39]

War is a striking rationale for an anthology of poets from both America and Britain, something of a novelty in itself, at a time when one of the countries was still non-belligerent. In contrast, a notice in *Seven* inviting submissions implied an absence of editorial motive bar one.

> The Exile's Press intends to publish an Anthology of work from American and English poets. These Poems may range from purely lyrical, non-social poetry to poems of social content—in other words a free field, with one exception. We will not consider verse which is Fascist in content, intention or appeal.[40]

The anthology finally included work by 34 poets, Americans (as far as I can judge) slightly in the majority. Few of the Americans are remembered today: Weldon Kees, Kenneth Patchen, Theodore Roethke, Winfield Townley Scott, Parker Tyler, and John Wheelwright perhaps. A number of them, Neville for example, and William Pillin, had been on the Federal Writers' Project. In contrast to this mixed bunch, the British contingent is historically cohesive. From *The New Apocalypse* it includes Dorian Cooke, Hendry, Nicholas Moore, Philip O'Connor, and Treece; the omissions are Norman McCaig and Thomas. Others included are Nigel Heseltine, H.B. Mallalieu, Keidrich Rhys, Lynette Roberts, Julian Symons, and George Woodcock. The most notable omission from the list is Roy Fuller. The contrast between the national representations owes, I think, to the limited scope (relative to the USA) of magazine publishing in Britain; the British contributors were largely contributors to the same few magazines such as *New Verse, Seven, Wales*, and *Twentieth Century Verse*.

'Crossing the Latitudes' closes with the prophecy of destruction visited on the destroyers. It also recapitulates the transformation of totalitarian symbols, previously noted, and again adds to it: the Communist clenched-fist salute, fingers now smoking like a gun, appears turned in on and against itself—like the revolution.

> Taken—the symbols that bore the need,
> spiritual and bodily deed:
> the right hand fisted, raised!
> smoking at the fingertips;
> saluting no amphitheatres of overalled men..
> but shielded faces and polished hats..
> the uniform solicitude of middlemen in cravats:
> without honour, reason or principle,
> to lay waste, who will
> their horror, to-morrow taste.

A restricted reading of this passage, predicated on Roskolenko's Marxist political disillusion, and focussed on the antimony of work clothes and business suits signalling the loss of revolutionary legitimacy when the party leadership substituted itself for workers' power, suggests that figured forth here is the rolling programme of Stalinist terror under which the cadres responsible for the purges are themselves purged in due course. Read thus the entire passage makes detailed sense. But this is because in writing of this sort figural detail acquires significance from textual location and contextual reference: as images they represent the content of the writer's thought process and in other contexts may signify differently. Hence I may suppose I find the same figure in "the business gentry" of the 'Introduction' to *The Exiles' Anthology*, where they are "the ghostly officers of the war [...] the realistic priests of property."

The editors, disclaiming "a set literary formula", issue what is in effect a manifesto against modernist manifestos because poetry is yoked with war: "Most of the contributors are bound together by something much more valid than the questing for the lacerated demobilized WORD, or the external exhuming of the language." Rather, poetry is itself at war—"with the clichés of the social and literary world." Having no literary programme is no different to following no party line.

For once the poet is comfortably a policeman. He polices with some Bohemian credulity the criminal acts of the politicos in power. Yet owing to the quality of his illegal imagination, he defies the civil servants and accepts no dictation. He has no party and no worthwhile master. He masters his art by inner comprehension, combining his sense of order with the radiance of his tortured ideas. He lives his images, his logic, his sensations and hallucinations, for they are the subjective properties of his theatre; as is war and language, love and decay—the objective earth for his illuminating spadework. Beyond Rimbaud is the literary grave, for it is beyond public address while being part of the *literary* wake.

Given the occasion the tone is flagrantly excessive, and moreover the notion of modernist literary experiment participating in its own obsequies was hardly apt to the situation of British poetry. But the editors' underlying premise is surely clear, that the onset of war represented the convergence of politics and art in terminal disorder. Thus what truly binds the poets together emerges at the close: they are all in the same boat.

> The illegal imagination is the Drunken Boat from which we chart
> the voyage, and amid the wreckage of schools, WORDS, programs,
> we start up the diesels and carry passengers.

The nautical imagery suggests Roskolenko's hand.

My account of Roskolenko's individual development as a poet will have shown, I hope, that his case is less strange than it first appeared to me. But does his case indicate any immanent development of poetry connecting the two avant garde moments with which his career intersected, the "Objectivists" and the "New Apocalypse", thus making him historically visible? No individual case, it goes without saying, can serve on its own to demonstrate such a filiation, or provide the range of evidence capable of sustaining an argument based in history. Roskolenko's own line of development was crucially via Crane, and with his first book this made his work seem of his time, but given the historical termini framing my question such a development is, if not downright regressive, recursive at least. But there is no reason why a historical development should follow a straight line, if something necessary to it has been overlooked. I can make this point as a question by asking why Crane's work was not included in

Zukofsky's "list of works absolutely necessary to students of poetry" in 'Program: "Objectivists" 1931'.[41]

In his 1931 essay 'American Poetry 1920-1930', from which the list was derived, Zukofsky devotes two pages to Crane, rather more than he allows some of the poets on the list. He was clearly anxious to do Crane justice. Like Symons, he is in two minds about Crane, and exempts 'O Carib Isle' from his negative verdict, finding that "but for a minimum of haze and a melody drummed by a kind of linguistic pedal, [it] leaves the sensationally classic and is, with distinction, of the senses."[42] More generally, classing Crane, for his use of metre, with the "new formalists", Allen Tate, John Crowe Ransom, and Malcolm Cowley, he finds him "emotionally preferable. He, at least, has energy."[43] These points weigh in Crane's favour, but in both there is a factor—Crane's metric—inextricable from what is found objectionable. Crane's energy is "too often pseudo-musical and amorphous in its conflation of sense values. His single words are hardly ever alone, they are rarely absolute symbols for the things they represent [...] The result is an aura—a doubtful, subtle exhalation—a haze."[44] Moreover, "Crane's music which is often Elizabethan drive—iambic in the grand manner—helps an indefinite language and prolongs verbal indecision past the useful necessity of meaning".[45] Zukofsky's point is that Crane's anglicised metric (something he deplored in Eliot and Stevens as well) is both pernicious and necessary; it encourages in him the proliferation of word combinations tending to "conflation of sense values" and "haze", yet is essential to whatever effect they achieve. Zukofsky is explicit on this point: without this music Crane's recent unrhymed poems, excepting 'O Carib Isle!', are "mystical, filmy. If fish were a dead metaphor, the sea-film they wear is the logic surrounding these poems, the result is rhetoric: 'noon's tyranny', 'sulphur dreams'."[46] What would Zukofsky have made of "aerial harvests"?

Energy in itself is not enough, but it may redeem 'conflation of sense values' from being mere rhetoric. It's a nice distinction. To be "of the senses" is preferable, as is a definite language; meaning (a necessity) can be useful to good writing also. Zukofsky's implicit judgement on Crane is that he was capable of writing well but not an example for study, and with Crane's death in 1932 it became final. But the judgement is specifically of Crane and, although Zukofsky's remarks reflect his ideas about the proper relation of words to things, it is based on the reciprocal relation in Crane of metric and figural exuberance. It does not transfer *in toto* from Crane to writing bearing his influence. Roskolenko, I think, found in Crane, via

The Case of Harry Roskolenko

the logopoeia of the Pound of *Lustra*, a means of using words to adjudicate ideology that Zukofsky's own methods could not supply, but any bearing of this on Thomas or the "New Apocalypse" is the subject of another essay.

NOTES

1   'Books Received', *Wales* 10 (October, 1939), 285.

2   James McAuley and Harold Steward, quoted in Michael Heyward, *The Ern Malley Affair*, Faber and Faber: London, 1993, 139. The hoax perpetrated by McAuley and Stewart on Max Harris, the editor of *Angry Penguins*, agitated Australian poetry in 1944; as an experiment intended to expose the credulity and lack of judgement of those who acquiesced uncritically in international literary fads it was meant to hold good as well for England and America, but although there were a few international reverberations once the affair became a cause célèbre in the Australian press, the hoax itself depended for its success on the local cultural situation. McAuley and Stewart seem to have thought that the worthlessness of the poems they attributed to the fictitious Malley, and hence of the literary fashion they were intended to represent, would be demonstrated—to their own satisfaction at least—by success in establishing belief in Malley's existence. Their reasoning therefore depended on certain assumptions about authorship (such as would forestall questions about the roles attributed to identity and intention, for example), but since these were shared by Harris and his fellow victims the hoax could be a success even while failing to demonstrate anything about the nature of poetry.

3   Roskolenko initially published as Harry Roskolenkier, abbreviating his surname in 1936. His party name was the even more abbreviated Harry Ross. Among other aliases he also used the name H.R. Crozier.

4   These dates refer to periods of collective self-manifestation, principally in group anthologies, rather than the historical persistence of a determinable style.

5   Roskolenko, *When I Was Last on Cherry Street*, Stein and Day: New York, 1965, 177. (Roskolenko attributes these words to Arne Swabeck, 'one of the more likeable leaders' of the Socialist Workers Party, in an account of his expulsion from the Party.) Biographical information about Roskolenko has been derived principally from this volume of memoirs and two others: *The Terrorized*, Prentice Hall Inc: Englewood Cliffs, 1967, and *The Time That Was Then*, The Dial Press: New York, 1971.

6   *The Terrorized*, 19. Roskolenko says that he visited Madison at the invitation of (female) graduate student. There is nothing in Zukofsky's reports to Pound (see below) to suggest that Roskolenko was more than a name on his check-list of aspiring proletarian poets associated with *New Masses*, except that they

were already in contact, whereas Zukofsky was having difficulty getting hold of the addresses of others. This may have been due to chance encounter at Madison, but for some this might smack too much of coincidence, since both were recent arrivals from New York, and part of the *New Masses* milieu. Roskolenko's recollections of the encounter, moreover, pitched so as to distance himself from Zukofsky, register historical knowledge (of 'a school of poetry') while disavowing personal association (he either can't recall or won't inscribe its creator's name). This, however, is Roskolenko's second reference to Zukofsky and Objectivism, and somewhat out of sequence in the chronology of his memoirs, since *The Terrorized* deals with the post-war period. Zukofsky is mentioned by name in *When I Was Last on Cherry Street*, in a summary of Roskolenko's early publication history, as the founder of Objectivism, and as calling Roskolenko an Objectivist. 'But I objected to being in any school.' 110.

[7] Barry Ahearn (ed), *Pound/Zukofsky, Selected Letters of Ezra Pound and Louis Zukofsky*, Faber and Faber: London, 1987, 96.

[8] Ahearn, 82. 'Mike' is Michael Gold, author of *Jews Without Money*, and an editor at *New Masses*.

[9] Louis Zukofsky, 'Program: 'Objectivists 1931', *Poetry* XXXVII, V (February, 1931), 268.

[10] In Zukofsky's theory '*minor units* of sincerity' correlate with the 'rested *totality*' (emphasis added) achieved in 'objectification (here enclosed in inverted commas to indicate that Zukofsky's use of this term is specific to his thinking about poetry). 'This rested totality may be called objectification—the apprehension satisfied completely as to the appearance of the art form as an object. That is: distinct from print which records action and existence and incites the mind to further suggestion, there exists, though it may not be harboured as solidity in the crook of an elbow, writing (audibility in two-dimensional print) which is an object or affects the mind as such [...] its character may be simply described as the arrangement, into one apprehended unity, of minor units of sincerity.' Zukofsky, 'Sincerity and Objectification, with Special Reference to the Work of Charles Reznikoff', ibid, 274

[11] 'Left!', *Left*, 1, 1 (Spring, 1931), 3.

[12] Boris J. Israel, 'Prose Canto XII. The Validity...', *Nativity: An American Quarterly* 2 (Spring, 1931), 50.

[13] Funaroff, ibid, 46; Roskolenko, Left, op.cit., 63; and Jack Conroy and Ralph Cheyney (eds.), *Unrest 1931*, Henry Harrison: NY, 1931, 90—the 'third annual volume of revolutionary verse'.

[14] Ahearn, 17.

[15] Ibid., 10. An English translation of *Literature and Revolution* was published in 1925.

[16] Stephen Halpert and Richard Johns (eds.), *A Return to Pagany*, Beacon Press: Boston, 1969, 304-5, 424. Roskolenko had, in fact, been a substitute drawbridge operator on the Harlem River bridges.

[17] *When I Was Last on Cherry Street*, 125. Roskolenko's politics were shaped by his experience of working class politics in Hamburg. Trotsky's supporters considered themselves a principled Left Opposition to Stalin's policy of socialism in one country, and the heirs to revolutionary legitimacy within the international communist movement, even when expelled from their own national Communist Parties. It was not until 1938 that they felt it necessary or feasible to establish an independent international organisation, the Fourth International.

Trotskyist organisation in the USA began in 1928 with the expulsion of James Cannon and Max Schachtman from the American Communist Party for their endorsement of Trotsky's 'Criticism of the Draft Program of the Communist International', a copy of which Cannon had brought back from the Sixth World Congress in Moscow. They were ready to start publishing *Militant* at once, and founded the American Communist League. American Trotskyism had considerable industrial strength in some regions, but was politically weak, and prey to internal dissent about the correct line to take on the Soviet Union. When the Socialist Workers Party was founded in 1938, after a decade of tactical entryism and amalgamation with other Marxist groups, it soon after lost some of its best intellectual leadership—Schachtman, and James Burnham—following an internal dispute about the Russian-Finnish war. Roskolenko himself had been expelled at the Party's founding convention.

For official accounts of these events see James P. Cannon, *The History of American Trotskyism, From its Origins (1928) to the Founding of the Socialist Workers Party (1938)*, (1944), second edition, Pathfinder Press: New York, 1972, and George Breitman (ed.), *The Founding of the Socialist Workers Party: Minutes and Resolutions 1938-39*, Monad: New York, 1982.

[18] Halpert and Johns, 500.

[19] Alfred Kreymborg, Lewis Mumford, and Paul Rosenfield (eds.), *The New Caravan*, W W Norton: New York, 1936, 661. The jibe against the Communist Party is in the context of its turn towards the politics of the Popular Front. At the Second American Writers' Conference in June, 1937, Joseph Freeman complained 'There are delegates here who criticise Communists, liberals, this congress, and anyone else who has endorsed the People's Front.' (Henry Hart (ed.), *The Writer in a Changing World*, Equinox Cooperative Press: New York, 1937, 235.) Roskolenko was one such delegate, and Freeman was responding to his objection to the Conference's Popular Front line: 'One must be in favour of destroying capitalism, not in prolonging it with efforts for a literary people's front.' (ibid., 234). At another session Roskolenko, again acting as an irritant, asked 'Why has Leon Trotsky's book *Literature and Revolution* been removed

from circulation in the Soviet Union?' The reply, from H. W. L. Dana, was that it was 'out of date because of the creative work of Soviet writers' (ibid., 228). The sub-texts here are the issue of proletarian literature and, as well, the new Soviet literature of socialist construction celebrated by A. A. Zhdanov at the 1934 Soviet Writers' Congress and, ultimately, the policy of socialism in one country. Roskolenko may have hoped to be answered with the bluntness of Carl Radek who, speaking at the 1934 Congress, said that 'Trotsky's assertion that proletarian literature is impossible is based…on a denial of the possibility of building socialism in one country'. ('Contemporary World Literature and the Tasks of Proletarian Art' in H. G. Scott [ed.], *Problems of Soviet Literature*, Martin Lawrence: London, 1935, 132.)

[20] 'Parallels of Darkness', *Sequence on Violence*, Signal Publishers: New York, 1938, 18.

[21] 'This is what Lewis Mumford, author of 'Culture of the Cities' says about the book', undated publisher's announcement for *Sequence on Violence*. The leaflet also includes a statement by Gorham Munson, and reproduces Paul Rosenfeld's 'Introduction' to the book.

[22] *Sequence on Violence*, 27.

[23] See the version in Thomas Moult (ed.), *The Best Poems of 1937*, Jonathan Cape: London, 1937, 47.

[24] See Henry G. Alsberg, 'Foreweard', *American Stuff: An Anthology of Prose and Verse by Members of the Federal Writers Project*, Viking Press: New York, 1937, vi.

[25] *When I Was Last on Cherry Street*, 155.

[26] *Sequence on Violence*, 53.

[27] Ibid., 43.

[28] Ibid., 14.

[29] The contemporary notoriety of this image of the rose is attested by J. F. Hendry who, however, attributed it to Mussolini's brother Arnaldo, 'whose aesthetic delight in bombed Abyssinians "opening like a rose" is well-known.' (Writers and Apocalypse', *The New Apocalypse*, 1940, Fortune Press: London, [1940] 13.) It is also mentioned in most modern histories of Fascist Italy, for which the common source is G.T. Garratt's 1938 Penguin Special *Mussolini's Roman Empire*. Garratt, the *Manchester Guardian* war correspondent in Abyssinia, cites Vittorio Mussolini's *Flying over Ethiopian Mountain Ranges*, 'the purpose of which is to have Italian youth learn to be above War's sorrows, seeing only its beauties. Il Duce's twenty-year-old son found the War a period of 'magnificent sport'—e.g. 'one group of horsemen gave one the impression of a budding rose unfolding as the bomb fell in their midst and blew them up. It was exceptionally good fun." (op. cit., Penguin Books: Harmondsworth, 1938, 102 n.1.)

The Case of Harry Roskolenko

This passage evokes the experience of time-lapse cinematography in which the lives of plants are speeded up and made visible to us in the twinkling of an eye. It is also exemplary of the aestheticisation of politics by Fascism discussed by Walter Benjamin, with reference to Marinetti's 'manifesto on the Ethiopian war, whereby it 'expects war to supply the artistic gratification of a sense perception that has been changed by technology' ('Epilogue', 'The Work of Art in the Age of Mechanical Production' (1936), in *Illuminations*, (Edited with an introduction by Hannah Arendt), Jonathan Cape: London, 1970, 234, 235.) Roskolenko's figural reinvention of the rose as an emblem of atrocity signifying Fascist Italy is the opposite of this, its position at the end of the series of totalitarian insignia ('and the rose'—yet another to add to the list) marking out for attention his intervention in the field of contemporary political myth.

[30] Heywood, 139.

[31] *Sequence on Violence*, 15..

[32] I am grateful to Herbie Butterfield for this information.

[33] 'Hart Crane', *Twentieth Century Verse* 8 (Jan-Feb 1938), no pagination. I suspect that Symons had rather more than pathos in mind when he yoked Thomas with Crane, and that what more was at stake was twisting words into shapes. Symons' considerable admiration for both was mixed with recognition of the exceptionality of their writing: he thought that Crane worked 'outside the possible limits of poetic language' (ibid.), and that Thomas' language was 'as pure... as language can be this side of our intelligence.' ('Words as Narrative', *Twentieth Century Verse* 1 (Jan 1937), no pagination.) These remarks are not so much intellectual reservations as extenuating phrases in the face of what is taken as self-evident achievement, so that when Symons also concedes that 'the reader... may reasonably complain that he sees no connection more than verbal between the various parts of Mr Thomas' poems' he can go on to say 'There is no solution to this problem, except the solution to be found in Mr Thomas' future writings'. (ibid.) Subsequently, while still not denying Crane's 'genius', Symons wrote that the 'poems of Hart Crane... were a phenomenon from which no good could breed'. ('How wide is the Atlantic? Or Do you believe in America?', *Twentieth Century Verse* 12-13 [Sept-Oct 1938], 84.) It's tempting to wonder if he had anyone in particular in mind.

[34] See Henry Treece, *Dylan Thomas, 'Dog Among the Fairies'*, Lindsay Drummond: London 1949, 51-53. Despite Thomas's denial, given to him in person, Treece nevertheless thought it 'probable that Thomas...came across a small section of Hart Crane's work...and in such work discovered a focal point for his own writing.'

[35] See *When I Was Last on Cherry Street*, 158-59. Treece and Roskolenko began their correspondence in 1939, the year of publication also of Thomas's first

book to be published in the USA, *The World I Breathe*. Treece reviewed *Sequence on Violence*: 'These poems establish him as one of the fine voices of our time'. (*Seven* 6 [Autumn 1939], 31.)Roskolenko reciprocated by reviewing Treece's *38 Poems* and *Towards a Personal Armageddon*: 'he has gone into the bone and blood of the self, and not into the factories or into the rhetoric of political illusions to substantiate the tight eloquence of his verse.' (*The New Republic* 104, 13, No 1, 374 [March 31, 1941], 444.) The final paragraph of the review recapitulates, without acknowledgement, several points made by J. F. Hendry in 'Writers and Apocalypse'.

[36] Hendry, Treece, Letters to Roskolenko in the Arents Library, Syracuse University.

[37] 'Writers and Apocalypse', 9.

[38] Ibid. For an account of Hendry's developed understanding of myth see his 'Myth and Social Integration', in Hendry and Treece (eds.), *The White Horseman*, Routledge: London, 1941, 153-79.

[39] 'Introduction', Helen Neville and Harry Roskolenko (eds.), *The Exiles' Anthology*, The Exiles' Press, in collaboration with The Press of James A Decker: Prairie City, Illinois, 1940, unpaginated—hence subsequent quotations will not be noted.

[40] *Seven* 4 (Spring 1939) [55]. Here, in addition to Neville and Roskolenko, Florence Becker and John Wheelwright are named as editors of the press. Alan Wald mentions that Wheelwright withdrew from the press after quarrelling with Roskolenko; as Wheelwright remained a staunch member of the Socialist Workers Party the quarrel may have been political. (*The Revolutionary Imagination: The Poetry and Politics of John Wheelwright and Sherry Morgan*, University of North Carolina Press: Chapel Hill, 265, n. 19.) Both Becker and Wheelwright were contributors to the anthology

[41] The listed poets were Pound, Williams, Moore, Eliot, Cummings, Stevens, McAlmon, Reznikoff, and (by implication) Rakosi, and Zukofsky himself. For a discussion of the list's significance see my 'Zukofsky's List', in Rachel Blau Du Plessis and Peter Quartermain (eds.), *The Objectivist Nexus*, University of Alabama Press: Tuscaloosa, 1999, 275-85, 338-40.

[42] Zukofsky, 'American Poetry 1920-1930, *The Symposium* 2 (1931), 68.

[43] Ibid., 66.

[44] Ibid., 66-7.

[45] Ibid., 67.

[46] Ibid., 68. Zukofsky goes on to say that 'Crane is not unique erring on the side of mysticism', and then cites Elinor Wylie. When he revised the essay for inclusion in *Prepositions* (1967), his collected critical essays, this citation was deleted, but

the remarks about it retained, with apparent reference now to Crane. This is unfortunate if it encourages us now to locate Zukofsky's objections to Crane as centrally concerned with mysticism. Zukofsky also elicits a contrast between both Crane and Wylie and John Donne, to whom 'the idea was also his feeling tone and was also a particular metaphysical concept of his time'. (ibid., 68-9.) In Zukofsky's own time, of course, also Roskolenko's, poets were more apt to consider particular political concepts.

ZUKOFSKY'S LIST

Crozier contributed this essay to *The Objectivist Nexus, Essays in Cultural Poetics*, ed. Rachel Blau DuPlessis and Peter Quartermain, The University of Alabama Press 1999.

1

There is surely no gainsaying the fact that the Objectivists are an enduring embarrassment to criticism and poetry alike for the sole reason that they disturb an ordinary understanding of history as chronology. They appear to flout the law of contradiction by their ability to occupy two positions at the same time in our cognitive map of poetry in the twentieth century, for they are equally of the 1930s and the 1960s. I state the problem of the Objectivists' historical standing in terms of its effect on us in order to draw attention to its obduracy, for it has been with us since their return to public view in the 1960s.[1] Since then it has been routine to see them as necessarily filling an abhorrent vacuum (not previously detected), the poetic lost generation or missing link between the modernism of Pound and Williams and the "New" American poetry of 1945-60. Quite where the gap is supposed to occur, of course, is altogether another matter, whether in the continuum of critical attention and esteem or in the sequence of poetic production. Certainly, in the sequence from Pound and Williams it is not necessary to postulate a gap before Olson and Duncan, but to acknowledge this to be the case is precisely to confront our embarrassment in its most acute form: our necessitarian version of what the Objectivists stand for historically, following their historic re-emergence, restages contradiction by making them at once the problem and its solution. There would be no problem, needless to say, had their re-emergence been a matter merely of critical rediscovery, or had they re-emerged as revivalists of a period style; but, as we know, critical rediscovery followed their re-emergence as poets of late maturity. And this is the key to the embarrassment that they have induced ever since, for with this second flowering they re-emerged discontinuously, it would appear, from a prior history that nevertheless— for it was there to be investigated—provided the only terms in which they could be thought. They were interviewed half to death as witnesses to their own pasts, so that it should not be wondered at if, resistantly, they drew attention to the integrity of their lives and careers. Inconvenient ancestral ghosts, their flesh-and-blood existence made them unaccountable.

I exaggerate, of course, but for a purpose. If we continue to be embarrassed it must be on our own account because we have been unable to describe for the Objectivists a position in history that accords them the status of agents. In the 1930s they were not around long enough to leave a lasting impression, yet in the 1960s, and attached to their prior history, they appear belated. The passage of time, with its telescoping effect, is not quickly going to improve matters on our behalf. If they will not fulfil the intermediary role invented for them because they have affronted us as an historic anomaly since the 1960s—and it is apparent that they need not—their situation remains that between their two epochs they are (what amounts to the same thing) either squeezed out of history or set in its margin as a special instance. The reason for this is not far to seek: historical and chronological belatedness are not the same thing ("confessional" poetry is a prime example of the former), and it is our sense of history as chronological incrementation that the Objectivists disturb. A history fully predicated of the Objectivists, however, is somewhat farther to seek, and would not consist of the bare chronicle of their self-manifestation in the 1930s, for it would need to account for the significance of their disappearance from the chronological record as more than a terminus of events, and it would need also to implicate them fully in the more familiar history that includes Pound, Williams, Olson, and Duncan. Such requirements, admittedly, imply considerable claims on the Objectivists' behalf, for they entail major adjustment of our received history (already undermined to disclose that explanatory gap), on behalf of which we feel the embarrassment we do in tacit acknowledgement of their claim on our attention. We should not continue to deal with them (aided and abetted by versions of the seamless unities of their separate bodies of work) by superimposing and conflating their different epochs, covering contradiction in the dust of history.

The argument required by the counter-history I propose, and the evidence to be gathered, fall outside the scope of this essay, which will nevertheless sketch the outline of such an argument in the course of an examination of a single item of evidence. Of immediate concern, therefore, is what the premises of such an argument might be, what view it takes of the historical context in which the Objectivists emerged. That context, of course, will be a construction, but given its proper context, it will be claimed, the term "Objectivists" might be understood to denote a much wider historical field than its recent use has documented, so that—speculatively at least—the identity "Objectivist" does not merely designate the four-man team (Rakosi, Reznikoff, Oppen, Zukofsky) that was defined in the 1960s. Such different denotation, feminist critics and historians might be pleased to note, would take off the pressure to bolt on Lorine Niedecker as an honorary fifth Objectivist, and avoid depriving her of her own idiosyncratic history. (Admirers of Basil Bunting, strangely enough, with the exception perhaps of Donald Davie, have not attempted to affiliate him in this way, probably because in the England of the 1960s, which bracketed him with Hugh MacDiarmid and David Jones, a myth of native ancestry and longevity answered to various local needs.)

The Objectivists' historical context brings us directly to the question of Objectivist theory, implicit in the classification of poets as Objectivists. Here we should not be concerned with the belated rationalizations of the term of the 1960s and after, overdetermined as they are by reminiscence and eager hindsight, but with the theory (insofar as it was such) indicated and transmitted by Zukofsky in his role as collective mediator, publicist, and specifically, in a word, as the Objectivists' *editor*. What needs to be registered about this, in addition to Zukofsky's reluctance to theorize—much advertised, but more important than it—is that the reluctance was theorized: the critic was secondary to the poet. What we read as theoretical statements by Zukofsky are promulgated as axioms and taxonomies, the specific terms of which are defined by illustration. The terms "sincerity" and "objectification", that is to say, do not remain in the conceptual domain, although they are concepts of particulars (poems and their elements), but are referenced in the work of Reznikoff. We may suppose that in these instances, in which he is not redeploying Poundian categories, Zukofsky's terms derive from his own poetic concerns, that they state his poetic aim and method, for of course they are not conceptual categories for analytical purposes. Were they so they would not require demonstrative illustration. But for analytical purposes Zukofsky catalogues the properties of poems in triads which indicate that his theory, at the formal level of composition and reading, is a development of Poundian axioms. Pound's phanopoeia, melopoeia, and logopoeia are rendered as image, cadence, and idea. (Or, in a later formulation, with the pleasures of reading in mind, as sight, sound, and intellection.) Zukofsky's development from Pound becomes clear if we correlate terms that are distinctively his own with those adapted from Pound, and place sincerity with image, objectification with cadence, for it is then necessary to suppose that "idea" has been in some way subsumed by both. It is important to emphasize at this point that Zukofsky is not merely applying or extending Pound's earlier theory; he retains Pound's theoretical axioms, which were a contribution to the study of poetry's formal properties, but subsumes them to a larger conceptual structure designed to accommodate questions of value as well. There is an ambition here to go beyond matters of craft, although Zukofsky's theory functions as well to preserve and consolidate modernist gains in technique, but to understand it we need to see it as an intervention within a specific historical situation. It is at once the counter-offensive and the rearguard defence of the younger modernists.

II

Situations are constantly being modified by agencies we also understand to be determined by them. With this in mind, we might see Zukofsky's Objectivist theoretical intervention as acting against the drift of events in order to assist the real direction of historical development, and indeed quite directly so by virtue of actions purportedly in a pragmatic mode. The attractions of such dissimulation are readily apparent, for theory can give an account of poems in terms of itself, it can instill preferences, but it cannot know poems directly or make judgements about them. The material contingencies of practice will always cause it to exceed theory; the most theory can then do is draw attention to those unpreconceived effects for critics to judge of. Zukofsky's historical situation made dissimulation possible because it was so unlike Pound's: whereas Pound, pioneering his way out of the wilderness of Victorian culture, had recourse to *a priori* principles derived from an ahistorical notion or innovative practices, Zukofsky could cite the example of his contemporaries' achievements. This active Poundian legacy provided him with admirable cover as that discriminator of values, the editor. And there is no doubt that, in adopting this role, Zukofsky performed an important service, underwriting the canon of modernist poetry as we still, to a great extent, have it today. Nevertheless, modernist theory, as part of his inheritance from Pound, was inadequate to the task of justifying that canon, let alone enforcing it. Indeed, it had been deployed elsewhere to become a cultural program, in consequence of the tactical inflections it received from Eliot, or, recalled as Imagism, it received a token assent as a primitive hygienic regime. All very well to patronize its limitations if Glenn Hughes' revivalist *Imagist Anthology 1930* was taken for its up-to-the-minute embodiment.[2]

To speak of Zukofsky as having underwritten the present-day canon of modernist poets is not, needless to say, to claim that he instituted it. Far from it. What he proffered was a list, something far short of the canonical, but instead current, provisional, appropriate to the moment. And of course the perception of what such a reading list should essentially prescribe, the sense of what constituted the historical ensemble of contemporary relevance, was not peculiar to him. It comes to us with an air of familiarity not because we recognize names from the canon but because our scholarship enables us to reconstruct systems of mutual esteem. Canonicity and historiography are not, however, to the present point, and need to be set aside if we are to address the significance of Zukofsky's list in relation to the Objectivists—who, it needs to be recalled, are neither canonical nor the subjects of a sufficient history. We need to attend, instead, to what is idiosyncratic in Zukofsky's list in order to detect how poets who are for us canonical are positioned there in a quite other order of values. It is indeed the presence of certain canonical modernists on his list, there perhaps indeed as Objectivists, the argument here outlined proposes, that is basic to a historical understanding of the Objectivists.

If I have been slow to introduce the piece of evidence—Zukofsky's list—which I consider exemplary for the historical argument I have in mind, it is because, as will by now appear obvious, I do not suppose that its significance can be yielded inductively. Its significance lies not so much in what the poets cited have in common as in how they are grouped together. Prefatory remarks have not served to signify this setting aside of inductive method by tendentious deferral but were designed to indicate the range of problems this evidence can be applied to. What remains, before the evidence is finally produced for inspection, is to indicate its situation in relation to Zukofsky's dissimulated theoretical project.

In a letter to Pound dated 8 September 1930, Zukofsky indicates the connection as "aesthetic criticism" of four essays he has written: 'Henry Adams: A Criticism in Autobiography,' then being serialized in *Hound & Horn*; 'Ezra Pound: His Cantos,' published in French translation in *Echanges*; and 'American Poetry 1920-1930' and 'Sincerity and Objectification,' published the following year in *Symposium* and *Poetry* respectively (Pound and Zukofsky 41). It is in this group of ostensibly disparate essays, rather more than in the editorial statements he contributed to the "'Objectivists' 1931" issue of *Poetry* and the 1932 *An "Objectivists" Anthology*, that we will more profitably look to delineate Zukofsky's theory.[3] Taken as a group they will be found to deal, respectively, with an exemplary poetic intellect, an exemplary poem, the current achievement of American poetry, and the work of a largely unknown poet (Charles

Reznikoff) whose work exemplifies the qualities in poetry which need to be known for purposes of critical judgement. (It will be recalled that in defining these qualities Zukofsky was integrating, in terms of larger and smaller units, Pound's threefold distinction of poetic properties.) Zukofsky's method throughout these essays is to draw attention to particulars, and this is consistent with a recognizable theory of knowledge and communication as well as, by implication, a critique of dominant cultural practice. In keeping with this method is the device of the list.

Of immediate concern is 'American Poetry 1920-1930', which was explicitly a sequel to René Taupin's *L'Influence du symbolisme français sur la poésie américaine (de 1910 à 1920)* (Paris, 1929).[4] We need to note both the method of Zukofsky's approach to his topic and the strategic possibilities it provided. Zukofsky's method implies that his sequel to Taupin's book is not simply its continuation, and this is not merely because the question of influence is consistently discounted, specifically, where he finds Taupin thinking in terms of poetic generations, and what he regards as "evolutionary implications" linking one generation to the next, Zukofsky prefers to "study the progress of individual work rather than its use in an 'evolution' of poetry" (61). Focus on individual poets, rather than poetry in general, allows room for critical censure without requiring Zukofsky to undertake a general survey of his period. The essay is not a critical balance sheet drawn up at the end of a poetic decade, and indeed its sense of timing is quite different. Accepting Taupin's notions of a "first generation" and a "younger generation", Zukofsky's strategic purpose is to combine them, and so he refuses to see the first generation (Pound, Williams, Eliot, Marianne Moore) as a "gang-plank for a younger generation to step onto" (61). Zukofsky's sequel to Taupin is thus the occasion to insist that poets of the first generation continued to develop or progress after 1920 (and thereby detach them from imagism; indeed, "they never started merely with the image") and hence that their relation to the younger generation is that of contemporaneity rather than influence (61). Citing Pound and Joyce, he suggests that the question of influence might more appropriately be explored in terms of the relations between contemporaries.

We can understand all this as "aesthetic criticism" because it is insistently evaluative, with Zukofsky's list as the outcome of a complex and a wide-ranging act of judgement. The theory entailed by his criticism is evidenced by the axioms that direct and justify his observations and judgements, and by the different occasions this essay and the other three address. Theory provides both tactics and strategy in these essays, and the absence of systematic theoretical exposition should not be taken as evidence that Zukofsky's thinking is without either system or the capacity to explain itself.

III

In 'American Poetry 1920-1930' Zukofsky's theoretical position is invested in the poets who provide his point of departure: "For bearings this essay returns to the several poets it started with" (72). They were those members of the first generation (but not, for example, H.D., "whose later work… suffers from an Anglicized dilution of metric and speech value") whose work had continued to progress, and certain members of the younger generation (61). His "portmanteau bibliography of poetry after 1920 is brief" (72). I now give it in the form in which it was reprinted in *Poetry* (there are minor differences) as the headnote to 'Program: 'Objectivists' 1931' as the "list of works absolutely necessary to students of poetry" (268). This is Zukofsky's list:

> Ezra Pound—*XXX Cantos* (Paris, 1930); William Carlos Williams—*Spring and All* (Dijon, 1923); Marianne Moore's *Observations* (New York, 1924); T.S. Eliot's *The Waste Land* (New York, 1922) and *Marina* (London, 1930); E.E. Cummings' *Is 5* (New York, 1926); references to earlier volumes of Cummings; Wallace Stevens' *Harmonium*; Robert McAlamon's *North America*; Charles Reznikoff; and *The Exile Nos 3 and 4*, edited by Ezra Pound (Chicago, 1928). (268)

However judiciously compiled, this is self-evidently a working list, for the contemporary student, and it requires some elucidation before we can either comment or interpret its historical significance. Today's student will not find copies of *Exile* readily at hand, but with this citation Zukofsky is directing readers to poets of the new generation without books to their credit; specifically, he is referring to himself ('Poem beginning "The"' in issue no. 3) and to Carl Rakosi ('Extracts from a Private Life' in issue no. 4).[5] Their inclusion, together with that of McAlmon, and perhaps of Cummings, marks the positive deviation of Zukofsky's list from our own canon. Its negative deviations, both from the contemporary canon and our own, are possibly less obvious, in the former case at least. Zukofsky was swiftly rebuked by the proprietor of *Poetry* herself in the next issue. Harriet Monroe denounced the "theoretic scheme" that left so many "poets of the last two decades consigned to outer darkness": Robinson, Lindsay, Frost, Masters, Sandburg, Jeffers, Millay, Lowell, Wylie, and the "once-revolutionary imagists."

More significant exclusions from our point of view, once it is borne in mind that the list is of poetry published during the 1920s, include Crane, Tate perhaps, but also the Eliot of *The Hollow Men* and *Ash-Wednesday*. What caused Zukofsky particularly to approve 'Marina', which he republished in *An "Objectivists" Anthology*? Can this question be rephrased to ask, instead, if it is feasible to categorize Eliot with other Objectivists? The line of reasoning behind such a question will be obvious, but it should be approached with the necessary caution that three of the poets in Zukofsky's list—Cummings, Moore, and Stevens—did not appear in either of Zukofsky's "Objectivists" compilations. Additionally, it may be noted that Pound's contribution to "'Objectivists' 1931" was blank space: "Mr. Pound gave over to younger poets the space offered him" [Monroe], 'Notes' 295). This might suggest that Zukofsky's view of his editorial project, and that of Pound, who had sponsored it, were somewhat different.[6] We are, of course, concerned with Zukofsky's, since the term "Objectivists" was his, and will recognize that the term was used at one time or another to describe most of the poets on his list as well as a considerable number of others of the younger generation whose names have altogether lapsed from memory.

But more than this, for having cited his list of works Zukofsky adds that the poets named seem to him "to have written in accordance with the principles heading this note" (268). The derivation of that statement of principles, after Zukofsky's reading of the dictionary and Spinoza, indicates the close alliance of his theory and poetry. In '"Recencies" in Poetry', his 'Preface' to the 1932 Anthology, Zukofsky felt it necessary to point out that the lexical definitions of the noun "objective", including his own "use of this term extended to poetry," which comprised the statement of principles in 'Program: "Objectivists" 1931', were transcribed ("slightly reworded") from his poem 'A'-6 (9).[7] The optical and military senses of the noun—as an objective glass ("the lens bringing the rays from an object to a focus") and as "that which is aimed at"—correspond, surely, to those qualities sought in poems under the terms "sincerity" and "objectification" (10). They also correspond to those aspects of nature differentiated in the distinction between "natura naturata" and "natura naturans" encountered in the scholium to Proposition XXIX of the first part of Spinoza's *Ethics*.[8] In 'A'-6 the military usage of the second sense of "objective" is not alluded to (as indeed it is not normally implied when we use the word in this way; only the dictionary gives the military prior claim on this sense), and in its extended use in relation to poetry, with Spinoza in the background, the term "objective" brings together things seen sharply and intention toward things in that mode in a synthesis which adjusts the creative powers of the poet and those of history. I quote Zukofsky's statement of principles as cited by him in '"Recencies" in Poetry', but note a significant variation of wording: the version of 'A'-6 given elsewhere in the Anthology reads "naturans" rather than "nature as creator" (10).

> An objective—rays of the object brought to a focus,
> An objective—nature as creator—desire for what is objectively
>   perfect,
> Inextricably the direction of historic and contemporary particulars
>
> (10)

"Nature as creator," Zukofsky's final form of words, glosses "natura naturans," which for Spinoza is synonymous with God as a free cause, as distinct from everything else which derives from God's nature or attributes. William Hale White annotated this passage in the *Ethics* by citing the Scholastic idea of the oneness of God and the world which was yet not their absolute identity.[9]

Spinoza knew all about lenses, but both Christians and Jews have tended to doubt whether he knew much about God.[10] He tends to attract those whose faith has failed, such as White and Zukofsky. But how do the principles stated by Zukofsky, derived (it would appear) from a version of natural theology, apply to the other poets on his list? How might they apply, for example, to the belief in revelation of the Anglican Eliot? How do they square, for that matter, with Zukofsky's Marxism? Only the first question needs an immediate answer, which we can approach if we consider that whereas Zukofsky has derived some form and substance of thought from Spinoza he has not retained its meaning. The desiring creative nature, or the desired perfection of creation, is not eternal but historic and contemporary, and exists independently as poetry.

IV

If we return to Zukofsky's statement of principles, in either of its forms, we can observe that it follows a returning curve from the object, to the perfect, back to the particulars. In 'Program: "Objectivists" 1931' particulars are glossed as both things and events, Marianne Moore's "Egyptian pulled-glass bottle" and the Russian Revolution. This sequence instates the received object, as a particular thing or event, within the perfect. Quite how the sequence unfolds and folds back on itself is not without its ambiguities: "inextricably" lacks a verb to modify, so that by ellipsis it cannot be certain which of "desire" and "perfect" is relative to "direction"; nor is the sense of "direction" certain, even as we follow the trajectory of Zukofsky's thought. Just as we move and are moved by desire, so Zukofsky's particulars both have and receive direction. These ambiguities are intrinsic, just as is, within the complex mediation of Spinoza's thought, the double focus of "objective", which is both gathered to and projected from the subject. Now, while I am fairly sure that within the phrase "the direction of historic and contemporary particulars," the historic and contemporary themselves inextricably linked, we may detect the hope of the communist, our attention should remain on "particulars," and the modes of knowledge and communication associated with them.[11] It is in relation to this term that other poets on Zukofsky's list can be thought of as having "written in accordance with" his principles, or that those principles can be seen as not exclusively appropriate to his own writing.

In Spinoza's thought, as Zukofsky might render it, God is a particular from which other particulars derive their being and which exists in them. In the same way, sincerity and objectification are particulars distinguished by scale and position. To distinguish between things and events, historic and contemporary particulars, is not, it would appear, to distinguish between kinds of particulars but merely to emphasize one quality of particulars rather than others. We might recognize all four qualities in Marianne Moore's Egyptian bottle.

But it is a characteristic of particulars, as of God, to exist in the present, where—unlike God in the popular notion of him—they exhibit change. Contemporaneity stands in contrast to the past, not history, and the present is stuffed with husks of the past. When Zukofsky praises Henry Adams for remaining young, we are reminded, perhaps, of Cummings. So a poetry of particulars might be understood as a poetry of history's manifestation in the present. Such a complex understanding of contemporaneity might well yield a principle common to the poets on Zukofsky's list. Indeed, in 'American Poetry 1920-1930', quoting from Marianne Moore's 'New York,' Zukofsky says of the first generation of his poets that they "did not stop with the monolinear image; they extended it to include 'a greater accessibility to experience'" (61). However, neither contemporaneity not accessibility to experience, as far as poetry is concerned, is a matter of disposition; they require constructive achievement. In Pound the monolinear image gives way to "the poetic locus produced by the passage from one image to another. His *Cantos* are, in this sense, one extended image" (73). In analogous ways Williams and Moore are seen to have coordinated multiple images as complex structures.

Images, we may suppose, are the particulars that make up poems and from which the complex particular that is a poem is produced—or at least, that this is so in the small body of work that comprises Zukofsky's list of American poetry in the 1920s. But how, we may well ask, is an image produced in language from the historic and contemporary particulars of the age? I think it is in relation to this question that Zukofsky's most stringent criticism of contemporary work is deployed, in precise relation to a sense of the specificity of meaning to particularized words. Words are particulars, as opposed to general lexical items, when spoken; they achieve a meaning specific to the particular occasion of their annunciation (though no doubt words may be spoken over and over again without losing their conventional generality and imprecision: this was, after all, one of T.E. Hulme's great themes) from performative features such as gesture and intonation. Zukofsky's criticism throughout 'American Poetry 1920-1930' is focused on prosodies and graphic devices capable of providing the written word with performative equivalents to "clarify and render the meaning of the spoken word specific. The things these poems deal with are of their world and time, but they are 'modern' only because their words are energies which make for meaning" (79).[12] It is in this context of prosodic inventiveness that we can understand Zukofsky's coolness toward the later H.D., and Stevens and Eliot as well ("like Eliot, [Stevens] has purposely led his rather submerged intellectual excellencies... to a versification clambering the styles of English influence"), on account of the metrical tug in their verse toward "anglicised" regularity (65).

It appears, then, that in 'American Poetry 1920-1930' Zukofsky provided the articulate demonstration of Objectivist principles in action, and that they can sufficiently explain both the exclusions and inclusions based on them. On this showing the statement that the poets on his list write in accordance with common principles is fully justified in terms of the principles themselves, and those principles define the term "Objectivist." But two questions remain to be posed, the first of which is crucial to the historical argument alluded to previously, but one which requires the second if it is to be properly answered. Can the poets on Zukofsky's list usefully be considered as Objectivists? Do Zukofsky's Objectivist principles adequately encompass their work? Some readers may have registered as intransigent modernist backwardness the primacy allotted to speech values by Zukofsky, even though his principles, his criticism, and his theory are all concerned with writing. If so, Zukofsky nevertheless does appear, even while resisting some applications later made of it, to endorse Saussure's primary distinction between langue and parole. His poetics of speech and music (the lower and higher levels of poetry in his later formulation of it) thus reveals a blind spot in his theory, which performs a disappearing trick with the dance of the intellect among words, as Pound defined logopoeia—that metonymic capacity of poetic language to mark words and phrases with contextual inflection as it shuttles between different registers and codes. It might be said that while Zukofsky had an ear for particular words, he had no time for particular jargons. (We might recall his reported rebuke to Pound in 1939, when he was seeking audience with sundry political crackpots in the United States, "Whatever you don't know, Ezra, you ought to know voices" ['Statement' 55]. But theoretical blind spots are prone to be negated by practice, and although we find little or no irony—of the sort encountered in Moore and Cummings, or in the earlier Pound and Eliot—in Zukofsky's writing, his method disposed him to be, like Pound and Moore, and McAlmon as well, a collector of quotations, of particulars of writing, and to build from them. Moreover, if Zukofsky is not disposed to dwell on the ironies of contemporary life, are they not a shared preoccupation of Rakosi and Oppen? If we would not withhold the term "Objectivists" from them on that account, why might we not apply it, in the light of Zukofsky's conception of their common principles, to the other poets on his list? I propose this as the question best suited to frame the early history of the Objectivist poets.

NOTES

[1] I mean both that commercial publication first made some of their work generally accessible (Oppen, *The Materials*, 1962; Reznikoff, *By the Waters of Manhattan: Selected Poems*, 1962; Zukofsky, *All: The Collected Shorter Poems*, 2 vols., 1964, 1965; Rakosi, *Amulet*, 1967) and that they were subject to group configuration: see, for example, *Contemporary Literature* 10.2 (Spring 1969) Special Number: The 'Objectivist' Poet.

[2] For Zukofsky's opinion of Hughes's anthology, see 'American Poetry 1920-1930'.

[3] For convenience of reference the reader may consult the versions of these essays in Zukofsky's *Prepositions*, with the caution that there 'Sincerity and Objectification' appears as Part II of 'An Objective' and has been purged of reference to Reznikoff.

[4] It seems unlikely that Zukofsky would have taken note of Taupin's book were the author (who taught French at Columbia) not personally known to him. The notion that modern poetry in English should go to school in France has been around at least since the 1890s (cf. Arthur Symons, *The Symbolist Movement in Literature*, 1899; and also the cases of Stuart Merrill and Francis Vielé-Griffin); its attraction for American modernists (most amiably stated by Harold Rosenberg, 'French Silence') no doubt owes much to the denial of any umbilical link to English culture. But although Taupin provided Zukofsky with 'American Poetry' as a cultural entity, he more usefully afforded him two points of theoretical resistance: influence as a category of literary history, and Imagism as the content of the decade 1910-20. For Zukofsky's opinion of Taupin's book see 'Imagisme'.

[5] Rakosi had also published four poems in *Exile* 2 (Autumn 1927).

[6] This is not the place to go into the details of Pound's relations with Zukofsky and other 'younger poets', but it is worth noticing that by 1933 Pound had qualified his enthusiasm for Zukofsky's project. 'A whole school or shoal of young American writers seems to have lost contact with language as language... in particular Mr Zukofsky's Objectivists seem prone to this error' ('Notes' 253; Pound nevertheless included Zukofsky and Oppen in *Active Anthology*). Pound (unlike Williams, however) seems to have been determined to keep poets of the younger generation at arm's length, and to have assigned to Zukofsky the role of convening them; this did not accord with Zukofsky's notions (a) that individual members of a generation could develop and (b) that relations between generations were concretely relations between contemporaries. The thesis of my essay is that Zukofsky used the term 'Objectivists' to refer to poets of both Pound's generation and his own, and that his editorial work was intended to make just this connection.

[7] The slightly different form of words used for the headnote statement of principles in *Poetry* was as follows. 'An Objective: (Optics)—*The lens bringing the rays from*

an object to a focus. (Military use)—That which is aimed at. (Use extended to poetry)—Desire for what is objectively perfect, inextricably the direction of historic and contemporary particulars.'

8 Zukofsky read the Everyman's Library edition of the *Ethics*, translated by A. Boyle (I am indebted to Mark Scroggins for this information), and would have found the terms 'natura naturata' and 'natura naturans' rendered as 'passive nature' and 'active nature'. Such interpretation obscures the finer verbal distinction by grammatical inflection of the Latin, which is more successfully brought across into English by Spinoza's contemporary, Dryden, in the preface to *Annus Mirabilis* (1667). '*Wit writing*, (if you will give me leave to use a school distinction), is no other than the faculty of imagination in the writer...*Wit written* is that which is well defined, the happy result of thought, or product of imagination' (14). The distinction was first made in the twelfth century by Averroes in his commentary on Aristotle, *De Caelo* (for medieval scholastic philosophy Aristotle was the philosopher, and Averroes his most important commentator), but for Dryden it was a commonplace to be turned to witty advantage (note the pun on 'school'). Spinoza appears to have revived it briefly in order to establish the proper relation of intellect to nature ('that which is contained in the intellect objectively must of necessity be granted in nature,' *Ethics*, I, Prop. XXX) by attributing the intellect to 'natura naturata' (I, Prop. XXXI). Romantic theory used the distinction somewhat differently; Coleridge, for example, refers to 'the essence, *natura naturans*, which presupposes a bond between nature in the higher sense and the soul of man' (*Biographia Literaria* I: 257). Epistemologically Spinoza is closer to Locke than to such romantic notions of the creative powers of the imagination, but in considering Zukofsky's use of Spinoza we would do well to bear in mind that historically such ideas stood between him and Spinoza.

9 Translator's note, *Ethic*, trans. White 30.

10 White's note draws attention to the need to distinguish between God and his creation, creator and created. But Spinoza's definition of God as 'a being absolutely infinite' (*Ethics and 'De Intellectus Emendatione'* I) incorporates everything with God in a way that sidelines theological disputes about limitation of God's power by reason or free will. Santayana, in his introduction to the translation Zukofsky read, makes clear that Spinoza was considered dangerous because he removed moral sanction from religion. 'The scandal consisted in the fact that Spinoza denied final causes, or purposes at work in nature, and that, in their ordinary sense, he denied the immortality of the soul, free-will, and moral responsibility. What came to turn these doctrines (which might have passed for simple materialism) into positive blasphemy was that he identified nature with God, and taught that all things, whether in the eyes of men they were good or evil, mean or noble, were integral parts of the divine being' (vii).

Zukofsky's List

[11] My editors suggest that I explain. The appeal of the *Communist Manifesto* to the workers of the world that they should unite to cast off their chains was, of course, a message of secular hope: the workers had *nothing* to lose and a world to win. But this is not quite what I have in mind when I use the phrase 'the hope of the communist'. For Western communists in the 1920s and 1930s the Soviet Union was both a cause to be defended and a beacon of hope: Soviet industrial development bore out Marx's account of the contradictions of capitalism, as did—closer to home—the depression. The hope of the communist appears, therefore, as a disposition projected in a positive mode ('I have seen the future, and it works'—Lincoln Steffens) and with strong negative reinforcement when setbacks occurred. Thus later in the 1930s the note of hope in communist representations of the popular struggle against fascism (Andre Malraux, *L'espoir*, for example, or Montague Slater, *Haunting Europe*) is likely, by its historical innocence, to strike the contemporary reader as pathos. These are European examples, and may be without American equivalents; indeed, it may be that the element of hope detectable in Zukofsky's sense of *direction* may set him apart from other American communists. The contrast I have in mind is with the American communist cult of proletarian literature (a blatant case of theoretical backwardness), which, whatever hopeful premises underwrote its politics, involved tactical deployment of themes of abjection, misery, and squalor.

[12] For further remarks on the performativity of poetic language in Zukofsky's theory, see my 'Paper Bunting'.

Carl Rakosi and The Library of America

A birthday celebration feature on Carl Rakosi was put together by Philip Coleman (School of English, Trinity College, Dublin) for the Spring 2004 issue of *Metre*. The contributions were by Philip Coleman, Michael Heller, Ron Callan, Nicholas Johnson, Kit Fryatt, David Miller, Maurice Scully and included the following essay by Crozier.

The Library of America "is dedicated to preserving America's best and most significant writing in handsome, enduring volumes, featuring authoritative texts", according to the statement printed on the dust-jackets of those volumes. To be authoritative a text needs more than editorial intention and execution; the reciprocal assent of the scholarly community also has a role to play. In this essay I want to consider what "authoritative" means in the case of the selection of Carl Rakosi's poems in the Library's anthology *American Poetry: The Twentieth Century, Volume Two: e.e. cummings to May Swenson*. (The poets are presented in the order of their dates of birth, this volume covering the years 1894–1913). In the case of an anthology so broad, inclusive, and representative in scope (it runs to over a thousand pages, includes token examples of Blues and popular song lyrics, and many African-American and women writers) it can be asked as well if the accolade "authoritative" is confined to the proper choice and use of copy texts, or if it might also extend to the selection of texts—especially if preservation involves more than durability. The question is not meant to license carping about exclusions and omissions: I hope it will be clear that any reservations about the selection of Rakosi's poems have been influenced by questions about the editorial treatment of his texts.

In the 'Foreword' to his 1986 *Collected Poems* Rakosi explains his decision not to organise the book chronologically, either by assembling poems in their order of composition, or by gathering together previous collections. He eschews such standard editorial formats because "the presumption underlying chronological sequence is that a literary development and some kind of psychological progression or evolving take place". He does not deny that such may be the case, but having already said that "tracing my development as a poet" does not interest him, he argues that any development or progression "can only be partial because a poet in the course of his life makes repeated leaps ahead and unwanted reversions", although "he does not make them on purpose or for a purpose (that he is aware of)". Unconventionally, therefore, but with Wordsworth and Whitman as available precedents, Rakosi prefers to gather his poems into arrangements although, in his case, the categories chosen (the separate sections of *Collected Poems*) are of the moment, even (in the light of other arrangements he has made of his work) provisional. "It seemed to me more creative and interesting to organise the poems as if I were making up a book for the first time, with the parts before me, the individual poems." Those parts, he says, constitute neither a large-scale "composition" nor a simple "aggregation"; rather, "the larger and perhaps different meanings they have when viewed in this way, is to be found, when it is there, in the arrangement".

What Rakosi values are the individual poem and the increment of meaning that may ensue when it is grouped with others as part of an arrangement. These arrangements are not series (the 'Americana' section, for example, includes poems such as 'The Founding of New Hampshire' not previously published as part of what might once have been taken as a developing 'Americana' series: indeed, this poem predates the earliest 'Americana' poems by a matter of decades); nor, for that matter, are they a microchronology. When Rakosi speaks of his poems as "the parts before me" we should take him at his word, thinking of them as spread out not like the parts of a jigsaw puzzle, or a clock, but as the parts of an as yet speculative whole. For Rakosi, as he posits himself in the 'Foreword', his poems are free of any entailments of textual history, as is his body of work as a whole. His *Collected Poems* is offered as neither monument nor record, but as its own creative act. One point needs to be added. In explaining what he has and has not done in the making of his book Rakosi has no need to mention his dealings with individual poems—of course, because in it they have no history—nor does he except, in passing, when he mentions the possibility of a chronological variorum. Such an edition could only exist in the realm of hypertext, and would show that many of Rakosi's poems have had very chequered pasts indeed.

Whatever its rationale, and despite its covert operations on Rakosi's past as a writer, *Collected Poems* must be viewed as authoritative as representing the author's latest considered view of his text as a whole, and it will remain so until the second and third volumes of his *Collected Works* have been published. The Library of America editors, however, do not slavishly adhere to the convention of following an author's last revisions and corrections, although in the case of their choice of work by Rakosi they might very well have done so for all the difference it makes. This may be just as well, for the bases for their choice of texts are firmly historical, while leaving ample scope for editorial discretion. In the rationale heading their 'Note on the Texts' everything finally turns on an unexamined notion of what constitutes the "authoritative" as the ultimate basis of choice, so that their editorial decisions, in other words, are to be taken on trust:

> The choice of text for each of the poems selected... has been made on the basis of a study of its textual history and a comparison of editions printed during the author's lifetime. In general, each text is from the earliest book edition prepared with the author's participation; revised editions are sometimes followed, in light of the degree of authorial supervision and the stage of the writer's career at which the revisions were made, but the preference has been for the authorially approved book version closest to the date of composition. Texts from periodicals, anthologies, and posthumous sources have been used only when a poem was not printed in one of the author's books during his or her lifetime, or when such a book version is not authoritative.

Here I should declare my interest. These principles might be admirable from my point of view, as editor of Rakosi's *Poems 1923-1941* (1995), were they not so hedged round with qualifications ("in general", "sometimes", "preference"), which serve to obscure their underlying purpose.

Date of birth produces some strange bedfellows: it is difficult to think of Charles Olson, whose career began in the 1940s, as the poetic contemporary of Hart Crane, whose career ended in suicide in 1932. Yet both are here. From one point of view literary and historical coherence are sacrificed to eclectic inclusivity: it would be interesting to have Robert Lowell and John Berryman in the same volume as Crane, but they are too young, just as it would be interesting to have had cummings in Volume One with Ezra Pound and Marianne Moore—again, too young. But so what? It wouldn't matter—this is a multi-volume anthology after all, encyclopaedic in its treatment of twentieth-century American poetry—if you could have your cake and eat it. The text on the front and back flaps of the dust-jacket claims that the anthology "restores" an era which ended with World War II. "New schools and definitions of poetry seemed often to divide the literary scene. This was the era of the Harlem Renaissance, the Objectivists, the Fugitives, the proletarian poets. It was also an era of vigorously individuated voices—knotty, defiant, sometimes eccentric". Study of textual history, preference for the text closest to the date of composition, both serve the purpose of restoring a literary era, but here could only achieve this (of course) if the era's poets were all conveniently born in the same two decades. Furthermore I wonder if the copywriter has looked at the product. After some cross-checking I can find just one proletarian poem, by Joseph Kalar. Two other "proletarian poets", Edwin Rolfe and Isidor Schneider, are scarcely represented as such, with poems selected from works either too late, in the former case, or too early, in the latter, to qualify. If proletarian poets did divide the literary scene, and such a case might well be made, the evidence for it won't be found here.

There's precious little evidence, for that matter, of what Rakosi was up to before 1945, and what there is resists identification as such. My edition of Rakosi's early poems may not have been available to the editors when they were at work, but even so in the case of his early poems they have chosen to set aside "preference… for the authorially approved book version closest to the date of composition". Their practice thereafter seems inconsistent with this, and it is a moot point what distinguishes the "stage of the writer's career" Rakosi had reached when he published revised versions of these poems in 1967, which the editors accept, and the stage he had reached in 1986 when he published revised texts of other poems which they reject. At what point in the intervening years did the author's views cease to be authoritative?

We can only address the editors' reasoning, and its possible significance for their choice of poems (as opposed to texts), by considering each of their textual decisions and their cumulative effect. The textual source for most of the poems chosen is *Amulet* (1967), the book which announced Rakosi's return to writing and publication after a long silence. The poems, in order of appearance, are 'The January of a Gnat', 'Amulet', 'Figures in an Ancient Ink', 'The Lobster', 'Lying in Bed on a Summer Morning', 'Young Girl', 'Americana 3', and 'To an Anti-Semite'. The fifth, sixth, and seventh of these, and part of the third, were new work. 'Discoveries, Trade Names, Genitals and Ancient Instruments', and 'Two Variations on a Theme', are from *Ere-Voice* (1971). 'Instructions to the Player' is from *Ex Cranium, Night* (1975), and 'The Avocado Pit' from *Collected Poems*. Much the same selection might have been made from *Collected Poems*: there 'Two Variations on a Theme' appears with the title 'What's His Offence?'; the final lines of 'Lying in Bed on a Summer Morning' have been rewritten, and slightly expanded, so that direct address of a personified 'sky' is replaced by third person reference, and reference to El Greco is dropped; the second half only of 'Americana 3' has been kept, and rewritten in shorter lines, with the title 'Boot Hollow'. I can see no reason for thinking that these versions are either inferior to, or less authoritative than those in *Amulet*, purely on the basis of textual comparison.

I can, on the other hand, imagine some purist fanatic objecting to the carte blanche Rakosi has taken, since very early on, to recast, cut, and reconfigure his text, and to treat it as material or springboard for other poems. This was, more or less, my position when *Amulet* was published, and I have had to grow out of it. It is not the editors' position: their choice of text, after all, is based on historical principles in order, we must suppose, to situate poems (whenever feasible) with reference to the era which the volume notionally represents. In this respect, by not going back to the "book version closest to the date of composition", they have missed a couple of tricks.

'The Lobster' is probably Rakosi's signature poem, in the same way that 'The Red Wheelbarrow' is Williams's. (It is also, I think, much the better poem, if only because Williams's was not made to be free standing.) Its first book publication was in 1933, in Rakosi's first book *Two Poems*. Textually the 1967 version is virtually identical: the middle lines of the fourth and fifth stanzas have become stepped-down lines (this characteristic of Rakosi's later prosody, associated with voiced effects of direct utterance), and a line-space has been introduced before the final line to make closure more emphatic by emphasising the disjuncture of "swims / backwards". More importantly, the dedication "to W. Carlos Williams" has been dropped. The editors' decision not to restore this mark of contemporary poetic affinity seems perverse.

The decision not to use the original version of 'To an Anti-Semite' has more far-reaching implications. It was first published in the *Selected Poems* of 1941. The 1967 version drops the final stanza, "And now I find you / trying to drive the Jews / and Communists out of America!" The omission detached the poem from its era, of course, but I am not sure that it does not also change the poem's original meaning. The first stanza (both versions) reads "So you fought for the Jews / in the last war / and have become a patriot again!" Can we be certain that it is the same World War in each case? In what sense did America fight in World War I (the war referred to in the earlier version) "for the Jews"? In what sense was this somehow unpatriotic? (Isn't that what the irony of "become a patriot again" implies?) Isn't it likely that in the first stanza "the Jews", in the conspiracy-ridden world-view of the anti-Semite, originally meant something like "the bankers", so that semantically the speaker then deftly turns the tables against him in the omitted final stanza? These conjectures have been framed as questions lest they seem over-ingenious. Nevertheless it seems incontrovertible that the anti-Semite of the 1967 version is the less scary proposition, an ignoble braggart rather than a menace, who tells fibs about himself rather than lies about Jews.

The two other early poems require briefer notice; in both cases the earliest book versions are in *Amulet*. 'The January of a Gnat' was first published in the *Little Review* in 1925, 'Amulet' in *Poetry* in 1931, and at this stage Rakosi already considered it early work, suggesting to the editor that it be captioned as such—advice which was ignored. Changes to the former in 1967 were insignificant, hardly worth making, indeed; the poem remains substantially unchanged. It was, however, one of the first of his poems that Rakosi radically overhauled, probably in 1932, stripping out its verbal exuberance to make of it the pared down 'The Gnat'. In the case of 'Amulet', on the other hand, words and lines have been omitted, and qualifiers have floated from one substantive to another; only the final stanza remains intact. I consider the earlier version to be superior, slight though it is: the unusual words which so fascinated Rakosi ("camphor", "witchhazel", "clabber") are held in suspension, and also keep at bay courtly but detached observation. Nevertheless, as one of Rakosi's female portraits it is not one of his best.

My argument so far is that the editors have gained nothing by departing from the policy of giving preference to the "book version closest to the date of composition", but forfeited much. At the same time, where they have adhered to that policy, in the case of early poems given their belated first book version in *Amulet*, they have again gained nothing and (this is my opinion) lost some quality. Moreover, by ruling out periodicals and anthologies as sources, and relying on *Amulet* as the unique source for Rakosi's early work, they have restricted the field unduly. There may be a logic in this, derived from the notion of the authoritative text, but it hasn't been consistently applied, and when it comes to the test I think its application has been found wanting. If in 1986 Rakosi was at a stage in his career when revisions of work from the 1960s weren't authoritative, what does that say about the status of the revision in the 1960s of work from the 1920s and 1930s? If distance in time does not count, what does?

This question brings me to 'Figures in an Ancient Ink', in which the older poet contemplates his former writing. If I read it as a radical disavowal of the significance of the image, as something superficial, mere "patina", in favour of direct speech, here represented as such by the use of interrogatives—to the extent that I view it as Rakosi's renunciation of his earlier modernism—I would surely go too far. At the very least, Rakosi retains an attachment to what he formerly wrote, appointing himself in some sense as its curator but with responsibilities, unlike those of the scholar, not only to the text but also to his current identity as a poet. This is perhaps the best pattern for an understanding of Rakosi's treatment of his early work in *Amulet* but, if so, it entails no constraint for scholarship, and leaves the logic of the single authoritative text in tatters.

In 'The Islands', published in 1932 in the *Lion and Crown*, a Columbia University journal, Rakosi associates Greeks, Danes, and Saracens in an imagination of a European past to which he is linked. (He spent his young years on the banks of the southern Danube, so this is less far-fetched than it might seem). Their "image is an ancient / ink", in need of artificial light if it is to be seen, and what they have in common is that they are not Christian: "Athens the Greek hawk / was no parakeet" implies "Paraclete" as a quasi-homophone. These predecessors are "fellow-agents", like Rakosi they live and act in the world, and the implication is that he lives and acts in a world no less strange than that imagined in the poem. It ends with the lines "the strangeness / is my insulator / but my heart is sound". The "insulator" links back to "filaments" ("Light the filaments"), and I find myself wondering just when the Rakosi household in Kenosha first enjoyed the amenity of electric power, but in any case Rakosi's early poems evince a fascination with sources of artificial light. The important question, however, is what the speaker needed to be insulated from.

In 'Figures in an Ancient Ink' the older poet asks "What, am I in love then / with my own images, an Onan / wrapped in their protective strangeness? / shrinking from what failure?" At this stage in the new poem extended citation of the old one, abbreviated and locally reconfigured, has receded, and what remains of it is "strangeness", the merest trace, but no longer the strangeness of the European past so much as the strangeness ("unconnected images") of the older poem's images. (The difference is inscribed in the new poem's recycled title). On its heels enters anxiety about failure, as though a sound heart had proved insufficient. But for what: success as a poet? as a man? as an American? All that can be said with any confidence, I think, is that anxiety is here projected on to the persistence of Rakosi's early text. This makes for a complex poem, with different textual and temporal layers, just about self-sufficient for the purposes of meaning but, because of partial incorporation of its prior text, unable to stand free of it or to elude having its representation of it called into question. As far as 'The Islands' goes, 'Figures in an Ancient Ink' cannot be thought of as authoritative.

One doubt remains. Can Rakosi's textual history be so exceptional as to exacerbate uniquely the logic of textual authority? I suspect not. If not, then surely textual authority needs to be established on a case by case basis rather than by rote? Indeed, it might be asked why the editors of this anthology should concern themselves at all with the choice of authoritative texts (after all, on their principles anthologies are the place of last resort for that commodity) when what we require of an anthology are reliable texts of an authoritative choice of poems. Their emphasis on authoritative choice of texts seems to imply that choice of poems is the lesser issue. In the case of Rakosi and the Library of America it seems to me to be a very big issue indeed, for two very simple reasons: its anthology includes none of the early poems dealing with the immigrant and urban experience, and it passes over entirely the great, late poem 'The Old Poet's Tale'. Put another way, we have neither Rakosi the "Objectivist" nor Rakosi the poet of old age. Instead we have (again I quote the dust-jacket) what is described as "the aphoristic wit of Carl Rakosi". Really? I'd have thought Rakosi's wit was too metaphysical to be confined thus. Take the 1986 version of 'Lying in Bed on a Summer Morning'.

> A contrary air
>   It is gone.
> And by the blue sky,
>
>   clear as in Genesis,
>   holds.
>
> What is there between us?
> an abstract air…
> a state sans question
>
>   or inquietude.…
>   something light
>   as a country air
> yet serious as gold
> or man sui generis.

Diction, contrast, and the controlled pace of repetition and variation together perform the turns of language that allow the problem of being to be addressed with the composure of wit. (Mere serenity is witless.) Whatever the grounds for choice of text in this case, there can be no appeal to textual authority.

www.ingramcontent.com/pod-product-compliance
Lightning Source LLC
Chambersburg PA
CBHW060359030726
47497CB00003B/781